D1601254

Human Ecology in the Wadi al-Hasa

Human Ecology in the Wadi al-Hasa

Land Use and Abandonment through the Holocene

J. Brett Hill

The University of Arizona Press   Tucson

The University of Arizona Press
© 2006 Arizona Board of Regents
All rights reserved
∞ This book is printed on acid-free, archival-quality paper.
Manufactured in the United States of America

11 10 09 08 07 06 6 5 4 3 2 1

Library of Congress Cataloging-in-Publication Data
Hill, J. Brett (James Brett), 1960–
   Human ecology in the Wadi al-Hasa : land use and
abandonment through the Holocene / J. Brett Hill.
      p. cm.
   Includes bibliographical references and index.
   ISBN-13: 978-0-8165-2502-7 (hardcover : alk. paper)
   ISBN-10: 0-8165-2502-1 (hardcover : alk. paper)
      1. Human ecology—Jordan—Hasa Wadi. 2. Land use—
Jordan—Hasa Wadi. 3. Land settlement patterns—Jordan
—Hasa Wadi. 4. Landscape changes—Jordan—Hasa Wadi.
5. Environmental degradation—Jordan—Hasa Wadi. 6. Hasa
Wadi (Jordan)—Environmental conditions. I. Title.
GN696.J6H55 2006
304.2'095695—dc22

                                        2005018813

Portions of chapters 2, 5, and 6 were originally published in
"Time, Scale, and Interpretation: 10,000 Years of Land Use on
the Transjordan Plateau, amid Multiple Contexts of Change,"
in *Mediterranean Archaeological Landscapes: Current Issues,*
edited by E. F. Athanassopoulos and L. Wandsnider, 125–42
(Philadelphia: University of Pennsylvania Museum Publications,
2004). Reprinted by permission of the publisher.

To Anne

Contents

Illustrations

Figures

Table

Acknowledgments

A large part of the material presented here comes from ongoing work, and some parts of this book appeared previously in slightly different form in Hill 2004a and 2004b. I have many people to thank for their contributions to the successful completion of this research, starting with the faculty of the Department of Anthropology at Arizona State University (ASU). My doctoral committee was cochaired by Geoffrey Clark and Michael Barton and included Charles Redman and Steven Falconer. Other mentors at ASU include Katherine Spielmann, George Cowgill, Keith Kintigh, and Peter McCartney. Each has influenced my thinking on the ways archaeology should be thought and practiced. This work was also advanced with the help of several archaeologists in Jordan. Of special note are Burton MacDonald, Deborah Olszewski, Gary Rollefson, and Nancy Coinman. Whatever quality this work has achieved is owed in significant part to these mentors' assistance and guidance. Any errors that remain are my own responsibility.

Multiple institutions provided financial support for this research. The ASU Graduate Research Support Office provided a grant to assist my fieldwork while in Jordan. The American Schools of Oriental Research provided a Near and Middle East Research and Training Program fellowship to conduct research at the American Center of Oriental Research in Amman, Jordan. The Archaeological Research Institute at ASU provided a graduate research fellowship and, along with the Center for Environmental Studies at ASU, awarded numerous research assistantships. William Doelle and the Center for Desert Archaeology in Tucson, Arizona, have supported the development of this book and continuation of the research in comparative contexts. Without the combination of financial support and institutional resources provided by these organizations, this book would not have been possible. I thank all of the many undervalued staff who paved my way through the bureaucracy and offered their friendship along the way.

This book is Wadi Hasa Paleolithic Project Contribution No. 48, supported by grants from the National Science Foundation (BNS-8405601, BNS-9013972, DBS-9302853), the National Geographic Society (2914-84), the Chase Bank of Arizona, and the ASU Research Vice

President's Office (90-0729). It is part of ongoing research supported by a National Science Foundation Biocomplexity in the Environment grant for studies of Coupled Natural and Human Systems (BCS-0410269).

Many other people have stimulated my thoughts in ways too numerous to list. One of the finest things to come from graduate school is the friendship and insight gained from other students. I have been exceptionally fortunate in this regard, and I rank my colleagues among the best minds and best spirits I have ever had the good luck to know. Finally, these few words of acknowledgment are inadequate to express the gratitude I owe to my family for giving me their patience and encouragement year after year to pursue dubious dreams and adventures. My parents, Jim and Maribeth; sisters, Stephanie and Kim; brother, Kevin; and their families have supported me in every way. My darling wife, Anne, has constantly provided her unselfish support through this process.

Human Ecology in the Wadi al-Hasa

1

Land Use and Land Abandonment

A Case Study from West-Central Jordan

Amid mounting concern over modern environmental degradation, archaeologists around the world are demonstrating the long history of such processes and the way they have shaped current landscapes. A growing body of evidence shows how humans have modified their environment for millennia, and contemporary problems cannot be understood without an adequate sense of this ecological past and the role of humans in it. This book addresses the cultural and environmental factors affecting land use through history in a desert environment. It focuses especially on the evidence for different kinds of land management in areas of different ecological potential and in different political contexts. I use a combination of archaeological and environmental data to examine the human ecology of agriculture and pastoralism from the beginnings of domestication through the rise and collapse of complex societies in the Levant.

Studies of human ecology have grown more sophisticated with an appreciation of the dynamic and recursive quality of ecological relationships and the effect of cultural institutions upon them. The tendency to seek causes of cultural phenomena in the natural environment has been balanced by a growing appreciation of humans' role in shaping that environment. A fundamental principle underlying the research presented here is that many natural and cultural factors, interwoven in a complex history of change and response to change, have shaped the landscape (Crumley 1994; Wilkinson 2003).

This approach to landscape archaeology has provided important contributions to an understanding of the relationships between humans and their environment. It has also provided insight into the long history of such relationships and the ways they affect our modern environment. Increased attention to ancient human impact on the environment has produced a striking array of examples of how our ancestors made significant changes to their environment, sometimes with profound consequences (Redman 1999). The next phase of development in this realm of study must include explicit attention to the variety of social, economic, and ideological factors that contribute to decisions affecting land degradation.

The research presented here contributes to our understanding of the history of human ecology in the southern Levant, where current debates are complicated by research at different scales and by a lack of consensus on the importance of localized phenomena. As a case study, it provides a complement to other research in this region of mosaic environmental history. But it is necessary to move beyond case studies that simply document environmental degradation and to attempt to refine explanatory models of processes in human ecology. Through this study, I evaluate the utility as well as the limitations of one such model of the effect of political organization on land mismanagement.

One of the foremost questions facing scholars interested in human impact on the environment is why people engage in activities that are unsustainable, eventually leading to degradation and abandonment. I am particularly interested in the conditions wherein people are constrained by aspects of culture and society that structure the rationality of their decisions. In order to understand degradation and abandonment, it is necessary to understand the temporal, spatial, and cultural factors that structure the evaluation of costs and benefits in decision making. When, where, and by whom costs and benefits were experienced are essential aspects of understanding the rationality of environmental degradation.

The complexities of environmental exploitation as a cost-benefit calculation are discussed in chapter 2. There, I explore the theoretical strains running through recent discussions of land mismanagement that are required to understand processes in the Levant. I focus especially on elements of spatial, temporal, and social disassociation among the decision makers, the producers, and those who bear the future consequences of land use. Variability along these three dimensions of interaction affects both the type of relations that developed in the past and the ways the archaeological record is formed and interpreted.

Analyzing and interpreting the archaeological and paleoenvironmental record of the Transjordan plateau requires a diverse range of data and technological approaches. In my analyses, I use settlement-pattern data collected by three independent archaeological surveys in the vicinity of the Wadi al-Hasa (or simply the Hasa), a large canyon draining the western Transjordan plateau toward the southern Dead Sea. Hundreds of archaeological sites indicating loci of habitation and production have been documented in the Hasa area, testifying to the extent of past economic activities that led to degraded land resources.

These sites are located in areas ranging from high plateaus, with adequate precipitation to support woodlands and rainfall agriculture, to extremely dry, low deserts and canyons. I focus especially on sites dating to the Holocene span of agriculture and pastoralism and suggesting such economic activity. These sites offer a large, long-term sample of land use in an area that has been incorporated into numerous political systems but has often fallen at the margin of both political and ecological systems. This database provides the opportunity to evaluate land use at different temporal scales and in different environmental contexts through time.

A key component of this research is the consideration of past land use as it relates to the culture history, especially the political history, of the region. Chapter 3 provides a synthesis of the culture history of the Wadi al-Hasa based on a combination of regional archaeological and historical literature. The focus is primarily on the Hasa, but the history of this area has been strongly affected by regional and supraregional forces, and I also take these forces into consideration in reconstructing local culture history.

This culture history of the Hasa focuses especially on economic production and political organization. With regard to economic production, I emphasize elements that relate to agropastoral settlement and facilities, production technology, and evidence for the support of elite nonproducers. With regard to political organization, I emphasize evidence of decision-making hierarchy and elite demands for surplus production or other economic manipulation, as well as of resistance to elite demands. These references are woven into a discussion of the changing relationships among producers and decision-making authorities throughout the Holocene.

Just as the culture history of the Hasa has undergone many changes over the Holocene, the physical geography of the area has altered in dramatic ways. Chapter 4 is a reconstruction of the major changes in the Hasa landscape since the end of the Pleistocene. Two principal factors affecting landscape change in the Hasa have been climate and human activities. I consider them in relation to local and regional evidence for geological and biotic changes that have produced the dissected desert canyons and plateaus where there was once a large lake and aggrading floodplain. Understanding the changing landscape of the Hasa is important to the analyses here both as a foundation for land use in the past and as the cumulative product of developments in land use. The disappearance of the lake and floodplain, as well as of wildlife associated with them, has undoubtedly had profound effects on land-use strategies in the Hasa. The relationships among human activities and hillslope erosion, floodplain incision, and biotic declines are fascinating and complex processes that have contributed to this dramatically altered landscape.

A combination of cultural and natural conditions has contributed to distinctive patterns of land use that vary through time and among ecological zones. One trend, evaluated in chapter 5, is the abandonment of sites following a period of use. I address this trend using a series of statistics that measure spatial association or segregation among sites from one period to the next. I hypothesize that if land use in the Hasa led to the degradation of resources such as arable soils, sites would be moved periodically to new areas with less-degraded resources. Farmers and herders' periodic abandonment and relocation to new areas are evident in shifting settlement patterns through time. I use measures of segregation to demonstrate a statistically significant movement from one part of the Hasa to another in each archaeological period.

However, cycles of abandonment are not spatially uniform throughout the Hasa. In chapter 6, I demonstrate that cyclical abandonment was more common in areas more susceptible to erosion. Areas of settlement on the more stable upland plateaus have undergone less-frequent abandonment and have experienced more continuous occupation. I use spatial variability in land-use patterns in conjunction with evidence of relatively continuous cultural and climatic conditions to address the problem of equifinality in human-impact research. Controlling for multiple environmental factors through the explicit use of temporal and spatial variability strengthens our understanding of anthropogenic degradation.

In these analyses, geographic information system (GIS) modeling of erosion potential is based on the Universal Soil Loss Equation (USLE). The USLE is a formula for calculating the susceptibility of hillslopes to erosion based on sediment attributes, ground cover, climate, and land use. I combine information on ground surface and climate with archaeological indices of land use to model how exposure to hillslope erosion would have varied through time and in different areas of the Hasa. I use these models to evaluate how people in different ecological zones and in different political circumstances practiced cultivation and herding with respect to the potential for soil loss.

The potential for soil loss is critical for two reasons. First, if frequent site abandonment was related to erosion, then higher rates of abandonment should be associated with higher susceptibility to erosion. Second, it is hypothesized that land mismanagement is in part a function of political organization. One way to identify covariance among land mismanagement and the organization of decision making is to document the association of exploitation in vulnerable locations with periods of increased political hierarchy. I use evidence of differential exposure to erosion in different political contexts to evaluate the hypothesis that hierarchical decision making contributed to unsustainable exploitation.

Modeling erosion with GIS capabilities provides insights not easily obtained through more traditional methods of geoarchaeology. The use of computer modeling does not replace field analyses, but rather provides a complement to them (Hill 2004a). The GIS techniques employed here offer advantages in the manipulation of large quantities of data required to analyze multiple archaeological and environmental variables. Moreover, they provide a temporally and spatially complete analysis of hillslope erosion throughout the Hasa for the entire Holocene, which would be difficult, if not impossible, based purely on geomorphological analyses. In addition to the expense of a comprehensive geomorphology research program, there are typically gaps in local depositional sequences and difficulties in identifying and dating small-scale events and processes, which, though not visible in the sedimentary record, have been ecologically important.

The erosion models presented here offer a spatially and temporally complete look at land use and the exposure to one kind of environmental degradation faced repeatedly through history in the Hasa and elsewhere in the world. They provide compelling support for the hypotheses in some cases and offer insight into the shortcomings of these hypotheses in others. Equally important, they provide stimulus and direction for future research.

The Wadi al-Hasa

The Wadi al-Hasa and surrounding area exhibit evidence of both long human habitation and extreme environmental degradation. In addition to being one of the best archaeologically surveyed areas of Jordan, the Hasa has a number of geographical qualities that make it an ideal location to evaluate human/landscape relations over time. It is one of the largest drainage systems in the southern Levant and one of the only perennial watercourses draining the western edge of the Transjordan plateau. It is located in west-central Jordan about halfway between Amman and the Gulf of Aqaba (fig. 1.1). The Hasa runs from southeast to northwest, draining an area of approximately 1,740 square kilometers from the Transjordan plateau into the Jordan Rift Valley and the Dead Sea (fig. 1.2) (Donahue and Beynon 1988; Schuldenrein and Clark 1994).

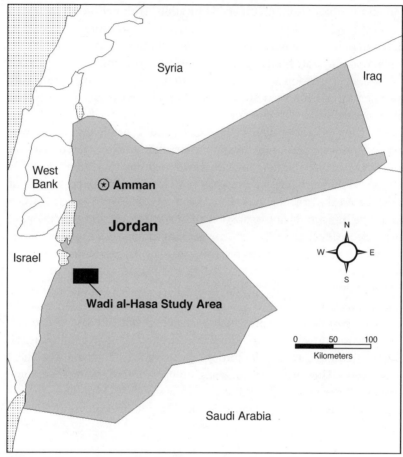

Figure 1.1   Location of Wadi al-Hasa on Transjordan Plateau

The Hasa is at the southwestern edge of the Irano-Turanian steppe vegetation zone and has highly variable precipitation, ranging from less than 300 millimeters of rainfall annually in the highest elevations (approximately 1,300 meters above mean sea level [amsl]), to as little as 60 millimeters in the lowest elevations (approximately 400 meters below mean sea level [bmsl]). It is only marginally productive for rainfall agriculture (Harlan 1988). Areas near springs and watercourses have been used successfully for irrigation farming on a small scale. The plateau grasslands are more productive for pastoralism, and the highest elevations are a productive environment for grain cultivation as well.

The Hasa drains an area of desert/savanna ecotone that is particularly vulnerable to even minor shifts in climate or exploitation pressure or both

Figure 1.2 Wadi al-Hasa
Landsat photo

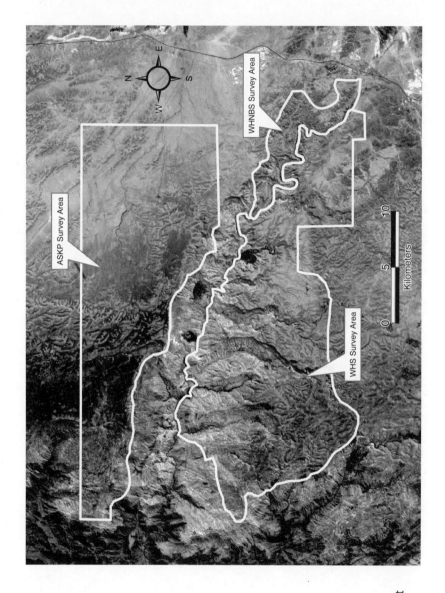

Figure 1.3 Wadi al-Hasa survey project boundaries

(Gophna 1995). Reduction in precipitation or removal of savanna flora can disrupt ecological relationships and lead to desertification more rapidly than in more humid areas. Tchernov and Horwitz (1990) argue that it is in semiarid zones, such as the Hasa, that environmental deterioration, either through a decline in precipitation or overgrazing, may lead to the most dramatic response among agropastoralists. In more humid areas, a small change will not result in rapid desertification. In more arid areas, a small change will not necessitate adaptive changes among populations already living in desert conditions.

The close proximity of relatively stable and productive plateaus to harsh and deeply dissected deserts, in combination with a history of fluctuating political power, makes the Hasa an ideal setting for the analyses in this study. The spatial and temporal variability among multiple factors known to be important in land management allows for control of individual factors in the evaluation of past environmental degradation.

The archaeological data consist primarily of information recorded by three large archaeological survey projects spanning the years from 1978 to 1993. These projects were the Archaeological Survey of the Kerak Plateau (ASKP) (Miller 1991; see also Mattingly 1996 and Mattingly et al. 1998); the Wadi el Hasa Archaeological Survey (WHS) (MacDonald 1988); and the Wadi al-Hasa North Bank Survey (WHNBS) (Clark et al. 1992; Clark et al. 1994) (fig. 1.3).

I use only the southernmost parts of the ASKP data that border the Hasa for comparative purposes. This data set is the closest geographical and cultural analog to the Hasa and provides a control mechanism for evaluating trends in the Hasa. In these analyses, I frequently distinguish between trends in the northern area, consisting of ASKP sites, and trends in the southern area, consisting of WHS and WHNBS sites. The objective of this distinction is to differentiate between behaviors in the relatively stable uplands of the Kerak plateau and those in the more varied terrain to the south. The ASKP was focused on the Kerak plateau, whereas the WHS and WHNBS were focused on the Wadi al-Hasa and its tributary canyons. Together, these survey projects recorded 1,664 archaeological sites in the study area.

I use these survey data, reflecting different settlement choices through time, along with information on terrain, soils, vegetation, and climate to understand how multiple factors have contributed to people's decisions about land use and how that land use has reshaped the environment. Chapter 2 takes a closer look at the natural and cultural processes that contributed to the rich archaeological heritage of the Hasa amid what is today a largely impoverished landscape.

2

The Costs and Benefits of Land Management through Time, Space, and Society

This chapter addresses the history, development, and current trends in the discussion of human impact on the environment, particularly in the southern Levant. Human degradation of the natural environment has received the attention of scholars since at least Classical antiquity (Hughes 1983; White 1967) and is a cause of growing concern in the present. Among the more pressing environmental issues around the world are degraded soil and water resources and the consequent declines in agricultural productivity. Agricultural and pastoral activities have often led to the erosion or depletion of soil critical to subsistence. The removal of vegetation due to such activities is also related to accelerated surface runoff, channel incision, lower water tables, and diminished stream and spring flow, particularly in arid and semiarid environments.

Such processes loom as imminent problems for contemporary populations, yet they have been ongoing for millennia in areas such as the Levant (Falconer and Fall 1995; Le Hourou 1981; Naveh and Dan 1973). Although anthropogenic environmental degradation dates back at least as far as approximately nine thousand years ago (9 ka) in some areas, the causes, locations, and responses to it have varied through time. There has not been a continuous, monocausal environmental decline in this region, but rather a series of shifting land-use practices, ecological decline, and modified recovery (Falconer and Fall 1995). In fact, a salient feature of both the ecological and the culture histories of the Levant has been their cyclical nature.

In addition to identifying episodes of anthropogenic environmental degradation through history, scholars have increasingly focused their attention on its causes and consequences. It is no longer sufficient to demonstrate that ancient humans impacted their environment. We have come to understand that human impact on the environment is ubiquitous in the past and that the more interesting and important questions have to do with variability in the process of human/environment interaction. Many different economic, social, political, and ideological factors affect human action as we go about obtaining sustenance from the Earth. Combinations of cultural elements have influenced the land-use decisions people have made, resulting in a wide variety of human impacts on the environment. Likewise, different environmental conditions have both enabled and constrained land use and have resulted in a variety of geological and ecological responses to human actions. Despite the potential for a great range of human-impact processes, a few general patterns must be considered.

Short-Term Benefits and Long-Term Consequences

One of the most important trends in decision making is the disjuncture between short-term benefits and long-term consequences (Redman 1992). People in the past often appear to have made land-use decisions for short-term gain that had detrimental long-term effects. In some cases, this pattern of decision making was probably rooted in ignorance, especially in situations where people were developing a new technology or exploiting unfamiliar environments (Butzer 1996; McGovern 1994; McGovern et al. 1988). In other cases, though, people were aware of the long-term consequences of activities such as deforestation or intensifying cultivation, yet they engaged in these activities to the degree that their lands were degraded and they were eventually forced to relocate to more productive areas. The reasoning behind this kind of behavior requires closer consideration from a number of perspectives.

First, what are the costs and benefits of land degradation? To understand the rationality of such a calculation it is necessary to understand both the actual and the perceived gains and losses. In some circumstances, the benefits of short-term gain may outweigh the long-term consequences in a real and practical sense. For example, in a case where immediate survival is at stake, long-term consequences may be rendered irrelevant in an individual's cost-benefit calculation. Such extreme cases are probably rare, but it is not hard to imagine cases where uncertainty about the future might cloud the issue of eventual consequences. In cases of political instability and insecurity, the rewards of this year's conservation efforts may be unpredictable, and calculations of consequence may be altered (Butzer 1996). From the human actor's perspective, consequences to be borne a century or more in the future may appear either uncertain or worth the benefit of many years of productivity in the meantime. There are many imaginable situations in which it may make perfectly good sense to degrade a landscape knowingly when the benefits are perceived to outweigh the costs.

Alternative attitudes toward land management may be more common in the past than we are aware of because our models and assumptions have traditionally been biased by expectations of more intensive, permanent settlement and agriculture. We may find that in past conditions of relatively low population density, mobility and extensive land use were more common. As we consider mobility at different temporal scales, we are likely to find that our conception of extensive land use is also scale dependent. Moreover, we must make clearer distinctions between emic and etic concepts of land use and abandonment.

To some extent, land degradation is a natural result of land use, and land abandonment is often considered a normal part of a subsistence strategy. Abandoning land for up to a few decades after a short period of slash-and-burn agriculture is a common and efficient practice in times and places where land is abundant relative to population (Netting 1986). Nelson (2000) argues that in the North American Southwest longer cycles of cultivation and abandonment, lasting up to hundreds of years, were practiced. This understanding of land use forces a reconsideration of our notions of abandonment. Some cultural orientations do not view such abandonment as failure, but rather as a normal part of the cycle of land use (G. Stone 1993). Thus, abandonment as a consequence of land degradation is not perceived as a result of bad management, but as a normal part of good management.

Periodic movement, as a fact and as a cultural ideal, is part of a natural connection to the landscape and the landscape of one's ancestors. The benefits of local land use are presumed to be temporary, and the consequences of land degradation are an expected and normal level of settlement mobility. The cost of degradation is culturally mediated by the expectation of settlement movement to a location where the cost of initiating a new round of cultivation is perceived to be less. The relative costs of intensification or abandonment are affected by ideological norms and social networks that facilitate movement (Netting 1993; G. Stone 1993).

Complicating analyses of costs and benefits are psychological factors arising from variability in decision-making frameworks and heuristic devices (Tversky and Kahneman 1974, 1981). Such variability affects both the ways that questions of risk are considered and the information-processing techniques that may lead to miscalculation of true costs and benefits. In the absence of precise methods of risk evaluation, people often use simplifying techniques based on past experience and available knowledge to estimate probable outcomes. Moreover, differences in the ways questions are framed may emphasize different aspects of probable outcomes, biasing perception of costs and benefits. Both heuristic techniques and decision-making frameworks are culturally mediated and may result in choices that appear rational from an emic perspective, but that have unanticipated consequences.

The discussion thus far underscores the ways in which land management is affected by human perceptions of reasonable choice. To a large degree, however, mobility and extensive land use at any scale are constrained by the availability of alternative lands. When landscape saturation occurs, alternatives become more limited, leading to increased sedentism and intensification (Netting 1993). Under conditions of population growth, sedentism, and agricultural intensification, circumscription by environmental degradation may ultimately lead to spiraling competition over a diminishing resource base and to increasing social complexity (Dickson 1987).

Conversely, the benefits and consequences of land use may become separated as a result of social complexity (Netting 1993:227). Understanding a second aspect of the cost-benefit calculation of land degradation requires that we ask who is benefiting in the short term and who is suffering in the long term. One of the most prevalent concepts employed in discussions of ancient land mismanagement is the separation of the motives of decision makers from those of producers in complex societies. Adams (1978) proposed a continuum of economic behavior ranging from strategies favoring flexibility, resilience, and long-term survival to strategies favoring maximization of short-term gain. Small groups left to their own devices in Mesopotamia developed a strategy of economic production that was diversified and sufficiently flexible to cope with environmental variability and uncertainty (see also Netting 1993:145). This approach emphasized pastoralism and was most pronounced at the periphery of Mesopotamian society. During periods of strong political centralization, this resilient strategy was undermined by elite efforts to maximize and stabilize production in order to produce and control greater surplus. The latter strategy emphasized floodplain cultivation and was most pronounced near the center of Mesopotamian society at the height of powerful political dynasties.

Adams draws attention to temporal and spatial variability in the type of strategy employed. The closer producers are to central authority, the more subject they are to elite pressures to maximize production. In contrast, producers on the periphery of the political system, especially mobile groups, will be difficult to control and more inclined to practice a resilient, context-sensitive local strategy. As centralized political control from distant capitals waxes and wanes, the emphasis on maximization will correspondingly increase or diminish. A key point in Adams's model is that the motivations of producers, who are focused on sustainable subsistence in conditions of local environmental variability and uncertainty, are not the same as those of elites, who are interested in competition and control of surplus in a much larger regional setting.

In addition, distant managers may not have adequate knowledge of local conditions to make appropriate and timely decisions about land use in the face of degradation or other changing environmental conditions. Alternatively, mismanagement may not be an unintended consequence at all, but may be part of a larger management strategy (McGovern 1994; McGovern et al. 1988). Elites may encourage overexploitation (which leads to environmental degradation) in order to undermine resistance and competition from local producers. Emphasis is again on a separation of decision makers' motives from producers' motives, leading to the forfeit of resilience and sustainability by the latter in favor of increased productive output advocated by the former. In short, the beneficiaries of short-term mismanagement are the elite decision makers, whereas the long-term consequences are borne by the local producers whose land resources are diminished.

Adaptation, Maladaptation, and Action

The development of systemic mismanagement and the inability to cope effectively with change owing to internal conflict between elements of society is a type of maladaptation according to Rappaport (1978). The specialization among components of a society that allow it to incorporate larger populations and regions into a state-level organization ultimately leads to a breakdown in the ability to manage numerous and diverse local problems. For example, the rise of bureaucratic institutions may facilitate food redistribution or defense in a developing complex society, but when new challenges are presented, those institutions are both unsuited to resolving the new problems and resistant to new institutions. Central authorities do not share the same motives or information as local producers and hence are unwilling or unable to make decisions that lead to sustainable land use. Instead, the demands of nonproducers—including civil bureaucracy, military, and religious elites, as well as attached craft specialists—place an added burden on agropastoral production. Centralized authority often facilitates increased production for a time to meet its demands, but it is inherently unsuited to respond to environmental degradation by curtailing or diversifying production (Redman 1999:212).

By examining the issue of land management at the scale of the social system, we gain a better understanding of actions that are apparently irrational at the level of the individual producer. Maladaptation occurs in the context of a system that has lost the flexibility to cope with change in an efficient manner (Rappaport 1978). The change can originate in an external phenomenon such as climate shift or foreign political challenge, or it can be internal to the system, resulting from declining productivity of agropastoral resources as they are overexploited. Because the decision-making apparatus of a complex society has become socially and sometimes spatially removed from the immediate problems of agropastoral production, it cannot efficiently cope with phenomena outside the range it was originally designed to manage. Thus, subsystem relationships that originally evolved as adaptive responses to a particular set of problems become too complex and overly specialized to respond flexibly to a different set of problems. What was once adaptive becomes maladaptive as environmental conditions change.

A key feature of this systemic view of maladaptation is that it operates at a different spatial and temporal scale than that for the individual actor. Social systems that have become sufficiently complex and internally specialized to be maladaptive would typically be regional states or empires covering large and often diverse geographic areas. The development of a complex society and the concomitant development of maladaptive traits are likewise processes that occur at a much longer temporal scale than the actions of individual agropastoral producers. The cultivation and herding activities associated with environmental degradation in the past typically operated at a seasonal or annual scale. Decisions involving field fallow, herd movement, and even settlement and abandonment occurred at the scale of individual events. The development of system maladaptation and the consequences of mismanagement often occurred at the scale of decades or even centuries. The importance of such scalar disjunction is twofold with regard to ancient environmental degradation.

First, the development of maladaptive organization and the consequences of mismanagement were probably often difficult to ascertain from the vantage point of the actors involved. Many aspects of land degradation and its causes are apparent to individuals working the land, but some slower processes may be difficult to appreciate for individuals without access to a record of historical observation. More important to archaeologists is the fact that the archaeological and paleoenvironmental record can be viewed at different scales with different results (Crumley 1994). It is essential to appreciate the different scale of individual processes versus system processes in our explanations. Explaining different types of processes necessitates an evaluation of the archaeological evidence appropriate to the scale of the process (Hill 2004b).

Although some processes occur at a scale ranging from individual events to several years, other processes may occur at much longer temporal scales. The concept of adaptation is frequently invoked in discussions of human ecology in general and has been proposed as one aspect of human impact on the ancient Near Eastern environment (Butzer 1996). Butzer proposes that although the landscape in the Mediterranean Basin has been degraded by human activities for several millennia, the diversified economic system prevalent in this region historically has been successfully adapted to a degraded environment.

In evolutionary terms, *adaptation* refers to the changing frequency of traits resulting from their differential reproduction (O'Brien and Holland 1992). Traits that are more successfully reproduced through time increase in frequency relative to those that are less successful. I focus here on the fact that adaptation is often a very slow process and is not an intentional act. Intentional acts can be selected for or against to the degree that they are reproduced through time, but the various factors that affect selection and that result in adaptation are often beyond actors' knowledge or control. A key point is that from an evolutionary perspective, adaptation is a result of cumulative selection through time. Adaptation and other evolutionary processes are not typically intentional or even perceptible to human actors engaged in everyday land management.

From this perspective, we should not expect to see evidence of people adapting to environmental conditions at the scale of individual management decisions. Instead, we should expect to see evidence of the cumulative effects of differential success in long-term patterns. Evidence of adaptation will most often manifest itself in archaeological perspectives that focus on century- and millennial-scale patterns. Many features of the Near Eastern landscape and land use are of such long duration, and archaeologists are uniquely situated to recognize patterns reflecting evolutionary processes. Adaptation has indeed shaped much of what we see in the archeological record because it is a cumulative record of thousands of years of behavior.

Understanding long-term processes, especially the differential success of a variety of land-use behaviors, is an important aspect of human-impact studies. Within the realm of archaeological explanation, evolutionary theory provides a useful set of concepts for understanding the patterns we find in the record of past lifeways. Within the realm of human ecology, evolutionary patterns in the archaeological record help us to understand long-term trends and consequences of behavior in different environmental circumstances. Evolutionary theory is particularly valuable to human-impact studies with regard to explaining long-term consequences. But explaining the archaeological record and the long-term consequences of cumulative behaviors is not the same as explaining variability in behaviors at any given time among specific people and social groups.

Much, if not most, land-use behavior at any particular time in history is not a direct result of evolutionary processes and cannot be explained as adaptation. It is instead contingent upon a variety of immediate concerns directed toward making the best choices from among numerous perceived costs and benefits. If we look at the actions of any particular set of settlers in the ancient Levant, we are as likely as not to find a number of activities that are either selectively neutral or negatively selected. Explaining the range of those activities requires consideration of all of the elements affecting immediate cost-benefit calculations as made by partially informed, politically constrained, and ideologically motivated actors in inherited environmental circumstances.

Understanding why people made the land-use decisions they did in the past requires recognition of individuals' evaluating their options and making decisions that seem to be best at the time. Their evaluations are oftentimes rational in a materialist sense, and their decisions are understandable in terms of the ecological constraints of their surroundings. Sometimes their decisions are understandable only in terms of the larger sociopolitical context of their lives and the demands imposed by a political economy. But part of understanding human action in a sociopolitical context requires recognition that people do more than make optimal decisions within that context. They have a wide range of options for their participation in society. They often participate in a limited or superficial way dictated in part by the presence of authority capable of enforcing compliance with larger-scale political designs. In the Levant, political authority has come and gone in numerous manifestations over the past several millennia, and the actual degree of control exercised in peripheral areas has fluctuated somewhat independently of elite ambitions. As a result, the correspondence between local activities and regional political formations has been imperfect. Understanding local activities requires examination of the immediate connections between individuals and the larger contexts within which they operate.

Making sense of ancient land-use behavior requires consideration of processes at different spatial and temporal scales. Individuals involved in planting, herding, settling, and moving on the Levantine landscape have done so with a variety of conscious and unconscious possibilities and limitations. The natural environment has changed in some significant ways at the local level, but has posed fairly consistent constraints on the suitability of different types of economic behavior over the course of the Holocene. The consistency of many environmental factors in the region has imposed selective pressures on behaviors through time and has resulted in specific adaptations to the natural environment.

The political environment has fluctuated dramatically on the scale of decades to centuries. The imposition of regional and foreign political authority has often affected land use by increasing both economic demand and the level of security and stability necessary for expanded production, especially on the desert margins. Increased demand has encouraged or forced expansion and intensification of economic activity in areas otherwise extensively managed by nomadic or seminomadic peoples. Such expansion, however, has often proved unsustainable and has subsequently declined. Moreover, there has always been a tension between elite authorities and local producers. At times, a relatively stable balance has been maintained for decades or even centuries. Sometimes such a balance has slowly diminished as elite interest in local conditions changed with global circumstances, such as new trade routes or extraregional political relations. At other times, economic activities have changed rather quickly as a result of technological innovation or the sudden collapse of political power. The resistance among local producers to elite demands is often a function of the elite political wherewithal to establish control in marginal areas. As elite control fluctuates, local resistance can become manifest fairly suddenly with the spread of new technologies, such as firearms or camel domestication, or with the rise of new ideologies, such as Islam.

Scale and Hierarchy in Explanation

A key to understanding land use and land degradation from an archaeological perspective is coming to grips with the issue of temporal scale. The processes described here occur at widely different timescales, and explaining such processes necessitates recognition of the importance of those differences. Employing explanatory concepts borrowed from theoretical frameworks as diverse as evolutionary ecology, political economy, and structure/agency requires some guiding principles. Probably the most familiar and well-developed discussion of temporal scale has taken place in the Annales school of history. The Annalist concept most widely cited by archaeologists is the temporal hierarchy from which the term *longue durée* is borrowed (Bintliff 1991; Braudel 1980; Knapp 1992). The other two levels of the hierarchy, the *conjonctures* and *événements*, are discussed less often in archaeology, but are nonetheless an important part of explanation. The *longue durée* refers to the long term, the *conjonctures* to the medium term or cycle, and the *événements* to specific events. There is, however, more to the temporal hierarchy than categorizing phenomena. At least two different strains of thought about time are worth exploring.

The first idea is that there are two kinds of time, linear and cyclical (Braudel 1980; Knapp 1992). Linear time is most familiar to us and is associated with progress. Cyclical time has become less emphasized in Western thought since ancient times, but has been an important concept in other cultures. Cyclical time is the time of ritual and is not progressive, but highlights the connection between past and present. There is more of a cyclical element to the longue durée and more of a linear element to the shorter timescales. Likewise, there is a more structured aspect of cyclical time and the longue durée, whereas the short term is affected more by random events. These differences lead to the second aspect of the temporal hierarchy that assists in reconciling different theoretical concepts: the hierarchy of explanation.

The hierarchy of explanation is the formal recognition that different processes work at different temporal scales (Braudel 1980; Knapp 1992; see also Bailey 1983 and McGlade 1995). It is essential to consider the temporal scale and to use appropriate variables and levels of detail for the process being explained. The temporal hierarchy has implications for both how we do research and how we resolve apparently intractable theoretical debates. The explanatory hierarchy dictates that completely different kinds of models are necessary at different scales of analysis. One important idea is that of indeterminacy: large-scale processes cannot be reduced to the small scale, and small-scale processes are not determined by large-scale processes. In other words, we cannot identify and explain a small-scale process and thereby understand the large-scale processes in which it is embedded. For example, we cannot explain the actions of a person constrained by and reshaping his or her social milieu, as in a structure/agency model, and thereby explain long-term processes such as the origins of agriculture or the rise of complex societies. These processes work at different scales and require different models and different levels of detail for understanding them.

Likewise, small-scale processes are not determined by large-scale processes. We cannot explain adaptations and maladaptations, as they are visible in the archaeological record, and purport to have explained why individuals acted the way they did at a particular time and place. Adaptation at the level of socioeconomic systems is not an appropriate explanation for the actions of individuals and interest groups. Yet archaeological data is often well suited to the study of long-term processes, and one of our most significant contributions will be developing an understanding of long-term processes and integrating the various temporal levels of process and explanation.

Archaeology offers an excellent vantage point from which to study anthropogenic environmental degradation. First, an archaeological approach allows us to view processes over a longer time span than that afforded by contemporary observation or historical records. Environmental degradation can occur quickly in some situations, but processes such as soil loss and water table decline often occur over multigenerational time spans, rendering them problematic for resource managers relying on human memory or short-term historical observation to recognize management consequences. Equally important processes such as soil recovery take even longer and remain poorly understood.

A second advantage of an archaeological approach is the ability to link environmental processes to human behavior. Correlating environmental changes with social, political, and economic behaviors helps us understand the causes and consequences of anthropogenic environmental degradation. Physiographic change at the Earth's surface occurs in a dynamic relationship with a range of natural and human variables. Although scientists have made significant advances in understanding the relationships among geological, climatological, and ecological systems, knowledge of human societies' role in cycles of change remains less developed. Archaeology offers insights into the interplay between behavior and environmental change, consequently leading to a better understanding of the variables shaping the Earth's surface over the past ten thousand years. Through understanding long-term and short-term processes and incorporating human agency in ecological systems, we can better explain human impact on the environment in the past and in the present.

Definitions and Concepts of Degradation

The term *degradation* has both geological and colloquial meanings that frequently overlap but are not necessarily the same. *Degradation* in geology is defined as "[t]he general lowering of the surface of the land by erosive processes, especially by removal of material through erosion and

transportation by flowing water" (Bates and Jackson 1984:131). In colloquial usage, the term indicates a reduction or corruption of quality. With
regard to the environment and ecology, degradation implies a decline in
utility or desirability of a landscape to living populations. The lowering
of a land surface by erosive processes often does result in such a decline
in utility or desirability. However, geological degradation is necessary to
the development of ecologically important landforms such as floodplains.
Likewise, ecologically important degradation such as soil-nutrient depletion or a decline in biodiversity may occur without notable lowering of
the land surface.

As noted earlier, concepts of land degradation and its consequences
for human action are culturally mediated and vary in different land-
management traditions. Blaikie and Brookfield (1987) discuss *land
degradation* as a perceptual term open to multiple interpretations depending on the use of the land. They focus primarily on the land's
economic uses and on a combination of natural and anthropogenic processes of degradation and recovery in the form of an equation (1987:7):

Net Degradation = (natural degrading processes + human
interference) - (natural reproduction + restorative management)

Emphasizing the concept of capability, their focus is on the use of the
land for production and on degradation as a social matter. Van der Leeuw
echoes this approach to degradation as a relative, socially determined idea
and offers the example of Greek farmers who were unconcerned with
large-scale erosion, but were quite upset by the encroachment of trees into
their grazing lands (1998:4–5). He proposes that there can be no absolute
definition of *degradation*, but that it can be understood in specific, local
circumstances.

Attention has also been brought to the matter of the intrinsic rights
of the natural environment and other living organisms, irrespective of
human cultural values (C. Stone 1993:19; White 1967). The difference in
perspectives on degradation may result in some confusion concerning
interpretation of environmental change in the past. For example, environmental scientists studying past degradation in Israel have referred to
the Islamic period, dating from the removal of Byzantine power to the
establishment of modern Israel, as "the darkest phase in the history of
Israel" (Naveh and Dan 1973:375). The evidence presented in favor of this
argument is a record of the decay of Roman and Byzantine infrastructure
and the abandonment of once productive lands. Many structures such

as irrigation works and terraces were not maintained during this period. Hillslope erosion was attributed to the collapse of terraces, and many farms reverted to desert or swamp. Yet nineteenth-century accounts of Palestine by Europeans exploring the land indicate that it was a vast, underpopulated area of grasslands, woodlands, and streams populated with abundant wildlife (Harlan 1988). These details would hardly seem to describe a degraded landscape to the average twenty-first-century environmentally concerned citizen. Such incongruity is likely related to variability in attitudes toward land management and abandonment.

Discrepancies in our understanding of land degradation are also undoubtedly related to long-standing differences in attitudes about our relationship and responsibilities to the land. Contradictory statements within the Western tradition of human/environment relations date back at least to the Old Testament (Hillel 1991; Redman 1999). Genesis gives directives to humans both to conquer and rule over the earth and to serve and preserve it. There is evidence of more detailed ideological guidance on many land-management issues in the Torah (Hüttermann 1999) and in Islamic traditions (Butzer 1994). These traditions indicate a concern with maintaining sustainable agriculture in a region of marginal productivity. Although land-use ideology in the ancient Levant was directed toward human dominion over the Earth, a long tradition of conservation management also clearly existed that probably resulted in part from past observations of anthropogenic degradation.

Just as there may be multiple motivations for land management, leading to the potential for conflict among different interest groups, there may be multiple ideologies of human responsibility toward the landscape. It is likely that human values have dictated our concepts of what is best for the environment, but there is recognition that what is best for humans largely corresponds with what is best for the environment. The rich grasslands and wildlife observed by nineteenth-century European explorers in Palestine were notable because they represented an underutilized environment available for cultivation and grazing. Likewise, the observed degradation in the Islamic-period Levant was identified in the context of European-shaped expectations of the land's potential productivity.

In the present analyses, I use the term *degradation* to refer generally to the declining abundance or availability of land resources to past human populations. Although I acknowledge the possible effects of a range of processes from lowering water tables to overhunting, I direct the bulk of my analyses at the role of agropastoralism in declining soil productivity. Environmental degradation caused by agropastoralists is owed primarily to the removal of vegetation and disturbance of the topsoil. Overgrazing and trampling by domestic herds, disturbance of soil structure by plow agriculture, and harvesting of plant fuels for various pyrotechnologies led to the destruction of much of the natural grass and woodland vegetation once common in this area.

Acting in combination, these factors augmented erosion by (1) increasing the impact of rainsplash through the removal of ground cover, (2) inhibiting infiltration and increasing the velocity of surface runoff through soil compaction, and (3) initiating positive feedback to these processes by removal of soil nutrients and the introduction of domestic goats and sheep, which together further reduced the ability of vegetation to recover.

Anthropogenic Environmental Impact in the Levant

Levantine archaeologists have documented abundant evidence of environmental impacts, including deforestation, overgrazing, and the denudation of hillslope soils resulting from agricultural, pastoral, and industrial activities spanning the Holocene (Falconer and Fall 1995; Naveh 1990). These impacts have resulted in diminished productive potential especially of the steeper terrain of upland areas. However, the magnitude and timing of processes that occurred over several thousand years are much debated.

Researchers at 'Ain Ghazal, near Amman, have argued for significant localized environmental degradation during the Neolithic period (9–7 ka), resulting in the abandonment of the first large population centers (Kohler-Rollefson and Rollefson 1990; Rollefson, Simmons, and Kafafi 1992; Simmons et al. 1988). They argue that devegetation surrounding this large Neolithic site led to erosion, declining agricultural productivity, and eventual site abandonment. Based on faunal evidence for the domestication and mismanagement of large goat herds, they suggest that overgrazing resulted in erosion in the vicinity of 'Ain Ghazal (Kohler-Rollefson 1988). Based on evidence of changes in building construction reflecting the declining size of wooden structural timbers and the declining production of lime plaster, they argue for deforestation of the area within a 7-kilometer radius of the site (Rollefson, Simmons, and Kafafi 1992; Simmons et al. 1988). They hypothesize that the abandonment of 'Ain Ghazal and other Neolithic sites in the southern Levant was in large part due to degradation of the surrounding landscape (Kohler-Rollefson 1988; Rollefson and Kohler-Rollefson 1989, 1992).

In contrast, Goldberg and Bar-Yosef maintain that Neolithic human impacts were localized and temporary, having no significant effect on society (Bar-Yosef 1995; Goldberg and Bar-Yosef 1990). They argue instead that wide-scale Neolithic abandonments in the southern Levant were due to climatic deterioration. They cite evidence from an alluvial terrace chronology in the Nahal Beersheva and from pollen-core analyses from the major drainage basins in the region to argue that anthropogenic factors became dominant in shaping the Levantine landscape only by the Chalcolithic period (6.5–5.3 ka), or later. The departure from expectations based on natural climatic cycles leads them to argue that humans began to dominate processes of environmental degradation by this time. They hold that prior to the Chalcolithic, communities experiencing environmental degradation could easily relocate to an area with adequate resources.

Researchers studying pollen from lake cores in the Levant find evidence of regional deforestation and a shift to economic species such as *Olea* (olive) in the Early Bronze Age (4.5 ka) in the Hula Basin (van Zeist and Bottema 1982) and in the Middle Bronze Age (3.7 ka) in Lake Kinneret (Baruch 1990). They argue, therefore, that it was not until the Bronze Age that regional deforestation occurred as a result of human activities.

Gophna, Liphschitz, and Lev-Yadun (1986; see also Liphschitz, Gophna, and Lev-Yadun 1989) argue that even during the Early Bronze Age, population densities were not high enough to cause significant damage. They compare estimates of the amount of land impacted by various human activities with the amount of land available for subsistence pursuits during the fourth millennium BP and calculate that there was enough surplus land to allow degraded areas to recover before they were resettled.

A comparative case in the Near East is found in the Deh Luran Plain of western Iran. In their study, Hole, Flannery, and Neeley documented a cyclical pattern of settlement and abandonment by Neolithic time periods dating to the Ali Kosh phase of 6750–6000 BCE (1969:364–68). Using evidence of site abandonment in conjunction with changing plant use, they argue for periodic soil salinization requiring relocation a few kilometers away. They note that this periodicity is on the order of fifteen hundred to two thousand years in marginal areas, but may have lasted longer in more favorable locations. Repeated soil exhaustion in the vicinity of early agropastoral communities resulted in a pattern of shifting settlement that lasted for several thousand years, while population remained small, and unoccupied areas remained available for new cultivation. They note, furthermore, that each stage in the development of domestication economies in that area contributed to positive feedback resulting in increasing dependence on cultivation and domesticated species.

The lack of agreement among the Levantine studies is due in part to differences of scale. Researchers focusing on archaeological site contexts find persuasive evidence of local degradation much earlier than do researchers focusing on regional phenomena. Localized resource patches were probably impacted first in ways detrimental to human use long before fluvial terrace development in distant wadis or pollen spectra in distant lakes registered regional deforestation. However, human actors, whose behavior we wish to understand, most likely responded to and were often constrained by local, rather than regional, conditions that were variable across space and through time.

A further source of disagreement among the models outlined here is a result of spatial environmental variability among the locations of research. The Levant is one of the most environmentally diverse regions in the world owing to its location at the junction of two continents and its highly variable climate. Danin (1995) identifies more than thirty different phytogeographical combinations and claims more than two thousand species in this relatively small region. 'Ain Ghazal, as well as many of the Neolithic sites thought to have been abandoned under similar circumstances, is located on the western edge of the Transjordan plateau in the greater Dead Sea drainage system. The terrace chronosequence established by Goldberg and Bar-Yosef (1990) is in Israel, draining to the Mediterranean. The most often cited pollen cores come from basins in the more humid central Levant, north of the other studies.

Archaeological research has shown that the Levant was also culturally diverse already by the Chalcolithic (Levy 1986) and Early Bronze Age (Dever 1995). Other researchers have demonstrated that the Levant during the Bronze Age was subject to a low level of political integration and comprised a distinct geographic and chronological mosaic (Falconer and Savage 1995). Social and political factors affecting the exploitation of environmental resources would not have been homogenous throughout the area. Studies in nearby regions have shown that erosion resulting from human activities varied at the local level, appearing at different times in neighboring valleys (Van Andel and Zangger 1990; Van Andel, Zangger, and Demitrack 1990). Under these circumstances, pan-Levantine assertions concerning ecological relations are probably oversimplified.

A greater understanding of various local situations is necessary before general claims can be made about anthropogenic environmental degradation in this region. Assertions that prior to the Chalcolithic or the Middle Bronze Age settlers in the Levant could simply move to another valley when faced with local degradation understates the importance, both ecologically and culturally, of thousands of years of environmental impact. The type and frequency of response to degraded environmental resources played a role in the development of Holocene ecological relations and human behavioral traditions. Moreover, variability in the processes of anthropogenic environmental impact is likely linked to variability in cultural development. Ignoring regional differences in degradation inhibits our understanding of those linkages.

The Wadi al-Hasa is a distinct regional setting with a relatively well-developed archaeological record. It thus offers an excellent opportunity for sharpening our understanding of variability in human/landscape relations, particularly for the later time periods of interest here.

Changing Land Use in the Levant

Changes in land use in the prehistoric and historic Levant involve the cyclical rise of large, centralized settlements, followed by their decline and a return to smaller settlements and dispersed, mobile populations. This pattern is exemplified by the rise of urbanism in the Early Bronze Age II and III, followed by its collapse and a return to diversified agropastoralism in the Early Bronze IV (Dever 1980, 1995). Similar changes occurred as early as the Pre-Pottery Neolithic B (Kohler-Rollefson and Rollefson 1990; Rollefson and Kohler-Rollefson 1989, 1992) and as recently as the early Ottoman period in the sixteenth century CE (Faroqhi 1997:443; Inalcik 1997:165–66).

As elsewhere, Levantine culture history is marked by cycles of shifting land-use strategies associated with changing natural and sociopolitical climate. Although the long-term basis for economic production in the Levant is founded on a diverse and flexible agropastoral system, periods of increased precipitation or increased incorporation into an international market economy or both have been characterized by intensified focus on large-scale agricultural production, especially of commodities such as olive oil and wine (Falconer and Fall 1995). Conversely, periods of decreased precipitation or more local market conditions have been characterized by a return to small-scale cultivation and increased reliance on transhumant pastoralism. This variability in human response to changing environmental and sociopolitical conditions has contributed to change in the type and scale of environmental degradation. Different land-use practices have resulted in fluctuating vegetation communities, different types and rates of erosion, and changing microenvironments.

Throughout millennia of variability in climate and political control, an underlying aspect of indigenous social organization has remained relatively constant. Tribal social organization has been an enduring feature of culture in the region since at least the Iron Age and probably much earlier. Although there have been repeated periods of domination by foreign powers superimposing other forms of organization on the region, tribal organization has continued as an important quality of society (Banning 1986; LaBianca and Younker 1995; Younker 1997). During periods of foreign domination, tribes played a part in the organization of resistance (D. Graf 1997a; Sharon 1975). When state power declined in the region, tribal organizations became dominant in local politics (Dever 1995; Kennedy 1991).

The presence of tribal or segmentary lineage social organization in this region has had consequences through history for land management. Cole (1985) notes that Bedouin tribes typically have a domestic mode of production that is not inherently inclined to the overexploitation of land. Surplus labor leads to leisure time rather than to surplus production because of the constraints of mobility and the fluidity of political power. There is relatively little utility or demand for surplus production in Bedouin society; consequently, agropastoral lands are not utilized as intensively as they are under other social-political forms. In contrast, he notes that in Saudi Arabia tribes traditionally guarded grazing lands and prevented overgrazing before the tribal system was abolished in recent times. The imposition of state government directing land use has disrupted the traditional management system and resulted in land degradation.

Atran (1986) notes that villages in Palestine have undergone different trajectories of land management depending on their social organization. Villages with more stable social fabric typified by long, continuous habitation have been more successful at resisting the fragmentation and loss of their traditional communal lands to nonlocal control than those with a more fluid tribal organization. Villages with a less-stable organization have suffered greater loss of control over their lands during recent political changes, as absentee landlords with different land-management motives have taken possession of once locally controlled communal lands. This distinction presents an interesting situation in the Hasa, where a large part of the population has long been Bedouin. Tribally organized Bedouin communities would have been particularly vulnerable to upheaval and the redirection of control over land-management decisions during periods of state domination.

Conversely, when state depredation became intolerable, Bedouin tribes would have been the most able to resist through abandonment and nomadic raiding from the desert to the east (see also Adams 1978). The Bedouin had a well-established, diversified, and easily mobilized economy to provide subsistence on the run. They had a well-developed social network to provide support in distant areas of retreat. And they were well adapted to survive in the protection of the eastern desert, where their state pursuers were ill suited to follow.

A detailed understanding of social organization and ethnic identification in the Hasa awaits more ethnographic analysis, but preliminary indications suggest important differences between people living in well-established villages on the plateau and those practicing more ephemeral strategies in the canyons and desert areas. The plateau villages and other locations of high agricultural production are typically inhabited by fellahin, or peasant farmers, who maintain strong ties to specific locations and invest in land capital such as orchards and terraces. In contrast, many people living in more recently established villages and camps and engaged in opportunistic farming identify themselves as Bedouin, or as immigrants from Egypt and Palestine.

Through history, a cycle of land use was created in which Bedouin tribes established themselves in grazing lands and small arable plots during periods of declining state control. When states established power in the region, the Bedouin lost grazing rights as more permanent settlements were established. At the same time, state authorities attempted to bring the Bedouin into a more settled life in order to control them more easily and to turn their energies to surplus production. When state demands became onerous, however, the Bedouin tribes rebelled, abandoned their settlements, and turned to nomadic pastoralism and predatory raiding on settlements. This cycle of state domination and Bedouin resistance associated with state decline was played out repeatedly through the history of the Hasa, as will become evident in the next chapter, which presents the culture history of the area.

The analyses presented here are designed to evaluate the relationships among costs and benefits of land use in the Hasa. The major axes of these relationships are the temporal and social separation that dictates who pays the costs and who reaps the benefits of management decisions. A clear understanding of human ecology in the Wadi al-Hasa requires recognition of the different processes operating at different scales and the different cultural factors affecting perceptions of land and its rational use. Both adaptation and individual action are visible in the archaeological record, but they explain and are explained by distinct processes and phenomena. Likewise, both land management recognizable to contemporary Western eyes as rational and land management based on alternative values are visible in the archaeological record. Understanding variable methods of land management in the context of the opportunities and constraints perceived by decision makers in the past elucidates the processes by which people make rational decisions that lead to undesirable consequences.

3

History of the Hasa

From the Origins of Agriculture to the Collapse of Empires

The human history of the Wadi al-Hasa and its surrounding area begin in the Lower Paleolithic, hundreds of thousands of years ago. However, the present analysis is directed toward the Hasa as a humanized landscape, and it was probably not until the origins of sedentism and a domestication economy in the early Holocene that humans became a major force affecting the landscape in irreversible ways. Thus, this discussion of culture history in the area is focused on the periods from the Neolithic through the Ottoman period. Although it is customary to address equivalent spans of time in the Paleolithic without great concern for a sacrifice of resolution, it is not common for archaeologists dealing with more recent periods to cover so much.

I take a relatively long-term perspective in this analysis, first, because many of the processes of interest, including landscape and land-use change, are often long-term processes. They take centuries or millennia to occur, and repeated cycles of such change are often required to detect patterns of interest. Second, the archaeological documentation of Holocene occupation in the Hasa consists primarily of survey data collected by MacDonald (1988), Miller (1991), and Clark and colleagues (1992, 1994). This data set is quite extensive both spatially and temporally, and is appropriate for a broad view of long-term changes in land use.

The extensive nature of the data is a strength with regard to the perspective of the current research. The availability of information about site type and location spanning many periods permits evaluation of change through time in a way that more detailed work on a particular period would not. However, a consequence of such long-term analysis is that no particular period can be dealt with at the level of detail that will satisfy specialists for that period. The information available for the Hasa is often not adequately specific to address subdivisions of time critical to debates in particular areas. It is not my desire to ignore such subdivisions. There simply is not enough known about them in the Hasa to make such distinctions at the present time.

This overview of the culture history of the Hasa is a synthesis of published historical and archaeological thought. It is an economically and politically focused background against which to compare and contrast specific aspects of land use as they appear in the archaeological record. The history of the area is presented chronologically from earliest to latest according to standard temporal distinctions of Levantine archaeology (MacDonald 1988; Miller 1991).

The Neolithic

The Neolithic is generally recognized as the first archaeological period during which people began to settle into sizable agropastoral communities of some endurance (Bar-Yosef and Belfer-Cohen 1989; Childe 1971; Kuijt and Goring-Morris 2002; Mellart 1975). Beginning approximately 10 ka, people in the Near East began to aggregate into settlements and rely increasingly on domesticated plants and animals. Sizable Neolithic sites have been excavated to the north and south of the Hasa. Sites are located in areas as diverse as the Zarqa valley, where 'Ain Ghazal is found in a mild, semiarid climate (Rollefson, Simmons, and Kafafi 1992; Simmons et al. 1988), to the stony cliffs and desert washes around sites such as Beidha (Kirkebride 1966) and Basta (Gebel et al. 1988; Nissen et al. 1987), both located in the sandstone desert near Petra. Relatively little is known of the Neolithic in between these large sites (Kuijt and Goring-Morris 2002). One Pre-Pottery Neolithic site of significant potential in the Hasa is the site of Khirbet Hammam (WHS 149) (Macdonald 1988; J. Peterson 2000, 2004; Rollefson and Kafafi 1985) at the downstream edge of the WHS study area. Khirbet Hammam appears to be a village site with architectural remains including walls and plaster floors. First described by Glueck (1939) as a large site with standing ruins, it is now quite disturbed at the surface by plowing. Recent excavations by J. D. Peterson (2004) indicate, however, that there are extensive buried deposits still intact.

In 1999, an additional Pre-Pottery Neolithic site, named el-Hemmeh, was discovered along the north side of the Hasa channel (Rollefson 1999). Subsequent excavations there indicate substantial architecture, including walls and plaster floors, as well as economic plant species such as *Olea* (olive), *Pistacia* (pistachio), and *Poaceae* (grasses including barley and wheat) (Makarewicz and Goodale forthcoming; N. Goodale, personal communication, January 2005). Although other Pre-Pottery Neolithic sites have been recorded and there were undoubtedly more sites from this period in the past, most remains appear to be smaller upland sites and lithic scatters. Given the number of large Pre-Pottery Neolithic sites in other parts of the Transjordan plateau, it is puzzling that there is not more record of this period in the Hasa. If the Pre-Pottery Neolithic settlement component in the Hasa were oriented around the floodplain, as suggested by Khirbet Hammam, el-Hemmeh, and other sites in the Levant, a large part of it probably was removed in subsequent erosion.

Whatever Neolithic settlement did exist in the Hasa was undoubtedly on the scale of villages to small individual farms. The largest Pre-Pottery Neolithic villages in Jordan had populations no larger than two to three thousand people (Rollefson, Simmons, and Kafafi 1992). A subsistence economy focused on farming and animal husbandry with a substantial input of wild resources was the most likely economic system (Bar-Yosef 1995; Rollefson, Simmons, and Kafafi 1992). Although there appears to have been an important ritual component to life and some specialized production activities, there was probably not a great deal of social or political hierarchy and hence not very much potential for land mismanagement resulting from organizational maladaptations associated with centralized authority (Kuijt and Goring-Morris 2002). It is very unlikely that much surplus production was required or that any kind of coercive behavior on the part of elites would have been effective. The seeds of hierarchy were surely present in communities numbering in the hundreds to thousands, but most people probably had some flexibility of movement and participation, and their interactions with the environment would have been voluntary and not a result of political coercion.

Nonetheless, the mere presence of aggregated populations practicing land cultivation and grazing would have had a marked effect on the landscape of the Hasa. If practices such as those at 'Ain Ghazal were followed in the Hasa and settlements of several hundred people were present, it is reasonable to expect that they would have impacted the landscape. There is currently little direct evidence for the scale of impacts predicted by Rollefson and Kohler-Rollefson. Evidence of rapid colluvial deposition separating Late Pre-Pottery Neolithic B and C components at el-Hemmeh, however, indicates substantial erosion during the site's occupation (N. Goodale, personal communication, January 2005). There is no reason to think that the vegetation and soils in an environment such as the Hasa would have been more resistant to the pressures of a Neolithic village than those in a more humid environment to the north.

There is an even smaller Pottery Neolithic presence recorded in the Hasa, and most extant collections of this period came from poorly preserved or now destroyed sites. A few Pottery Neolithic ceramics were identified by the WHS, and one of those sites (WHS 524) (Bossut, Kafafi, and

Dollfus 1988; MacDonald 1988) appears to have been a valley-bottom village and may still hold some promise of buried materials. It is difficult to know if this absence represents an actual hiatus of occupation or if it is also a result of geomorphic changes in the valley floor. Banning (1995; Banning, Rahimi, and Siggers 1994) argues that Pottery Neolithic sites in northern Jordan were often smaller and were dispersed along valley floors, where they are now buried. If the Hasa floodplain has changed substantially, those sites might be largely gone now rather than buried. Bossut, Kafafi, and Dollfus (1988) noted that WHS 524 was largely buried by colluvium, which they speculated was a result of deforestation above the site. They also noted that the site would have extended farther onto the terrace 20–30 meters above the current channel before that surface was removed by erosion.

A marked drought has been noted in numerous independent paleoclimate records (Bar-Matthews et al. 1999; Goodfriend 1999; Rossignol-Strick 1999) and would have been a major factor affecting site abandonment and general settlement movement during the Pottery Neolithic period throughout the southern Levant. In a related model, climate patterns shifted from a monsoonal to a Mediterranean precipitation pattern (Bar-Yosef 1995; Goodfriend 1999; Simmons 1997). Such changes undoubtedly affected settlement in the Hasa as well and may have initiated changes in vegetation, hydrology, and erosional processes.

The Chalcolithic

The Chalcolithic period is somewhat better represented in the Hasa, but still quite poorly understood in this part of Jordan. Although the Chalcolithic has been an archaeologically productive period in nearby areas (Henry 1994; Lee 1973; Levy 1986, 1995), it remains a potentially interesting period for research in the Hasa. Evidence for specialized pastoralism and the rise of the first chiefdoms has been found in the Negev, a few kilometers to the northwest (Levy 1983a, 1986, 1992, 1995). The northern Negev has been the location of some of the most significant Chalcolithic studies in the Levant for decades (e.g., Gilead 1995; Levy 1983a, 1992). Large villages in hierarchical settlement patterns have produced evidence of extensive landscape modification in the form of checkdams and other runoff-control devices. One reason offered for the rise of specialized pastoralism in the late Neolithic and Chalcolithic is that it was necessary to take herds farther from agricultural lands to prevent degradation by overgrazing and trampling (Kohler-Rollefson 1988; Levy 1983b).

Evidence for craft specialization and the production of prestige goods provides notable markers of more hierarchical organization and of perhaps the rise of elites. It has been suggested that the Chalcolithic was a turning point for human ability to cause large-scale environmental degradation in the Levant. Goldberg and Bar-Yosef (1990) propose that this was the first period for which enough social hierarchy existed to cause differential motivations with regard to landscape management.

Although it is commonly acknowledged that there was a great deal of regional differentiation in the southern Levant during the Chalcolithic period, some continuity is recognized between the Chalcolithic and the preceding Neolithic cultures across the region (Joffe 1993). For this reason, the Chalcolithic has been characterized as the end of a sequence of cultural development that began in the Natufian period.

Chalcolithic remains recorded on the Transjordan plateau so far are more ephemeral than those of the Neolithic, consisting of encampments and small farms for the most part (Hanbury-Tenison 1986; Henry 1994; MacDonald 1988). The nearest analog that has been studied in some detail for Chalcolithic settlement in the Hasa is the Wadi Hisma, approximately 100 kilometers to the southwest (Henry 1994). In the Wadi Hisma, Chalcolithic settlement of the Timnian complex has been extensively documented. Sites there indicate a transhumant settlement system in which nomadic pastoralists herded caprines in a manner similar to modern Bedouin and supplemented their subsistence with hunting and gathering. The late Neolithic and Chalcolithic were probably the beginnings of fully nomadic pastoralism in the southern Levant, and this type of subsistence was probably concentrated in the more arid parts of the region.

Chalcolithic sites in the Hasa typically resemble those described in the Wadi Hisma in that they are usually small series of oval stone enclosures with sherd and lithic scatters (MacDonald 1988). Sites such as WHS 308, WHNBS 231, and WHNBS 399 were designated farms or domestic clusters by the survey crews who recorded them and may indicate substantial permanent or semipermanent occupation. In the absence of subsurface investigation, it is difficult to say much more about this period in the Hasa. The most reasonable speculation at present is that the Chalcolithic period in the Hasa was also typically composed of small seasonal or semipermanent settlements focused on horticulture and pastoralism, with some attention still given to wild resources. Given current uncertainty about the state of the Hasa valley floor during the Chalcolithic period, it remains a possibility that horticulture or larger-scale agriculture was more commonly practiced than in the Wadi Hisma.

Although the possibility remains that significant parts of the Chalcolithic record in the Hasa were removed by subsequent degradation of the floodplain associated with it, those elements that have survived are consistent with a dispersed, small-scale settlement system. There is currently no evidence for village-scale settlement of the kind associated with the Beersheva-Ghassulian complexes to the north and west. Considerably more evidence for Chalcolithic settlement remains in the Hasa than for the Neolithic, yet none of it indicates aggregated settlements such as the Neolithic villages of Khirbet Hammam (WHS 149), el-Hemmeh, or WHS 524. It is probably safe to infer that the remaining archaeological record is representative of the Chalcolithic settlements of the Hasa.

A dispersed small-scale settlement system during the Chalcolithic would not likely have incorporated elements of political complexity such as those proposed for other parts of the Levant during this period. Nor would such small, dispersed settlements have presented the same kind of ecological problems as large aggregated villages. Nonetheless, the sheer number of sites during the Chalcolithic period is worth considering with regard to the human ecology of the Hasa. The Pre-Pottery Neolithic is currently represented by only five to six sites suggesting any kind of sedentary occupation, and only two of these sites are villages. Likewise, the Pottery Neolithic is represented by only two sites suggesting sedentary occupation, and only one of these sites is a village. The Chalcolithic sites recorded in the Hasa comprise ten to twelve locations of somewhat sedentary occupation.

The currently documented Chalcolithic sites in the Hasa probably represent a fraction of those that once existed. First, only approximately two-thirds of the area has been surveyed. Of that, the area of the south-bank survey was covered by sample transects, leaving large portions unexplored. Second, as discussed later, it is likely that many Chalcolithic sites were destroyed by subsequent erosion of the valley floor and the surrounding wadi sides where these sites are most common. Finally, if nomadic pastoralism was a major aspect of economic activity in the area, the ephemeral nature of such sites makes them poorly visible in the current record.

If, in fact, people focused on a pastoralist economy were exploiting numerous sites in the Hasa, they and their herds may have posed problems for the soils and vegetation of the area. Fall, Lines, and Falconer (1998) note that the emergence of specialized pastoralism may have had broader environmental impacts in the southern Levant than the larger aggregated settlements of the preceding Neolithic. Similarly, Grigson (1995) proposes that declining numbers of cattle relative to ovicaprids from the Chalcolithic to Early Bronze Age in desert fringe areas may signal degraded agricultural environments.

The Early Bronze Age

The Early Bronze Age is better known than earlier time periods in Jordan, and it is a period during which we see important developments in the history of the Levant. One of these developments is the rise of urbanism in the form of numerous walled cities (Richard 1987). Large, aggregated populations existed in many parts of the southern Levant, including nearby locations such as Bab edh-Dhra and Numeira (Rast and Schaub 1974) only a few kilometers north of the Wadi al-Hasa along the Dead Sea, and at Arad (Amiran 1978) in the eastern Negev. Although most of the largest sites from this period are in the Jordan valley and the western Levant, significant settlements are also found on the Transjordan plateau (Richard 1987; Schaub 1982), and numerous settlements from this period can be found in the Hasa (Clark et al. 1992; Clark et al. 1994; MacDonald 1988; Miller 1991).

There is some debate as to the nature of the Chalcolithic/Early Bronze Age transition (Amiran and Gophna 1985; Braun 1989; Hanbury-Tenison 1986; Joffe 1993), but there was a shift in material culture and settlement patterns when an overextended Chalcolithic system collapsed during a period of pronounced drought. The development of an Early Bronze Age society is usually associated with an influx of new settlers from the north (Braun 1989; Gophna 1995), the influence of Egyptian interactions (Esse 1989; Joffe 1993; Kempinski 1989), and indigenous change among the surviving populations in the area (Hanbury-Tenison 1986; Schaub 1982). The net results were an expansion of settlement in many areas and the rise of a distinct social and political hierarchy. This hierarchy is reflected in a three-tiered settlement hierarchy, city planning, craft specialization, and large-scale interregional trade relations (Amiran and Gophna 1989; Richard 1987).

Such changes in society would have affected settlement in the Hasa at least indirectly. However, there is no evidence of a large, centralized authority controlling the Hasa in the Early Bronze Age, and evidence from other areas indicates that a great deal of autonomy still existed in smaller rural communities such as those typical of the Hasa (Falconer and Savage 1995). At least thirty-five sites in the Hasa suggest some kind of settled occupation. Ten sites have been identified as villages, and eighteen as farms, hamlets, or domestic clusters. There was a noticeable shift in Early Bronze Age settlement pattern in the Hasa from small sites near major wadis to larger and more dispersed sites in upland areas. Papalas (1997) also notes a shift toward a greater variety of site types, including a distinction between habitation sites and special-purpose ritual sites. This was also the first period in the Hasa during which evidence for the fortification of sites is found, with three *qasr*/forts and numerous tower/tombs recorded as having significant Early Bronze Age components.

Although other parts of the southern Levant were experiencing increased contact and perhaps conflict with Egypt during the Early Bronze Age, there is not much evidence to suggest that Egyptian coercion or exploitation played a large part in economic production in the Hasa at this time. It has been argued that elites controlled production around Early Bronze Age cities in other parts of the Levant (Amiran and Gophna 1989), and the presence of larger communities, elaborate tombs, and defensive structures may signal some kind of elite hierarchy in the Hasa. However, Joffe (1993) proposes a political system directed by a council of elders without strong social stratification, and if elites did exercise control over exchange with outside powers from Egypt and Mesopotamia, this control probably did not extend very far into the countryside (Falconer and Savage 1995).

No excavation has yet been done of Early Bronze Age sites in the Hasa, and detailed reconstruction of the society there awaits such investigations, but it is probably safe to infer that ecological problems associated with centralized authority and surplus production were not an important factor in landscape change in this area. Conversely, a dramatic increase in settlement number and size occurred in the Hasa during the Early Bronze Age. There was still a significant pastoral component to economic production at this time, and as settlement shifted to the plateau, it may have been oriented more around dry farming of the better-watered uplands. The plateau is typically a more stable zone geomorphologically because many areas have gentler slopes. Consequently, agropastoral activity on the plateau may have been somewhat less problematic in terms of erosion. The plateau remains a productive area for farming and pastoralism even today after more than five thousand years of occupation.

Van Zeist and Bottema (1982) use pollen analyses from the Hula Basin to the northwest of the Transjordan plateau to argue for regional deforestation due to an increase in economic species such as *Olea* (olive) during the Early Bronze Age. Baruch (1990) shows a similar change in pollen cores from the Dead Sea, much closer to the Hasa. The expansion of upland Early Bronze Age settlement in the Hasa may correspond to an expansion of arboriculture in this area as well. Upland areas of the plateau are currently the most common location of orchards in the Hasa, and there is no reason to expect that such a regional phenomenon would be absent from this area. Moreover, the Hasa may not have been as heavily wooded as other areas, and, hence, the development of orchards would not have required as much removal of native trees.

Harlan (1985) uses archaeological, paleoenvironmental, and historical evidence to postulate an environment in a pluvial cycle of aggrading channels and abundant vegetation during the Early Bronze Age in the southern Ghor and on the Moab plateau adjacent to the Hasa. Donahue and others (Donahue 1985; Donahue, Peer, and Shaub 1997) likewise cite evidence from Bab edh-Dhra and Numeira just to the north of the Hasa to argue for aggrading alluvial fans with springs and streams at higher elevations. The settlement evidence from the Hasa does not indicate extensive use of a fluvial environment. There is relatively little Early Bronze Age settlement at low elevations in the Hasa, a well-vegetated aggrading fluvial system, where one would expect to find it. However, if the Hasa valley bottom and its tributary correlates were aggrading during this time period, there may be unidentified buried Early Bronze Age material there. If the Hasa valley bottom has been incised in a manner similar to the Wadis Kerak and Numeira since the Early Bronze Age, low-elevation materials would have been eroded.

The Middle and Late Bronze Ages

I treat the Middle and Late Bronze Ages together in this discussion because they are similar in most ways and because both are somewhat weakly represented in the Hasa archaeological record. The Middle Bronze Age in the Levant saw a return to urbanism, political complexity, and the importance of international relations following a hiatus in the Early Bronze Age IV period (Dever 1987; Ilan 1995). However, there were differences in settlement and land use in the Middle and Late Bronze Ages (Dever 1987; Hopkins 1993).

Middle and Late Bronze Age urbanism was focused primarily in the northern valleys and coastal regions of the Levant. Few large Middle and Late Bronze Age sites are located on the Transjordan plateau, and, in general, desert fringe areas settled in the Early Bronze Age were much less so in the subsequent Bronze Ages (Dever 1987; Hopkins 1993). Urbanism during the later Bronze Ages was directed more toward trade and tribute to Egypt (Bunimovitz 1995; Ilan 1995; Sauer 1987). Although there are indications of earlier Egyptian forays into the Levant, the Middle and Late Bronze Ages saw a great deal more influence from that region. At times, this influence was in the form of invasion and the demand for "gifts" and other forms of tribute (Leonard 1989). There is, likewise, the first appearance of influence from northern Mesopotamia during this time period (Ilan 1995). In general, both trade and tribute demands were directed toward large urban sites to the west of the Transjordan plateau.

Egyptian sources make numerous references to the nomadic peoples of the Transjordan plateau and attempts to deal with them (Hopkins 1993). The Shasu pastoralists were particularly troublesome to Egyptian attempts to control Palestine militarily. However, it appears that the plateau was at the edge of Egyptian control and that much of the population there was at least seminomadic and difficult to regulate. However, Bienkowski (1992a) cites Egyptian occupation during the Late Bronze Age as a major reason for the decline of settled occupation. Kitchen (1992) argues for invasions of Moab (Kushu) and Edom (Seir) by both Ramses II and Ramses III during the Late Bronze Age. He notes Egyptian interest in Jordan as early as 1900 BCE during the Middle Bronze Age and numerous Egyptian influences on art in Transjordan throughout this period.

The archaeological record indicates considerably more settled agricultural life on the plateau to the north than to the south. It was probably during the Late Bronze Age that the polities known as Edom and Moab began to form to the south and the north of the Hasa, respectively. The Wadi al-Hasa itself frequently would be a line of demarcation between these regions in subsequent centuries. Although quite closely related in their history and geography, these two regions developed somewhat differently in their early years (Bienkowski 1992a; Knauf 1992).

Edom appears to have remained largely nomadic during the Late Bronze Age, while Moab had already begun the return to more aggregated settlement and perhaps political hierarchy (Bienkowski 1992a). This pattern is manifest in quite different records of settlement to the south and north of the Hasa. MacDonald's (1988) south-bank survey recorded no village sites with Middle Bronze Age components and only one village of the Late Bronze Age. Neither MacDonald's south-bank survey nor Clark and colleagues' eastern Hasa north-bank survey (Clark et al. 1992; Clark et al. 1994) recorded anything identified as a farm or hamlet from these periods. Bienkowski (1992a) argues that there is really no significant Late Bronze Age settlement in Edom. In contrast, Miller's Kerak plateau survey recorded eight Middle and Late Bronze Age villages or towns on the southern part of the plateau, as well as numerous undifferentiated structures and one qasr/fort (Miller 1991).

Much of the difference seen in the records of Edom and Moab is probably attributable to different land types in the two areas. Moab has been referred to as the breadbasket of Jordan, whereas Edom is viewed as a more marginal agricultural area (Knauf 1992). In general, Moab is characterized by larger expanses of relatively low-relief land that experiences adequate rainfall for agriculture. In contrast, Edom is characterized by a hillier topography with less-stable soils, many deep canyons, and less rainfall. Differences in agricultural productivity are undoubtedly an important part of any explanation for the differences in settlement history during this period. Yet, as a simple explanation, these differences are problematic because the same differences existed in previous and subsequent periods when Edom was occupied by sedentary agriculturalists.

Other factors that may have contributed to differing land use include relations with Egypt and the possibility of different environmental conditions than those of adjacent periods. Hopkins (1993) indicates that Egyptian concern with Bedouin raiders during the Late Bronze Age was focused on the Shasu, who were identified with Edom. Regional distinctions at such an early date are difficult, but the populations of Edom and Moab may have maintained different relations with Egyptian powers. If raiding for profit was an important part of the Edom economy, mobility may have been essential to avoid reprisal. Hopkins argues that a lack of centralized authority favored a return to pastoralism during the Late Bronze Age. He posits that a system of peasant/pastoralist integration became untenable during this period because of political instability in the area and that formerly settled people turned to pastoralism for subsistence.

Changing environmental conditions may also have affected land use during this period. There is evidence that the Middle and Late Bronze Ages experienced somewhat less rainfall than the highs of the preceding Early Bronze Age (Bar-Matthews et al. 1999; Frumkin 1997; Neev and Emery 1995). If Early Bronze Age agriculture in the uplands of Edom was predicated on high precipitation, a decline in precipitation may have rendered agriculture untenable until other factors led to a renewal at a later time. However, climate change would fail to account for differences in land use between Edom and Moab, both of which probably experienced climate change in similar ways.

It is also possible that early agropastoralism had an adverse effect on the productivity of upland soils in Edom. It seems unlikely that such impacts would have precluded further use of upland soils considering that they are still productive today, but perceptions of declining productivity in key areas may have affected decision making. Agropastoral technology and its effects on the landscape in southern Jordan during this period remain largely unknown.

Detailed understanding of the factors affecting settlement in this area awaits subsurface investigations that currently consist of only minimal testing (Bienkowski et al. 1997). Still, it is probably reasonable to infer that a combination of factors, including political instability and environmental conditions, together influenced decisions to pursue a more mobile pastoralist economy in Edom that is now only poorly represented in the archaeological record. Middle and Late Bronze Age pastoralists appear to have been even less sedentary than previous populations that practiced pastoralism. Historical records indicate a large enough presence to warrant significant military concern (Hopkins 1993), and yet these pastoralists, unlike their predecessors in the Chalcolithic, left very little record of camps or architectural installations of any kind (MacDonald 1988).

Even though the Middle and Late Bronze Ages are periods during which we begin to see evidence of political interference in economic decision making in Transjordan, there is not much reason to think that surplus demands or other aspects of centralized authority affected the Hasa. Current evidence indicates a dispersed, if not small, population over much of the area and relatively little day-to-day outside manipulation of economic production. The villages that did exist in southern Moab during this period were mostly small and probably also oriented around production for local subsistence. However, the Middle and Late Bronze Ages may be the first periods during which political instability and the fear of conflict became a factor affecting economic decision making.

The Iron Age

The Iron Age represents a high point in both early settlement of the Hasa and scholarly interest in the region's archaeology. It is the first period in which we see abundant evidence of large-scale settlement throughout the area and the rise of institutionalized political hierarchy with local centers of power. It is also of great interest to scholars because it is the period in which the biblical kingdoms of Edom and Moab were described for the first time historically.

Although many early Iron Age components have been recorded during survey of the Hasa, there is some debate as to the validity of those findings. Twenty-nine sites were recorded in the Hasa with sherds identified as Iron Age I in date. However, some scholars have argued that those dates are probably inaccurate because they are based on comparisons with pottery from Palestine, and no local stratified deposits from this period have yet been identified (Bienkowski 1992a; Bienkowski et al. 1997; Hart 1992). Efforts to test potentially stratified deposits in the Hasa have revealed no in situ Iron Age I components at two locations where they were recorded during survey (Bienkowski et al. 1997). Furthermore, other larger and better-excavated Iron Age sites in the region have revealed no Iron Age I components (Bienkowski 1992b). Bienkowski and colleagues (1997) argue that Iron Age I settlement in the Hasa was limited or nonexistent and that the early Iron Age was still a period of nomadic pastoralism on the southern Transjordan plateau. Nonetheless, small-scale testing at two of twenty-nine sites with Iron Age I potential is far from conclusive, and MacDonald maintains that there is Iron Age I settlement in the Hasa (personal communication May 1998). In either case, it is probably safe to infer that whatever settlement existed during this time period was relatively slight in comparison to the subsequent Iron Age II period.

Whatever the state of settled habitation, the period from at least 1000 BCE was marked by the rise of tribal kingdoms (LaBianca and Younker 1995; Miller 1992) that were frequently in conflict with the Israelites to the west (Bartlett 1983, 1992). Edom was conquered by David of Israel in 990 BCE and subsequently paid tribute to David's armies. There was, likewise, intense conflict between Moab and Israel, and the famous Mesha stele is one of the earliest historical accounts of Moab and the fight for independence from Israel (Liver 1967). The Mesha stele is also significant for its description of the public works undertaken by the king, including the construction of city walls, cisterns, and roads (LaBianca and Younker 1995). Most of the evidence for such construction activities in Moab occurs to the north of the present study area, but the population of the Hasa was undoubtedly affected by demands from both Israelite invaders and local elites for surplus production.

Considerable attention has been paid to the form of political organization found in Edom and Moab during the Iron Age. These polities are traditionally referred to as kingdoms, based on Old Testament descriptions (Bartlett 1992; LaBianca and Younker 1995; Millard 1992; Miller 1992). *Kingdom*, of course, is not a common anthropological designation, and recent attempts have been focused on a more meaningful and comparable analysis of the structure of political relationships. Some scholars refer to *chiefdoms* or *state-level society* in the Iron Age (Finkelstein 1995; Knauf 1992; Miller 1992). But Miller is generally suspicious of biblical accounts of the grandeur of early kingdoms in Moab. Others emphasize the tribal character that underlay temporary, higher-order political developments (LaBianca and Younker 1995; Younker 1997).

Likewise, there is some debate about the origins of political complexity during this time period. Some scholars argue that most developments were indigenous (LaBianca and Younker 1995), but others argue that a local tribal system was overlain by a secondary state supported by foreign powers (Knauf 1992). There is general agreement that some kind of institutionalized political hierarchy appeared in Transjordan during the Iron Age and that there was an underlying tribal social system that persisted throughout this period.

Major Iron Age sites of the period include Buseirah (Bennett 1983) just to the south of the study area and al-Mudaybi and Dibhan just to the north (Herr 1997). Within the study area, 187 sites with some Iron Age component were recorded. Of those, 109 sites have evidence of agropastoral activity, and 41 were classified as towns or villages. In addition to 33 farms and domestic clusters, 6 qasr/fort sites and 13 towers were recorded. The Iron Age clearly represents a tremendous increase in settled, aggregated life as well as attention to defense.

By the late Iron Age, the Hasa and surrounding areas had come to the attention of Mesopotamian powers. Prior to this time, Assyrian involvement in the area did not extend as far south as the Hasa (Millard 1992). By 796 BCE, Adadnirari had subjugated Edom, and after 732 BCE Edom and Moab became tributary kingdoms to Assyria (Millard 1992). By the early seventh century BCE, Tiglath-Pileser and his successor, Esarhaddon, exacted tribute and labor from Edom and Moab (Bennett 1983). And in 668–631 BCE, Assyrian military forces entered the area under Ashurbanipal (Bienkowski 1992a). These early Mesopotamian ventures forced military service and tribute from populations in Transjordan and established vassal states in the area.

Early incursions, however, were for the purpose of intimidation rather than destruction (Bennett 1983; Millard 1992). Millard goes further to argue that as Assyrian vassals, polities such as Edom and Moab fought each other less than they had as independent kingdoms and thus were more stable. He points out that Edom and Moab enjoyed peaceful relations with Assyria and a degree of autonomy as long as they paid their tribute. The Assyrian presence led to political and economic stability, and the demand for regular tribute encouraged a more settled economy to meet it (Bienkowski 1992a; Millard 1992; Weippert 1987).

By the end of the Iron Age, in the mid–sixth century BCE, Neo-Babylonian invasions began to disrupt all of the southern Levant. The destruction of Israel and Judah at this time generally marks the end of the period, and similar attacks were waged in Transjordan (Bennett 1983; Knauf 1992). Nabonidus attacked and destroyed parts of Moab in 582 BCE and Edom in 552 BCE (Bartlett 1979; Knauf 1992). Bartlett argues that despite Neo-Babylonian destruction, some areas such as Edom were not depopulated, and the remaining populations were eventually incorporated into subsequent Nabatean society. Sauer (1987) goes further to argue that Edom faired well during the Neo-Babylonian destruction of Palestine, and Herr (1997) notes the expansion of Edom into the Negev after the decline of Judah. Others argue, however, that Neo-Babylonian interference in the area led to the decline of Transjordan states and that the Persian withdrawal of eastern power from the area in 400 BCE led to the disintegration of Moab and Edom (Knauf 1992; Smith 1990). Notably, many Arabs were described as free from taxation during this period (Bartlett 1979). Accordingly, only one possible Persian period ceramic has been noted in surveys of the Hasa (Mattingly 1996). Whatever population may have remained in the area was probably less sedentary, but the lack of Persian period ceramics may have more to do with our understanding of ceramic styles from this period than a total absence of settlement.

A few observations of other Iron Age developments are worth noting. Mayerson (1994d) compares the Arabian frontier to other historical frontiers and concludes that most Iron Age forts were probably defensive refuges in hostile country, subject to nomadic raiding, rather than military stations to control an organized enemy. Knauf (1983) and Kohler-Rollefson (1993) argue that it was probably during the Iron Age that camel pastoralism developed in the Levant, subsequently changing warfare and nomadic peoples' ability to occupy previously uninhabitable parts of the Arabian desert. Lindner and Knauf (1997) note the settlement of high, rocky terrain in relation to both defense and a desire to develop pastorally productive areas away from agriculture zones. Christopherson and colleagues (1996) use GIS erosion modeling to argue that agricultural terracing became a common technique to expand agricultural production into otherwise unstable terrain during the Iron Age II period.

Overall, the Iron Age was a period of dramatic change in the political and technological development of the Hasa. This period saw the rise of large-scale intervention in economic production as well as the technology to develop new economic resources. Both agriculture and pastoralism were able to expand into new areas, and the tension between sedentary and nomadic populations increased with the rise in both defense and mobility by the respective parties. Although specialized pastoralism may have developed millennia earlier, the newfound mobility and independence of pastoralists changed social and political dynamics in the area forever.

The Hellenistic Period

The Hellenistic period is only modestly documented in the Hasa archaeological record and may mark the return of sedentism and economic stability in the area. There remains, however, a general lack of evidence for early Hellenistic settlement and economy in the southern Levant (Smith 1990). Life in the area appears to have been typically rural and focused on subsistence agriculture and pastoralism, never having fully recovered from the Babylonian aggression (Berlin 1997; Smith 1990). Trade diminished during the early Hellenistic period, and Ptolemaic interest in the area was focused on the extraction of agricultural products and raw materials such as timber through a somewhat burdensome taxation (Smith 1990).

The Ptolemies made efforts to control Arabian trade monopolistically, but they had difficulty subduing southern Transjordan, including the Hasa. The area formerly identified with Moab was now divided into two districts, one being Gabalitis on the southern Moab plateau, which was disputed territory between the Ptolemies and the rising power of the Nabateans (Avi-Yonah 1977:41).

After the Seleucid Kingdom annexed southern Transjordan, the situation remained fluid, and Arab tribes in border areas were at least nominally under the authority of the Phylarchs (Avi-Yonah 1977:50–51). However, the Seleucids changed their attempts to regulate the area, and it was during the late Hellenistic period that conditions were suitable for the development of an autonomous Nabatean state (Smith 1990). The Seleucids encouraged trade and helped keep trade routes safe, allowing for the growth of cities along them. They also had a less-burdensome system of taxation than the Ptolemies and encouraged more self-determination along with Hellenization. The Nabatean state, with its clear Hellenic influences and strong focus on international trade, was largely a result of this improved political climate (Smith 1990).

Hellenistic presence in the Hasa is documented in twenty-nine sites showing some indication of settled occupation. Fifteen Hellenistic towns or villages have been recorded, with ten of those located on the Kerak plateau. Only eight sites are identified as farms, domestic clusters, or hamlets, and only five tower/tombs and one qasr/fort were recorded in the area. This was a low point for settled occupation between the Iron Age and the following Nabatean period. However, the Hellenistic period is considerably shorter in duration than the Iron Age and overlaps with Nabatean development. Smith (1990) notes that the lack of diagnostic Hellenistic sherds may be because local ceramic traditions were carried on during this period for which we have not adequately refined our understanding of pottery. Thus, the decline in settlement during the Hellenistic period may be more apparent than real and may be restricted to a short period following the decline of Persian influence.

The Nabatean Period

The Nabatean period, by contrast, is abundantly identifiable in the Hasa and marks the rise of the first local, autonomous, clearly state-level polity in the area. The Nabateans are famous for the spectacular monuments of Petra, approximately 75 kilometers to the southwest, and their presence was strong in the Hasa as well. One of the most notable Nabatean sites outside of Petra is located at Khirbet et Tannur (WHS 229) (Glueck 1937) on a steep summit in the center of the Hasa canyon. Other monumental sites in the area include Qasr edh-Dherih (WHS 253) (MacDonald 1988; al-Muheisen and Villeneuve 1992, 1994), Mhai (ASKP 436), and Nakhl (ASKP 420) (Mattingly 1996; Miller 1991).

The origins of Nabatea are somewhat controversial, and several authors have proposed differing views on the location of the first Nabateans as well as the manner in which the Edomites were related to them (Bartlett 1979; Bienkowski 1990; D. Graf 1997a). The early Nabateans were largely nomadic pastoralists who developed control over the Arabian trade that brought exotic goods from the east across the desert to the Levant and Mediterranean markets. Graf is skeptical of early accounts of them as completely pastoral and argues that they may have come from Mesopotamia and had some agricultural background. Bartlett makes a strong case for continuity between Edom and Nabatea and argues that the Nabateans were composed of desert tribes who encountered a diminished, but still settled, agricultural population in Edom. Through a process of intermarriage with Edomites and the adoption of local traditions including language, the growing Nabatean population incorporated the remaining Edomites.

Although it is clear that the Nabateans distinguished themselves through their control and development of large-scale trading between the East and the Mediterranean, they also oversaw an expansion of settlement and agriculture in places such as the Hasa (Hammond 1973:29–30). In the Nabatean pantheon, there was a significant emphasis on agriculture.

The goddess "Atagartis"—the deity of fertility, vegetation, and grain—was of great importance at the temple of Tannur in the Hasa (Hammond 1973:97). There was also a strong emphasis throughout Nabatea on the development of arid land agriculture and hydraulic technology to manage scarce water sources (Hammond 1973:72–73; Oleson 1995).

The development of agriculture during the Nabatean period was closely related to growth in population, but was also a part of the development of a strong social and political hierarchy. A hereditary monarchy was developed that lasted for more than 270 years, from the early second century BCE to 106 CE, when the area was annexed by Rome (Hammond 1973:15–38). During this time period, a great deal of investment was made in the construction of religious and royal monuments, public works, and defense. Nabatean monuments at Petra are the most elaborate and impressive in Jordan and among the most impressive anywhere in the ancient world. Nabatean monuments are likewise the most elaborate and impressive in the Hasa.

Nabatean public works, especially water-management devices, are common throughout southern Jordan (Hammond 1973; Oleson 1995), and it is likely that some of those recorded in the Hasa date to this period. These devices include numerous reservoirs, cisterns, aqueducts, and terraces. Other public works include city walls, roads, and caravansaries to serve transportation and trade on a large scale.

Defensive investments include the construction and maintenance of forts and watchtowers as well as the formation of a significant military force. A total of six qasr/forts and forty-one towers in the Hasa have Nabatean components, and MacDonald (1984) describes a system of defensive installations stretching from east to west, guarding the various tributary wadis entering the Hasa from high vantage points. Throughout most of the Nabatean period, the Hasa was well defended from foreign invasion, and several military campaigns are described in which Nabatean forces defended the area against attack from Seleucid, Jewish, or Roman forces (Berlin 1997; Bowersock 1983) and launched expeditions against neighboring powers in Judea (Hammond 1973:18, 28).

The Nabatean period in the Hasa was one in which local stability and security were fairly high and in which great demands for surplus agricultural production were generated. This combination led to an expansion in agricultural settlement. Forty towns and villages in the Hasa were recorded with Nabatean components, and a further twenty-four farms, domestic clusters, hamlets, and structure complexes document an expansion of agropastoral production into every part of the Hasa landscape.

The combination of improved hydraulic technology, political security, and surplus demand makes the Nabatean period an interesting time with regard to environmental impact. It is also the only time period during which such large pressures on agropastoral production would have been almost entirely locally generated. There is great potential for overproduction by a centrally organized state dependent on food production in an agriculturally marginal area. It is likely that some foodstuffs were imported during this time, paid for by tariffs and markup on trade goods, but there would have been unusual pressure on local producers to fill those demands so that wealth generated by trade could be utilized in other ways. Unlike most other periods in the Hasa, the Nabatean period represents a time when pressure for surplus production would not have been based on foreign or extraregional demand.

The Hellenistic and Nabatean periods have been described as among the most arid cycles of the Holocene, with consequences for Dead Sea levels and site locations (Donahue, Peer, and Shaub 1997). Yet there is no apparent contraction of settlement in the Hasa or removal from valley-bottom locations that might have been incising during a major drought. The construction of a retaining wall protecting Umm Hraga (WHS 725) (Copeland and Vita-Finzi 1978; MacDonald 1988) may indicate incision of the Hasa channel as early as the Nabatean period. In general, however, the valley bottom was fairly extensively utilized during the Nabatean period. The expansion of settlement, including valley-bottom locations, may indicate that the Nabateans developed a mastery of hydraulic engineering that allowed them to extend agriculture into desert margins during a drought. Conversely, it may reflect the fact that drought in the late centuries BCE was not as severe in this region as previously supposed (Bar-Matthews et al. 1999).

The Roman Period

The Roman period officially began in 106 CE, when Palma annexed Nabatea to the Roman Empire on the orders of the emperor Trajan (Hammond 1973:38). Nabatean civilization had already undergone economic changes as the traditional trade route from Petra to Gaza declined and population spread north on the Transjordan plateau (Bowersock 1983). There was an increased emphasis on agriculture, especially irrigation agriculture. There also was an increasing concern among the Romans for the defense of the Arabian frontier from the various Thamudic desert tribes, and the lack of Nabatean efficiency in this regard is cited as one reason for the Roman annexation (D. Graf 1997c). By the first century CE, Arab tribes were posing problems as they infiltrated the Negev and desert margins of Jordan. The Saracen nomads of the Arabian Desert were to become a preoccupation of both the Romans in Transjordan and of subsequent historians.

The subject of Roman military involvement in the Hasa is one of the most closely analyzed and debated features of the archaeological and historical literature about the area. MacDonald discusses the nature of the defensive fortifications in the Hasa and their relationship to the Via Nova Trajana, the road constructed under Trajan's authority and running the length of Transjordan (MacDonald 1984; MacDonald and D'Annibale 1983). Banning (1986; 1987), Parker (1986, 1987), Mayerson (1994c, 1994d), and D. Graf (1997b, 1997c) have debated the nature of Roman defense on the frontier in this region.

Using survey data from the Hasa, Banning has proposed a mutualistic system in which settled and nomadic people often maintained a cooperative relationship. In contrast, Parker has argued for more conflict between Roman interests and nomadic tribes. He argues that the system of forts along this frontier was originally designed to protect caravan trade and eventually developed into a "Limes" system to defend the frontier from nomadic raiders from the east. Mayerson dismisses archaeological data altogether and concludes from historical sources that Roman fortifications were not meant to control nomadic movements, but to defend the Romans and local populations from raiding. Graf takes an even more extreme view and argues that the Roman defenses were built to defend the Romans from the local population.

There are probably elements of truth in more than one of these arguments, and Roman military investments could easily have served more than one purpose. Moreover, the Roman period lasted for more than two hundred years. It is likely that problems varied through time, and the element of change during the Roman period is found in both Banning's (1987) and Parker's (1986, 1987) arguments. Mayerson (1994c) rejects the idea of a mutualistic relationship but accepts the idea that there were mutually beneficial relations at times. He acknowledges a limited amount of nomadic control in the area, but oddly describes the nomads as the aliens in this relationship (Mayerson 1994d).

Graf (1997b) describes a local population that became hostile to Roman military and imperial presence in the third and fourth centuries CE. He cites thousands of Thamudic and Safaidic tribal inscriptions as evidence that the local people were disturbed by excessive taxation and military conscription, as well as by the generally predatory acts of occupying forces. These inscriptions describe close relations with Nabatean powers and resistance to Roman authority. The Romans were reluctant to include Nabateans in positions of power, without any relief from their duties as Roman subjects. Resentment over the perception of injustice resulted in resistance and brigandage.

Regardless of the subtleties of their relationships, there was a significant Roman militaristic presence in the Hasa. A total of eight qasr/forts and twenty-three towers with Roman components were recorded by surveys in the area. The function of "towers" recorded in this area is somewhat problematic (Banning 1987), but there was a small increase in larger fortifications deemed qasr/forts. This military presence stands in contrast to only twenty-three towns or villages, a 43 percent decline from the Nabatean period. However, thirty-six farms, domestic clusters, hamlets, or structure complexes were recorded, representing a 57 percent increase in small, isolated settlements. This increase in dispersed settlement suggests that the local people were not particularly afraid of nomadic raiding during this time.

In many ways, there was continuity from the Nabatean to the Roman period. Twenty out of the twenty-three towns or villages identified with Roman components indicate prior Nabatean occupation. There is no reason to suspect major changes in agricultural or pastoral technology from the Nabatean to the Roman period that would emphasize the use of different lands. Roller (1983) suggests that some settlement shift may have been due to the construction of the Via Nova Trajana and the consequent development of a transportation corridor farther to the east than it had been.

The Roman period in the Hasa would have remained a period of intensive settlement focused on agropastoral production with a substantial commitment of that production to surplus. The support of a large military presence, major public works, and political elites would have continued to be an economic pressure on the landscape resources of the area. Historical records suggest that this pressure was intensified as tax and manpower demands were increased (D. Graf 1997b). Though Nabatea as an autonomous political entity had disappeared, Nabatean ethnicity and personal identity were still present in the region throughout the Roman period and were elements of Arab nationalism and resistance (Hammond 1973:38–39; D. Graf 1997b). The human population and their attitudes toward the landscape were probably fairly continuous from the Nabatean period, but the imposition of a large foreign power affected settlement location and type as well as production demands. Throughout the Roman period, interest in this area was based on maintaining the flow of Arabian trade in eastern commodities that was developed by the Nabateans, and so the region remained an important part of the empire (Fiema 1991).

The Byzantine Period

The Byzantine period was marked by a great deal of continuity with the earlier Nabatean and Roman periods. However, it was a time during which transformations were set in motion that would have long-lasting effects. If the transition from power in Rome to Constantinople had any bearing on Transjordan, it was to consolidate the empire's focus in the east. As in neighboring parts of southern Palestine, the Hasa underwent an expansion of settlement, and based on the number and distribution of sites at this time, the period represents a peak of population and desert agriculture in the area. In the Negev and Sinai, similar trends were attributed to the spread of Christianity, public security, and prosperity (Mayerson 1994a).

The survey record of the Hasa indicates a 96 percent increase in town or village settlement to a total of forty-five, whereas the number of farms, domestic clusters, hamlets, and structure complexes remained fairly constant at thirty-one. Population estimates are not warranted with the limited data at hand; based on the number of sites indicating settled occupation, however, the Byzantine period may have had the highest population until the modern era. Nine qasr/forts and seventeen towers with Byzantine components suggest a continued strong military presence in the Hasa. However, Mayerson (1994a) notes that in neighboring regions, local communities made arrangements with Bedouin sheikhs for protection from local tribes without involvement of the imperial government. Rosen and Avni (1993), commenting on pastoralist sites in the Negev, indicate that nomads had a strong dependence on settled communities. They argue that the close proximity of pastoralist sites to the Byzantine Empire through several centuries indicates a relatively close peaceful relationship and nonsignificant threat.

Relatively little distinction has been made among phases of the Byzantine period in the Hasa, and this is a notable quality of many discussions of Byzantine archaeology in the Levant (Parker 1999). However, where such distinctions exist, the data suggest that there was a decline in settlement activity by the late Byzantine period. Such a decline would be consistent with the general observation that both population and imperial interest in the area began to decrease by this time (Fiema 1991; Kaegi

1992; Patrich 1995). Fiema attributes this decrease to a shift in the local economy away from international exchange and caravan traffic toward agriculture and local exchange. With the diminishing importance of the Arabian trade network, Byzantine powers found less reason to invest in the area, and it fell into economic decline.

Though there was substantial cultural continuity throughout the Classical Age of the Hellenistic through Byzantine periods, after the annexation of Nabatea southern Transjordan was mainly of interest to the Mediterranean powers as a conduit of exchange and a boundary zone to the empire. Developments in the Hasa during the Roman and Byzantine periods, unlike in the Nabatean period, were not a local phenomenon. Major Nabatean sites probably continued to be used, but rather than the construction of new communities and religious centers, Roman and Byzantine investment was focused more on transportation and the defense of trade. The spread of Christianity throughout the Byzantine Empire undoubtedly had effects on Arab culture in the Hasa, and evidence of Christian institutions is found from this time period (MacDonald and Vibert-Gogue 1980). It is possible that changes in the nature of ideas concerning the relationship between humans and the environment followed from this transition (Redman 1999), but this possibility remains speculative in the absence of more detailed data on specific attributes of land use. Nevertheless, it is worth considering that the imposition of new ideas in a region with a long ideological tradition of land management may have had notable effect on human-ecological relations in the region (Hüttermann 1999).

Probably the greatest effect of Roman/Byzantine control over this region was in terms of stability. The establishment and maintenance of large-scale political security in the area undoubtedly affected economic development on a local level. Regardless of whom defensive installations were meant to protect, several hundred years of stability and the absence of large-scale destruction allowed for the expansion of economic activity into marginal areas. By the end of the Byzantine period, the Hasa and southern Transjordan had fallen from importance in the empire, and security collapsed, against both international threats and local raiding.

Goldberg and Bar-Yosef (Goldberg 1995; Goldberg and Bar-Yosef 1990) describe geomorphic evidence of erosion in the Negev that may be owing in part to anthropogenic factors. They identify a period of sedimentation that is associated with upland erosion during the Byzantine period. This is the first such episode that may be attributed to the expansion of agricultural settlement rather than to climate change alone. Given that this period was a high point of agricultural settlement in the Hasa as well, it is possible that deposits such as Fill IV (Copeland and Vita-Finzi 1978) in the Hasa channel are analogous to Byzantine period deposits identified in the Negev. Fill IV appears to date from post-Roman times and may reflect the expansion of Byzantine settlement and upland erosion. The precise timing of this deposition remains to be demonstrated and might as easily date to the medieval Islamic periods or to the degradation of Classical period terraces and checkdams or to both.

The Early Islamic Period

For a brief period in the early seventh century CE, the region fell under the control of the Persian Sassanid Empire, which was then at war with the Byzantine Empire (Donner 1981). There is no archaeological record of this transition in the Hasa because it was so brief, but it must have had profound effects on the area. Donner (1981) argues that this brief occupation by the Sassanids changed people's view of the inevitability of Byzantine rule and that the Byzantines never firmly reestablished control over the area south of the Dead Sea and the Kerak plateau. Southern Transjordan, including the Hasa, was under the control of desert tribes such as the Judham and Lakhm. Many of the tribes that controlled this region remained loyal to the Byzantine Empire during the early stages of the Islamic conquest, and the Hasa in particular was the location of some notable events of that conflict.

The site of Mu'ta (Mauta, ASKP 304) lies just 3 kilometers to the north of the present study area. Mu'ta was the site of the first battle between Byzantine and Islamic forces in 629 CE, and it remains an Islamic pilgrimage site today (Donner 1981). Byzantine forces were victorious in that battle, but it was to be their last significant victory in this area. When Byzantine authorities learned that the governor of the Arabs at Ma'an, in southern Jordan, had converted to Islam, they allegedly took him to Hammam 'Afra (WHS 104) and beheaded and hung him (Schick 1994). In general, there was considerable resistance to the Islamic conquest, particularly among urbanites in the region. Mayerson (1994b) argues that no matter how unbearable the tax burden and religious differences with Constantinople, the citizens of 'Aila, in southern Jordan, could not have welcomed domination by the Bedouin components of the Early Islamic invasion.

During the early conquest, the Muslims focused more intensively on the nomadic and rural people who would have composed a large part of the Hasa population. Donner (1981) proposes that rural settlements were raided first by the Muslims because these settlements had regular contact and probably kin relations with Arab nomads and were thus already large-ly Arabized. The Muslims realized early that it was crucial to control the Arab tribes in the area because no Arabian town could prosper long when surrounded by hostile nomads. Although controlling the nomadic groups and directing their raids to the advantage of the conquest, Mohammed and his followers were not Bedouin and considered the nomads an inferi-or class of people who should be settled to become truly Muslim. The new conquerors preferred to give power to settled people rather than to the Bedouin, and it was a conscious policy to place nomads on empty lands and in settlements. Donner proposes that the early success of the conquest was owing to the unification and reorganization of tribal society.

From a Western perspective, the Muslim conquest may have seemed like the end of civilization, but there is evidence that in many cases it was neither very violent nor very different from Byzantine rule (Johns 1992; Walmsley 1991, 1997). The Islamic period in the Hasa, as in other areas, may be underrepresented in survey records because of a lack of knowledge about ceramic chronology during this time. Relatively few ceramics dat-ing to the Early Islamic period have been recorded in the Hasa, but Johns (1992) and Whitcomb (1992) argue that this absence does not represent an actual decline in population. A total of only twenty-three potential sites were recorded with evidence of significant Early Islamic components. Of these, only seven were recorded as towns or villages, representing an 84 percent decrease in aggregated settlement from forty-five during the preceding Byzantine period. Based on historical records, Johns argues, in contrast, that there was a thriving settlement system with prosperous agriculture on the Kerak plateau during this period. Likewise, Walmsley (1997) specifically notes that the area of the Hasa was fertile and prosper-ous in the ninth and tenth centuries CE and that agriculture and industry flourished during the Early Islamic periods in Jordan.

Hawting (1987) describes an early period of "Fitna," or time of trial, after the conquest during which there was political instability lasting until the establishment of the Ummayad dynasty in 661 CE. Much of the early conflict had to do with the disposition of conquered lands and the impo-sition of a new tax system. After a brief period of expansion and wealth accumulation through Bedouin raiding, there was a renewal of tension between nomadic and settled peoples as resentment grew over how con-quered areas were to be settled and taxed. Muslims and non-Muslims were, of course, taxed differently, but nomads were taxed differently regardless of religion (Donner 1981; Lambton 1985). In general, non-Muslims paid higher taxes, but the rate of taxation and the disposition of their lands were variable regionally and depended on whether they surrendered voluntarily or only after conquest. Early in the Islamic period, conquered people were governed mainly by local authorities who answered to the conquerors with taxes and little direct contact, much as they had during the Byzantine period (Hawting 1987).

The earliest Islamic dynasty was the Ummayad, who were Arabs and based their authority in Damascus, just to the north of Jordan (Hawting 1987). After only a few decades, the Ummayads fell to the 'Abbasids in 749 CE. Members of the 'Abbasid family were also Arabs who spent much of their early rise to power at Humayma, a few miles south of the Hasa in the Wadi Hisma (Kennedy 1981). The 'Abbasids subsequently moved their capital to Baghdad. Brockelmann (1948) notes that it was after this move that the Arabs lost their absolute sovereignty in Islam. There were several periods of political change as the locus of power shifted between the Levant, Mesopotamia, and Egypt, from the Ummayad period until the late eleventh century, when power fell to the Seljuk Turks of the Ayyubid period (Bosworth 1967; Peake 1958). Such shifts in power undoubtedly led to fluctuations in the security and political stability of Jordan, but more recent analyses indicate that this was a time of economic prosperity. Shaban has called this period the golden age of Islam, noting clear signs of prosperity and progress in all walks of life (1976:89).

Discrepancies in perceptions of the Early Islamic period are probably owing in part to differences of scale and focus of analysis. Considerable and growing evidence indicates periods of stability and prosperity, particularly in urban contexts (Johns 1992; Walmsley 1991, 1997; Whitcomb 1992). But there is also reason to believe that as the glow of the early conquest wore off and new tax systems altered society, unrest occurred in frontier areas such as the Hasa. Shaban (1976) describes in some detail how large landowners enhanced their wealth and evaded taxes at the expense of small landowners. During the years 775–85 CE, the Muslim tithe was one-tenth of produce, but then the rate was increased to one-third to one-half of produce. Many small landowners were forced to give up their holdings and join Shi'i protest movements. As the inequity of the tax burden between urban and rural sectors worsened, urbanism grew. Shortly after 892 CE, a system of tax farming was instituted in which rights to tax collection were sold to individuals. Partly as a result of this system, many small farmers were forced from their lands and joined nomadic groups. Accounts from Syria indicate that there was a great deal of conflict, and agricultural output declined rapidly, causing a food crisis in which the Fatimids had to beg the Byzantines for grain in 1054 CE. Thus, urban centers such as Pella and Kerak may have prospered more than rural areas, especially during the tenth and eleventh centuries, when rural producers suffered from elite demands.

Although the ceramic data from the Hasa may generally under-represent early Islamic settlement, the data still indicate far more Ummayad period material than 'Abbasid through Mamluk. Most Early Islamic sites in the Hasa were not distinguished by period, but nine Ummayad poten-tial settlement components were identified, whereas only one each from the 'Abbasid and Fatimid periods and four from the Ayyubid/Mamluk periods were recorded. This difference would support the idea that settle-ment in the Hasa declined over the course of the Early Islamic period. The large majority of Early Islamic sites in the Hasa are in locations with prior Byzantine occupations. The survey data from the Hasa, in conjunction with archaeological and historical data from elsewhere in Jordan, suggest that there was continuity from the Byzantine through the Early Islamic periods in many aspects of settlement and economy. But most settlement in the Hasa from this time probably dates to the early centuries after the conquest, before changes in the tax structure led many small farmers to abandon their holdings for a more nomadic existence.

The Christian Crusades to the Holy Land reached the vicinity of the Hasa during the Ayyubid period, when crusader castles were built nearby at Kerak and Tafila, just to the north and south respectively of the study area. During the twelfth and thirteenth centuries, the fear of conflict and the proximity of Western powers again in this region undoubtedly had some effect on the local populace, but there is no evidence of Westerners' presence in the Hasa, and their power may not have extended far into the countryside. Holt (1986) suggests, however, that the eastward shift of the Hajj road was a consequence of Crusader control over the areas around Kerak and Shaubak on the western plateau. Humphreys (1977) argues furthermore that the Transjordan plateau became increasingly important during the Crusader period because it was the main transportation route from Egypt to Syria that was not in Crusader control. He notes that al-though the area was not considered rich, it was strategically very impor-tant, and there was a trend toward centralization and militarization as the Ayyubids tried to rein in local principalities.

The Late Islamic Period

The beginning of the Late Islamic period, as defined in this area by MacDonald (personal communication, October 2000), is marked by the rise of the Mamluks of Egypt in the mid-fourteenth century CE. Both the Mamluk period and the following Ottoman period were notable for the renewed expansion of stability and prosperity in the fourteenth to sixteenth centuries (Adnanal-Bakhit 1982; Bosworth 1967). The Mamluks' primary capital was in Cairo, but their secondary capital was located in Kerak, and their interest in Transjordan undoubtedly was a factor in renewed stability in this area (Johns 1992; Peake 1958). The survey record of the Hasa indicates only four Ayyubid/Mamluk settlements. However, a total of seventy-four undifferentiated Late Islamic potential agropastoral sites were recorded, and it is likely that some of them date to the Mamluk period. This number represents a threefold increase over the total number of Early Islamic sites recorded. The lack of refinement in Islamic period ceramic chronology extends into this period, and it seems likely that more precise dating will reveal a greater number of settlements from this period.

In general, historians are inclined to praise the Mamluk administration for expanding security for farmers and the Hajj pilgrimage route, as well as for promoting a great cultural and artistic efflorescence (Adnanal-Bakhit 1982; Bosworth 1967). Adnanal-Bakhit notes that almost all towns, villages, hamlets, manors, quarters, and tribes of Jordan today were established by the sixteenth century CE. He also argues that most inhabitants of the region were settled in towns and villages or were seminomadic with agriculture as their main source of income. Toward the end of the Mamluk period, prosperity was somewhat threatened by the Portuguese diversion of international trade, and the brief decline in Mamluk control over this area was quickly filled by Ottoman authority in 1516 CE (Bosworth 1967).

The Ottoman period is the final temporal division recorded by archaeological survey in the Hasa. It is interesting that it is also one of the longest periods of ostensibly uninterrupted rule since the beginning of centralized authority in the region. Dating from the early sixteenth century to the early twentieth century, it lasted longer than any other state-level organization in the Levant except the combined Roman and Byzantine Empires. The Ottoman rulers were quite powerful and at times even efficient, but their longevity in this area must be attributed in some measure to a lack of competition. A large part of the Ottoman period in Jordan was typified by a lack of effective centralized authority and domination by local tribes outside the scope of Ottoman control (Faroqhi 1997; McGowan 1997; Mousa 1982). The time period from the late sixteenth century to the late nineteenth century was probably the longest period of social and economic decline since at least the end of the Iron Age and perhaps the

Middle and Late Bronze Ages. It represents in that regard an excellent, relatively recent view of this region during a state of abandonment and decay (Harlan 1985, 1988).

The early Ottoman period during the sixteenth century CE was evidently a time of renewed stability and investment in the Hasa and in Jordan in general. Much of the interest in the Hasa had to do with the defense of religious pilgrims on their way to Mecca. It was probably during this period that the Qal'at al-Hasa (WHS 1074) and the Hajj road (WHS 1073) were built, or at least significantly improved (MacDonald 1988; Peterson 1986). But there were also efforts to provide peace and better protection of peasants, resulting in increases in cultivated arable land, population, and urban development (Inalcik 1997). The Turkish authorities frequently tried to replace the feudal control of land with a standardized *cift-hane* or labor-land combination of taxation equal to 10 percent of economic value of yearly produce. Nomadic peoples were also encouraged to settle and extend cultivation during the early Ottoman period. These improvements in stability and the extension of cultivation have led Hütteroth and Abdulfattah (Hütteroth 1975; Hütteroth and Abdulfattah 1977) to call this the golden age of the Ottoman Empire.

By the end of the sixteenth century, however, Jordan was to fall into a state of economic and demographic decline that would last for more than 250 years. The cause of this decline included an imbalance between rapid population growth and limited food resources that led to land exhaustion, desertification, and epidemics (Inalcik 1997). But political and economic factors also contributed to the dramatic decline in settled life. Inalcik cites the avoidance of attack by passing troops, brigand bands, and caravans as major reasons for peasants' leaving their villages. He notes also that a particularly relevant reason for abandonment was to avoid paying taxes. One of the most effective means of avoiding excessive taxation was to threaten abandonment of the land. During times of famine, the Bedouin raided cultivated lands and destroyed fields, presumably in a form of mass protest. Sharon (1975) notes also that when the Bedouin began to acquire guns in the late sixteenth century CE, it became very difficult for the Ottoman authorities to control them.

By 1597 CE, the number of abandoned settlements was two to three times the number of permanently occupied villages (Inalcik 1997). Hütteroth and Abdulfattah (Hütteroth 1975; Hütteroth and Abdulfattah 1977) and Faroqhi (1997) show that many late-sixteenth-century settlements close to the desert fringe were given up, while those in hilly country survived much better. Hütteroth uses historical maps to show 45–85 percent abandonment of the Transjordan plateau during this period. Faroqhi uses this evidence to argue that abandonment was in large part owing to insecurity, and he notes that war demands weighed heavily on peasants. As centralized authority broke down and the tax base declined, provincial administrators and their tax farmers increased demands on peasants and craftsmen, leading to further abandonment.

The widespread abandonment of settlements on the plateau lasted until the late nineteenth century, when reforms in the Ottoman Empire began to spread to the more distant provinces (Mousa 1982; Quataert 1997). By the late nineteenth century, the sultan attempted to shore up the empire's Islamic foundations, and considerable investment was made to develop stronger ties to the Arab provinces (Akarli 1986). Part of the reform process involved the subjugation of nomadic tribes, and the armed forces began again to establish security for agricultural producers (Quataert 1997). Many nomadic peoples were either forced to settle or saw advantages to a settled life at this time. Those who remained defiant withdrew into the desert, and vast areas of land previously marginally cultivated or held by pastoral nomads saw an increase in settlement and agricultural production. However, Istanbul failed to replace the tax farmers, and agricultural tax remained controlled by local elites until the end of the empire.

In the Hasa, 110 sites with potential agropastoral components dating to the Late Islamic period were recorded. Of these, 31 were attributed to the Ottoman or late Ottoman period, and undoubtedly many, if not most, of the 74 undifferentiated Late Islamic sites also date to this time. Although only 3 Ottoman period villages have been recorded, 34 undifferentiated Late Islamic towns and villages, and a further 31 farms, domestic clusters, hamlets, and structure complexes have been recorded. Of these smaller sites, 14 were clearly Ottoman, and the remainder were undifferentiated Late Islamic. Given the abundant historical record of abandonment throughout Jordan during the middle Ottoman period, it is probable that most sites from this period date to the sixteenth and the late nineteenth to early twentieth centuries, when Ottoman authority was strongest in the region.

Although eleven qasr/forts were recorded with Late Islamic or Ottoman components, the majority of them are indicated only by a handful of sherds and probably represent squatter occupations of earlier structures. Only a few fortifications indicate Ottoman military presence, and they are concentrated on the Hajj road. It is likely that throughout much of the Ottoman period, military presence in the area was restricted to protecting the religious pilgrimage route.

The majority of Late Islamic sites probably date to the nearly two and one-half centuries of relative prosperity and stability of the Mamluk and early Ottoman periods. As noted earlier, this density of settlement represents a dramatic increase over the Early Islamic period. This increase was followed by an equivalent period of abandonment and retreat to the uplands of the western plateau as the threat of Bedouin raiding increased. It was during the early nineteenth century that European explorers began to penetrate this region and to describe it. Harlan (1985, 1988) uses these accounts to document a landscape largely depleted of human inhabitants but rich in natural flora and fauna. Early European accounts typically describe the plateau as rich grassland with large numbers of wild animals and abandoned villages. They describe the Hasa as an aggrading stream full of water and fish, where many village ruins were populated by birds and other game that Arab boys hunted with ease.

In other parts of the southern Levant, the Islamic period in general has been described as a time in which a great deal of land degradation occurred (Naveh and Dan 1973). Terraces and other agricultural improvements dating to the Classical periods were not maintained and fell into decay, which resulted in the loss of once productive agricultural resources and the erosion of upland soils no longer supported by well-maintained terraces. To the extent that such processes occurred in the Hasa, it is reasonable to expect that they occurred in large part during the centuries of Ottoman period abandonment.

Finally, in the last decades before the British Mandate and the beginning of the modern state of Jordan, there was a renewed expansion of settlement and economic prosperity that continues to the present time. With the development of improved military and transportation technology, settlement was once again expanded into desert fringe areas that had been controlled by Bedouin and only modestly cultivated for centuries. However, villagers were still often required to pay protection money to the Bedouin and were generally engaged in cooperative economic exchanges with them (Mousa 1982). In the meantime, many locals resisted Ottoman tax collectors and were hostile to their authority, resulting in the Kerak revolt of 1910 and the Arab revolt of World War I. The Arab revolt, including the capture of the railway station at Jurf ad-Darawish and the battle of Tafila in the Hasa, contributed significantly to the defeat of the Ottoman Empire in the war and thus to the end of the Ottoman period (Lawrence 1938). Following the British Mandate period, the modern state of Jordan was established, and the area was returned to local, state-level authority for the first time in more than a thousand years.

Cycles of Political Hierarchy

The preceding discussion is meant to provide a background against which to evaluate hypotheses of land management. As noted in chapter 2, it has been widely hypothesized that when political organization becomes hierarchically differentiated, the decision-making process is separated from the consequences of those decisions. Under conditions of centralized hierarchy, especially with geographically distant authority, the motivation and information to practice locally sustainable agropastoralism will be diminished. As a consequence, producers are pressured to overexploit resources, contrary to their own knowledge and self-interest. The Hasa area is an ideal location in which to evaluate this hypothesis. It is an area of generally marginal agricultural productivity that is susceptible to overexploitation with easily recognized results such as erosion. Moreover, it has been repeatedly subjected to political conquest by foreign rulers relatively uninterested in local inhabitants' long-term well-being. The primary reasons for conquest have typically been payment of tribute, establishment of a frontier buffer zone, and the maintenance of transportation corridors for trade and pilgrimage. Cycles of conquest have typically been followed by a return to decentralized local authority.

The implication of this hypothesis is that under conditions of increased hierarchy and foreign domination, we should see evidence of more exploitative, less sustainable land management. Evaluation of the hypothesis requires some clarification of concepts and how they are to be measured. First, what is political hierarchy, and how do we measure it? An abundant literature exists on the nature and development of political complexity that is not necessary to reproduce here. For present purposes, we can define *political hierarchy* as any political system in which the decision-making process is removed from local producers. In actuality, there may be no clear dividing line between hierarchical and nonhierarchical organization, but rather a continuum of increasing complexity. At a minimum, some type of chiefdom level of organization would probably be necessary to cause a separation between the decision makers and the producers in society. The systematic mismanagement proposed by the current model would be most problematic at the state level, where there are institutionalized, permanent differences between classes of society engaged in the various functions of management and production.

Chiefdom-level political organization has been proposed for neighboring areas of the southern Levant by the Chalcolithic period and has been proposed as a factor in anthropogenic environmental degradation at that time. However, in the Hasa there is currently no good reason to suspect such political complexity at this early date. The level of political organization most likely to result in land mismanagement did not occur until the Early Bronze Age at the earliest. Since that time, political hierarchy has been a feature of every identifiable archaeological culture in the area, rendering distinction between periods of hierarchy and nonhierarchy problematic. In its actual expression in daily affairs, however, political hierarchy waxed and waned repeatedly. Thus, the question becomes simultaneously theoretically possible and practically difficult to address. Theoretically, the fact that the actual manifestation of political complexity varied in time makes it possible to evaluate land management accordingly. Practically speaking, variability is difficult to distinguish within broad chronological periods.

The measurement of political hierarchy in the Hasa must rely in large part on inference from regional culture history. Inference of political hierarchy and its relation to land management must be made at the level of a few major distinctions over the course of history. Political organization in the Hasa can be divided into the following categories through time. The late-prehistoric Neolithic and Chalcolithic periods were characterized by increasing intensification of agropastoral land use under a fairly egalitarian political system. Small villages, hamlets, farms, and seasonal encampments were the norm, but decision making and land management were probably organized along family or segmented lineage lines.

The Bronze Age, Hellenistic, and much of the Islamic periods were characterized by the tenuous hold of chiefdom- and state-level authority over an agrarian populace largely independent in their daily economic practice, but subject to attack and tribute demands. During these periods, the Hasa came under the influence and even the nominal dominion of foreign powers who were often unable to maintain a physical presence in the area. Small seasonal and permanent settlements were occupied during these periods, but most economic activity was probably subsistence based, and decision making was largely in local, family, or segmented lineage hands.

The Iron Age, Nabatean, and perhaps Islamic periods such as the Ummayad and Mamluk were times when the Hasa was under relatively local, state-level authority. The Iron Age kingdoms of Moab and Edom were the first indigenous complex societies in the area with local centers of authority. Though Mesopotamian powers did make significant encroachments into the Hasa during the Iron Age, they were relatively infrequent, leaving most daily management decisions in local hands.

The Nabatean period includes a highly developed state with a nearby locus of authority and major centers within the current study area. Although state-level authority during Islamic periods such as the Ummayad and Mamluk was not truly local, it did have some indigenous characteristics. The Ummayad dynasty was of Arab ethnicity, with its capital relatively nearby in Damascus, in contrast to the preceding centuries of Roman and Byzantine rule. The early days of the Islamic conquest were marked by attempts to place authority in the hands of loyal followers of Mohammed rather than of the Byzantine administrators and military leaders whose loyalty, and often origins, were in distant regions of the empire.

The Mamluk period is notable in that nearby Kerak was considered a second capital of the Mamluk state, with a significant presence of authority only a few kilometers from the current study area. Throughout the Iron Age, Nabatean, Ummayad, and Mamluk periods, there were numerous prosperous villages and farms, and economic decision making was probably somewhat hierarchical. Regular tribute and tax demands would have been necessary to support elites.

The Roman and Byzantine periods as well as parts of the Ottoman period were marked by a strong foreign presence in the Hasa, with a significant interest in economic decision making. These periods represent the most centralized, hierarchical, and distant political authority to have ever maintained a strong presence in the Hasa. The Roman period was the first time that the Hasa was brought under the regular political control of a foreign empire that had the means or desire to maintain constant military and administrative presence. That presence continued uninterrupted through the Byzantine period and was characterized by relatively large population centers, agricultural production, and major investment in military and economic infrastructure. Economic production would have been strongly shaped by state demands and the necessity to support a large bureaucracy. Agricultural settlement was encouraged, and some production would have been oriented toward export for foreign markets.

During the early and very late Ottoman periods, Turkish authority in Istanbul also made significant efforts to encourage agricultural settlement and to maintain economic and military control over the area. During most of the middle Ottoman period, Turkish presence in the Hasa was minimal, and political power was more typically decentralized and local. Many villages and towns occupied during the early and late Ottoman periods were abandoned during the middle Ottoman period. Economic production during the peaks of Ottoman control was largely influenced by tax demands and the need to support a state bureaucracy. It was also affected by the manipulative practices of state-sponsored tax farmers who preyed on local producers for their own enrichment.

The political history of the Hasa can thus be divided into four rough categories of hierarchical authority:

Lowest—Neolithic, Chalcolithic
Medium Low—Bronze Age, Hellenistic, ʿAbbasid, Fatimid, Ayyubid, middle Ottoman
Medium High—Iron Age, Nabatean, Ummayad, Mamluk
High—Roman, Byzantine, early and late Ottoman

Two aspects of this categorization are notable. First, the division of earlier periods is less fine grained than later periods. For example, the Neolithic endured for thousands of years, whereas the Ummayad lasted less than a hundred. To some extent, this difference is a function of the different temporal resolution of the data at different times in the past. However, more variation probably existed in the political authority expressed in more recent periods than in earlier periods. Thus, for the purpose of differentiating degrees of political hierarchy, the variability in the lengths of periods is appropriate.

Second, there may have been more variability in political authority even during well-known periods such as the Roman and Byzantine than a simple categorization conveys. For example, foreign political concern with frontier areas such as the Hasa changed as larger military and economic interrelationships changed within periods of general domination by a single power. However, division into more, or more fine-grained, categories would not be warranted by the present data and would sacrifice the heuristic value of a simplified model.

I consider the analyses in chapters 5 and 6 in relation to these divisions among differing levels of political hierarchy with the aim of evaluating the role of political hierarchy through time in land management. But first I consider the landscape history of the Hasa as a complement to the culture history. Chapter 4 is directed toward a synthesis of how the Hasa landscape has changed through time as an economic resource.

4

The Evolution of the Physical Landscape

Just as human society has undergone profound change during the past ten thousand years, the appearance of the Wadi al-Hasa landscape and its surrounding area is dramatically different than it was at the beginning of the Holocene. This chapter provides an overview of what is known about those changes and what can reasonably be proposed based on current evidence.

For present purposes, the study area is divided into three geographic zones (fig. 4.1). First, the wadi, or gorge, comprises the floodplain and fluvial terraces on both sides that are present throughout the Hasa drainage system. These areas have been the locus of most agropastoralist activity focused on the water and soil resources of the fluvial system. Also included in the wadi zone is the lower portion of steep slopes that ascend from the floodplain to the surrounding uplands. The wadi zone ranges in elevation from approximately 815 meters amsl down to almost 400 meters bmsl, where it flows into the Dead Sea. The wadi slopes are the location of several archaeological sites and were also used for some agropastoral production. Due to the instability of soils there, however, and the difficulties inherent in irrigating plots elevated above the wadi channel, most productive activity has been restricted to livestock grazing and farming in the vicinity of springs that issue from the wadi sides.

The second zone consists of the upland plateaus primarily to the north and south of the Hasa drainage system and the upper parts of slopes above the escarpment. The plateau typically ranges from approximately 1,000 meters to 1,300 meters amsl. These plateaus currently have the richest agricultural production in the study area and among the richest in Jordan owing to their relatively high rainfall and rich soils. Although they do not appear to have been as intensively occupied during the early Holocene as the lowland areas, they have since become the locus of the great majority of permanent occupation in the study area. In addition to their higher productivity, the upland areas may be more easily defended from attack and have often attracted settlement during periods of political insecurity.

The third zone of interest is the easternmost part of the study area, where the plateau and the wadi bottomlands meet in the vicinity of an-

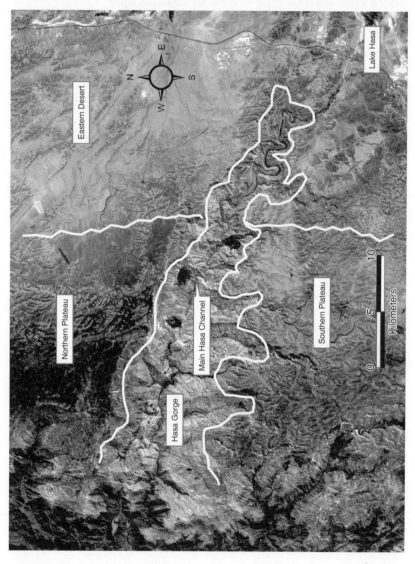

Figure 4.1 Approximate geographic zones discussed in text

cient Lake Hasa. Because the plateau slopes downward to the east as part of the Nubian-Arabian Shield (Bender 1974:21), and the Hasa drainage flows downward to the west toward the Wadi Araba and the Dead Sea, a zone is created in the upstream part of the drainage system that has elements of both plateau and wadi zones. It is at an intermediate elevation of approximately 815 meters amsl and is consequently quite arid, yet has modest topographic relief and broader arable soils than most wadi bottomlands (Willimott et al. 1963). The eastern Hasa has often been the locus of settlement activity. In some instances, economic activity has been focused on the area's productive potential, especially around the former lake and in the alluvial soils near the wadi channel (Clark et al. 1992; Clark et al. 1994; MacDonald 1988; Neeley et al. 1998; Olszewski et al. 1998). In more recent periods, activity has been focused on the suitability of north-south transportation in the relatively low-relief topography along this edge of the plateau (MacDonald 1988). The eastern end of the gorge has also been used as an entry point for transportation to wadi-bottom and lowland areas (MacDonald 1988).

Each of these zones has undergone different kinds and rates of change related primarily to climate and anthropogenic influences. I discuss landscape evolution in chronological order from the earliest to most recent changes, presenting evidence of the effects to each of the zones.

The Eastern Hasa

At the end of the Pleistocene, the area was affected by climate warming that signaled the end of that geological epoch. The geographic zone most intensively studied for the late Pleistocene and probably most dramatically affected by climate change at that time is the eastern Hasa. This area was dominated by a large lake and marsh system with springs along the shore (Schuldenrein 1998; Schuldenrein and Clark 1994). The extent of this lacustrine system has not been fully mapped, but archaeological and geoarchaeological research indicates that human activity was focused on the lake and its associated resources (Clark et al. 1992; Clark et al. 1994; Neeley et al. 1998; Olszewski et al. 1998; Schuldenrein 1998; Schuldenrein and Clark 1994, 2001).

The existence of an ancient lake in the eastern Hasa was first noted during a soil survey by Willimott and colleagues (1963), who perceived that the area was formerly an internally drained system. Since that time, Vita-Finzi and Copeland (Copeland and Vita-Finzi 1978; Vita-Finzi 1966), and Schuldenrein and Clark (Schuldenrein 1998; Schuldenrein and Clark 1994, 2001) have studied the alluvial and lacustrine deposits associated with the lake and the upper Hasa channel. Their efforts were directed toward the timing of the lake's disappearance and the formation of intermediate fluvial terraces between the upper lake deposits and the current channel. In addition, Schuldenrein and Clark noted tufas of ancient springs at the western edge of Lake Hasa that would have provided freshwater when water tables were higher than they are today.

The analysis of sediments and their positions indicate that a lake/marsh system extended from a western edge near the upper end of the Hasa gorge to several kilometers east of the Desert Highway. The eastern edge of the lake remains unknown at present, but, given the low gradient of the plain, it is likely that the lake could have extended 10 kilometers or more to the east of the Desert Highway for a total east-west dimension of approximately 16 kilometers (Willimott et al. 1963). The north-south dimension is equally uncertain, but Willimott and colleagues noted that the wadi floor attained a width of 6 kilometers to the east of the Desert Highway. More recently, Moumani (1996, 1997) has noted similar deposits, indicating a lacustrine setting a few kilometers to the south of the Hasa near Jurf ad-Darawish. Archaeological reconnaissance in that vicinity indicates extensive late Pleistocene human activity there as well (MacDonald 1999; MacDonald et al. 2001). Preliminary examination of LandSat photographs of the eastern Hasa and Jurf ad-Darawish area suggests that the lake systems in the two areas were closely related (see also Moumani 1996). Current evidence indicates that a system of lakes, at times covering several dozen square kilometers, dominated the eastern Hasa area during the late Pleistocene (Moumani, Alexander, and Bateman 2003).

Such a large, shallow lake system would have undoubtedly fluctuated in size and mineral content over time. During relatively dry periods, Lake Hasa may have been reduced to a system of brackish ponds and marshes with only a few springs providing freshwater (Schuldenrein 1998; Schuldenrein and Clark 1994, 2001). The onset of a warmer and at times drier climate during the late Pleistocene would probably have reduced the lake to this condition prior to its disappearance.

The Disappearance of Lake Hasa

The timing and cause of the disappearance of Lake Hasa are still somewhat in doubt, and at least two theories about this process have been proposed. Willimott and colleagues (1963) suggested that the internal drainage basin probably disappeared when it was captured by headward erosion of the Hasa channel (see also Clark et al. 1992). In other words, drainage at the western end of the lake would previously have been toward an internal basin to the east. As headward channel incision of floodplain sediments in the Hasa migrated upstream, it eventually incised the western edge of the lake, causing the lake to drain and water tables to be lowered. Drainage in the eastern Hasa was subsequently reversed to join the incised channel of the lower Hasa flowing to the west.

Since Willimott and colleagues' 1963 proposal, Schuldenrein and Clark (Schuldenrein 1998; Schuldenrein and Clark 1994, 2001) have offered an alternative hypothesis in which Lake Hasa was breached at a point somewhat downstream by the Hasa fault. Faults are present and visible in the vicinity they propose, and the general area is well known for tectonic activity in association with the Jordan Rift fault. It is conceivable that tectonic movement in the area of the western edge of Lake Hasa contributed to a breach of the basin's confines and consequently to the lake's drainage. At present, however, there is no evidence for a connection between tectonic movement in the late Pleistocene and the disappearance of Lake Hasa, and the proposal remains based on the coincidence of general evidence of faulting and the obvious disappearance of the lake.

Currently, the headward incision proposal is more parsimonious and hence more likely. The breach and drainage of the lake can be explained simply by the incision of the Hasa channel into the western edge of the basin. Based on determinations of the lowest elevations in the basin and the highest elevations of identified lacustrine sediments, Lake Hasa was probably not more than 20 meters deep (Schuldenrein 1998; Schuldenrein and Clark 1994, 2001). A high terrace that represents the highest floodplain in the wadi during the late Pleistocene was incised approximately 20 meters in its upper channel at some time in the early to middle Holocene. The incision documented by this high terrace would have been sufficient by itself to breach and drain the lake. It is also likely, however, that there was not much of a lake to drain by the time this incision occurred. After many years of climate change, the lake may have been largely evaporated by the time its drainage was captured (Schuldenrein 1998; Schuldenrein and Clark 1994, 2001). However, its incision would still have had significant consequences for the water table and springs.

Thus, a dominant feature of the environment in the eastern Hasa had disappeared or was greatly reduced by the early to middle Holocene. The lake would at times have provided water suitable for human consumption, but was likely brackish as it was exposed to relatively high evaporation and concentration of minerals. However, the presence of such a high water table would have increased the number of springs in its vicinity, such as those found at 'Ain al-Buhira (WHS 618) and Yutil al-Hasa (WHS 784) (Clark et al. 1994; Schuldenrein 1998; Schuldenrein and Clark 1994). In addition to these water sources, the lake and its environs would have been home to a wide variety of the plant and animal species utilized by hunter-gatherer and incipient cultivator populations in this region during the Epipaleolithic and early Neolithic. The disappearance of this large lake and its associated resources would have been a profound loss to human populations in the area.

The disappearance of Lake Hasa is thought to have begun in the late Pleistocene, 15–12 ka, following high levels as late as 18 ka (Schuldenrein 1998; Schuldenrein and Clark 1994, 2001). However, if the lake basin was intact until the early to middle Holocene, it may have retained pockets of water and life, and even been somewhat rejuvenated when precipitation levels were relatively high. If the lake basin remained intact until a later date, the pronounced increase in precipitation noted for the Pre-Pottery Neolithic, the Chalcolithic, and the Early Bronze Age may have caused it to again become an attractive resource for humans in the area.

Late-surviving lake remnants have been associated with the relatively high number of Neolithic and Chalcolithic sites recently found around the edge of Wadi Juheira Lake (MacDonald 1999; MacDonald et al. 2001). Notably, a Chalcolithic component was documented at an otherwise Middle Paleolithic lake-edge site in the eastern Hasa (Schuldenrein and Clark 1994), and numerous undifferentiated "late" (probably late-prehistoric or early-historic) lithics were recorded in the vicinity by the WHS project (MacDonald 1988). More recently, Olszewski (personal communication December 2004) has documented a late Pre-Pottery Neolithic B component at the lake-edge Epipaleolithic site of Tor al-Tareeq (WHS 1065).

The evidence suggests that Lake Hasa or related bodies of water may have existed in various manifestations, including patches of marsh oasis, until relatively recent times. The dissection of the lake basin by headward erosion of the Hasa channel would have made the retention of water during later periods less likely. However, an August 1981 LandSat photo shows a significant amount of water in part of the Hasa basin just east of the Hasa station and near a large phosphate-mining operation, suggesting that conditions were still conducive to ponding in the present era. This ponding is likely related to the mining operation, but it may indicate that a closed basin in this area can still retain winter precipitation through the dry summer.

Ecology of the Eastern Hasa

The plant and animal remains from archaeological sites dating to the late Pleistocene in the eastern Hasa indicate a steppe environment with a strong riparian component associated with the lake basin. Species of mammals recovered at the late Pleistocene site of Tor al-Tareeq (WHS 1065) include *Testudo* (tortoise), *Gazella* (gazelle), *Bos* (auroch), *Equus* (horse, ass, zebra), *Ovis/Capra* (probably ibex), and avifauna (Neeley et al. 1998). Faunal remains at the slightly earlier site of 'Ain al-Buhira are similar and include species such as *Struthio* (ostrich [eggshell]) (Olszewski et al. 1998). The equid, gazelle, and ostrich remains are consistent with an open grassland environment. These animals were undoubtedly an important resource for steppe hunter-gatherers throughout much of the late Pleistocene and early Holocene. Conversely, the pig and perhaps auroch remains are consistent with woodland or riparian vegetation that is their preferred habitat. The presence of a large body of water in the eastern Hasa would also have supported waterfowl, fish, shellfish, and a wide variety of plant species. Pollen profiles include *Typha* (cattail), *Salix* (riparian willow), *Alnus* (Alder), and *Quercus* (oak) (Schuldenrein and Clark 1994), but the predominance of nonarboreal taxa indicates an open steppe environment (Neeley et al. 1998). A diversity of animal and plant resources were a feature of the broad-spectrum adaptation of the Epipaleolithic and early Neolithic (Bar-Yosef 1995; Bar-Yosef and Belfer-Cohen 1989).

The disappearance of the lake and the decrease in precipitation associated with the Younger Dryas and the Holocene dramatically reduced the quantity and variety of resources available to humans. Paleoclimate records indicate that precipitation reached extreme lows by 13.2–11.4 ka during the Younger Dryas and levels comparable to the present by as early as 11 ka (Bar-Matthews et al. 1999; Goodfriend 1999). Current precipitation in the eastern Hasa is around 10 centimeters a year, falling almost entirely in the winter (Royal Jordanian Geographic Centre 1986). Such low levels of rainfall probably would not support the grasses required by large herds of animals. Nor would they maintain the lake and shoreline that was present during wetter periods. During dry cycles, utilization of the eastern Hasa would have been restricted to areas that could be watered from intermittent flow in the main channel and from the few springs and ponds that may have survived. A limited amount of low-intensity seasonal pastoralism was possible as nomadic groups moved through this area to and from resource patches in other areas.

An important natural resource to humans in the eastern Hasa during the late Pleistocene and the beginnings of sedentism and cultivation was lost during subsequent millennia of relative drought. It is likely that at times since the demise of Lake Hasa, climate shifts improved the potential habitability of this area. Although the eastern Hasa is currently quite arid and lacking in subsistence resources, one must travel only a few kilometers to the west to find plateau grasslands capable of supporting grazing animals. Periodic increases in precipitation that are well documented throughout the Holocene may have allowed the plateau grasslands to extend into the eastern Hasa. During these periods, pastoralists probably extended their land use into the newly open grasslands. Likewise, increased precipitation may have rejuvenated springs, streams, and ponds in the eastern Hasa, allowing for expanded agricultural production based on irrigation from renewed water sources. There is a distinct periodic fluctuation in the eastern extension of settlement throughout the Holocene that may be a reflection of fluctuating agropastoral resources in an east-west manner as precipitation levels changed.

The Hasa Gorge

The deep gorge that drains toward the Dead Sea to the west of Lake Hasa is a result of millions of years of downcutting through bedrock as the Transjordan plateau uplifted relative to the Dead Sea graben (Donahue and Beynon 1988). The bedrock bottom of the gorge was incised to its current state long before the archaeological presence of interest here and had undergone repeated cycles of incision and aggradation. For example, at Multaqa al-Widyan (WHNBS 192–96) there is evidence that the Hasa floodplain was aggrading in the early Upper Paleolithic (Olszewski et al. 1998). In situ archaeological materials there indicate that well in excess of 4 meters of fine-grained alluvial (and probably aeolian) sediments were deposited since the early Upper Paleolithic occupation. Likewise, there is evidence at Tabaqa (WHS 895) that the Hasa floodplain was aggrading at approximately 28 ka (Schuldenrein and Clark 2001) and continued to do so some time after the early Natufian presence in the Epipaleolithic (Olszewski et al. 1998; Olszewski and Hill 1997). A large early Natufian component at Tabaqa is buried by approximately 2 meters of fine-grained sediment.

There is currently no evidence of major sedimentary discontinuity between these occupational sequences at Multaqa al-Widyan and Tabaqa, and it appears that aggradation was virtually continuous from at least the early Upper Paleolithic until post-Natufian times. However, given the large-scale climatic fluctuations that occurred in the southern Levant during the late Pleistocene and early Holocene, it is very unlikely that a stable aggradational regime was maintained continuously for twenty to thirty thousand years. It is more likely that cycles of deposition and erosion occurred on the floodplain throughout this time period that remain poorly understood at present. Yet no stratigraphic evidence currently exists for large-scale episodes of incision like those that occurred later.

The Fluvial Terraces

The accumulated sediments of the late Pleistocene formed a paired high terrace whose remnants are visible virtually continuously on both sides of the Hasa gorge from the eastern end down to the western edge of the WHS study area near Khirbet Hammam. Although small remnants of this terrace are visible along the sides of the gorge in many places, they form sizable ledges in locations where they have been protected from the massive episode of erosion that subsequently removed the majority of the sediment of the abandoned floodplain represented by the terrace. These locations include especially the outside curves of large meanders in the gorge and at the confluence of the Hasa and its major tributaries, where the gorge widens considerably.

This high terrace has been designated the "Tabaqa" terrace, so named for the Natufian site associated with its upper strata near the confluence of the Wadi al-Hasa and the Wadi Ahmar (Hill 2001). The Tabaqa terrace is composed in its upper strata of finely laminated, light-brown silty sediments indicative of a low-energy fluvial/paludal system. Within these deposits are numerous dark organic layers, suggesting a marshy environment with abundant vegetation and relatively slow sediment accumulation (Olszewski et al. 1998). The Tabaqa terrace ranges in height from 35 meters above the wadi bottom at the Wadi Ahmar to as much as 60 meters in the western part of the study area. At its eastern end, where the terrace articulates with the lacustrine sediments of Lake Hasa, it appears to be as low as 20 meters.

The site of Tabaqa is actually located next to an ancient oxbow lake formed in a meander of the Wadi Ahmar just 200 meters upstream from its confluence with the Hasa (Olszewski et al. 1998; Olszewski and Hill 1997). The location of a large Natufian site in such a setting is indicative of the type of environment that existed there in the late Pleistocene. Natufian sites in the southern Levant are typically located near riparian habitat suitable to the broad range of plant and animal species upon which they subsisted. The oxbow lake at Tabaqa was probably part of a slow meandering stream in an aggrading fluvial system. The presence of numerous organic deposits indicates that this system was often a setting for abundant riparian vegetation (Olszewski et al. 1998; Olszewski and Hill 1997). Without further paleobotanical and zooarchaeological analyses, we cannot say in detail what types of flora and fauna lived there, but it is reasonable to infer that a broad floodplain with considerably more abundance and diversity of life was then found along the Hasa than at present.

The Tabaqa terrace represents a late Pleistocene environment that was dramatically altered when the aggradational regime was reversed and channel incision began to lower the water table and erode the floodplain. Since that time, the channel has been incised 20–60 meters, and nearly the entire ancient floodplain has been completely removed. The timing of this transition has been the subject of interest to geomorphologists working in the Hasa since at least the 1960s, when Vita-Finzi (1966) described the deposits there. It is of interest to the present discussion because it is clear from archaeological testing at Tabaqa that alluvial deposition continued long enough after the Natufian occupation to accumulate 2 meters of additional sediment. It is important with regard to the Holocene environment to know when the Tabaqa floodplain began to incise and the Hasa gorge began to take on its present characteristics.

I evaluated the relationships among terraces in the Hasa system using archaeological evidence recovered during surveys (Hill 2001). I originally hoped that relocation of Neolithic, Chalcolithic, and Early Bronze Age sites from the MacDonald (1988) and Clark and colleagues (1992, 1994) surveys would reveal stratigraphic evidence with which to bracket the end of the Tabaqa terrace aggradation and its subsequent incision. Based on the published data, I relocated several Pre-Pottery Neolithic sites and all of the Pottery Neolithic and Chalcolithic/Early Bronze Age sites associated with the wadi channels. I examined a total of fifteen Neolithic and Chalcolithic/Early Bronze Age sites with respect to their positions on fluvial terraces, but could identify no verified in situ components that were buried by fluvial deposits of the Tabaqa terrace.

A notable pattern did emerge, however, in regard to site locations. All fifteen of the in situ Neolithic and Chalcolithic/Early Bronze Age components evaluated were located on or above the surface of the Tabaqa terrace. The additional Neolithic site of el-Hemmeh was unknown at the time of this reconnaissance, but its location on a terrace at least 50 meters above the current Hasa channel is consistent with other findings (Makarewicz and Goodale forthcoming). Remnants of the Tabaqa terrace large enough to support architectural remains are fairly infrequent, but they often do hold Neolithic or Chalcolithic/Early Bronze Age sites. No verifiable in situ remains from these periods have been located below the level of the Tabaqa terrace surface even though the huge majority of relatively level land is found along lower terraces. In addition, virtually every archaeological period postdating the Chalcolithic is represented by sites at lower elevations.

From a geological standpoint, surface materials lack the positive implications of buried stratified indices. Dated materials on the surface of a fluvial terrace are only an indication of the latest possible date of terrace formation and carry no logical implications regarding the maximum age of the surface. However, from a behavioral standpoint, the implications of patterning in the archaeological record may be significant with regard to interpreting the landscape options available to people in the past.

For example, the extant surface of the Tabaqa terrace represents a very small proportion of the present land surface in close proximity to the wadi channels. It is therefore extremely unlikely as a statistical matter that all Neolithic and Chalcolithic/Early Bronze Age sites were randomly located on that surface. Archaeological site location is, of course, never random, but predicated on such concerns as access to resources (e.g., water, agricultural land) and defense. Given what is currently known about settlement in the Neolithic through Chalcolithic periods, it appears unlikely that people would have chosen to settle only on the ledges formed by isolated high-terrace remnants. Archaeological evidence from elsewhere in the southern Levant indicates that people chose settlement locations close to water sources and floodplain farmland. Bar-Yosef (1995) emphasizes the greater occupation of floodplains during the Pre-Pottery Neolithic as economic focus shifted to cultivation. Banning and colleagues (Banning 1995; Banning, Rahimi, and Siggers 1994) note that late Neolithic settlement in northern Jordan emphasized dispersed sites on bottomlands, where they are now buried. Gilead (1995) and Levy (1983a, 1983b, 1986) note that Chalcolithic settlement in the Negev is focused on nucleated valley settings, and a number of large Chalcolithic sites there are located in valley bottoms. Hanbury-Tenison (1986) suggests that Chalcolithic settlement was situated in open settings with easy mobility for pastoralists. These locations are typically either in valley-bottom locations or on high saddles, and he notes that no consideration seems to be given to defensive locations.

Late-prehistoric settlement locations in the Wadi al-Hasa are on a terrace that is currently high and relatively removed from the present floodplain. They are partway up steep, often unstable slopes, with awkward access to agropastoral resources either on the floodplain below or on the plateau above. Sites are typically overlooked by hills and steep slopes and would be difficult to defend from above. These settlement locations are difficult to explain in the current landscape. If they were focused on modern floodplain resources, one would expect some evidence of them to be located on lower terraces or on low spurs, of which there are many in the area.

The Tabaqa terrace currently consists of small patches of level terrain that are not irrigable with gravity-fed technology from the channel 20–60 meters below. In the past, these terrace remnants may have been subject to different hydrological conditions that made them irrigable from springs or runoff. If that were the case, however, there would have been a variety of such locations at different elevations throughout the drainage system. The fact that every site associated with the watercourse from the Neolithic through Chalcolithic/Early Bronze Age periods is at the level of the Tabaqa terrace suggests that lower-level surfaces were not viable settlement locations.

Based on the position of Neolithic remains on the surface of the Tabaqa terrace, this terrace had ceased aggrading by approximately 9 ka. The next best age of deposition in the Hasa comes from a single radiocarbon date of 3.95 ka, 1 meter below the surface of the Hasa terrace at the present valley floor. The intervening five thousand years of the early-middle Holocene represent a critical period of valley-floor evolution and cultural development in the Hasa. Yet practically nothing is known of this time period.

A lower terrace at approximately 20–25 meters above the current channel can be located at several places, including site WHS 428 and across the wadi from WHS 149 (Khirbet Hammam). This terrace is not continuous throughout the drainage, but several isolated remnants are possibly contemporaneous, and the terrace may correspond to Copeland and Vita-Finzi's (1978) Fill II. The mapping and dating of this terrace remain intriguing future research endeavors because it represents an important but poorly understood intermediate period in the Hasa valley-floor history.

A fruitful comparison may be drawn between the development of the Hasa valley-floor morphology and that of neighboring wadis a short distance to the north. Donahue and colleagues (Donahue 1985; Donahue, Peer, and Shaub 1997) have documented valley-floor changes of the middle Holocene at the wadis Numeira and Kerak a few kilometers to the north of the Hasa and draining from the Transjordan plateau to the Dead Sea. At both of these locations, they found evidence that the wadis underwent a long period of slow erosion and aggradation during the early Holocene, resulting in a gentle, bowl-shaped profile. This slow development was interrupted by a period of rapid downcutting of 28–50 meters in the Early Bronze Age IV period. This period of downcutting resulted in extensive erosion of lateral areas as well as a steep-sided lower profile of the channel bottoms. Donahue, Peer, and Shaub were aided in their precise dating of this sequence by large and well-documented Early Bronze Age sites adjacent to and severely affected by these changes. To date, no such documentation exists for this time period in the Hasa, but the similarities among the drainages warrants consideration of a similar process in the Hasa.

If the Hasa floodplain was similarly slowly eroded during the early Holocene and aggrading during the Early Bronze Age, the intermediate terrace below the Tabaqa terrace may date to this time. In places, the profile between the Tabaqa and intermediate terrace is more bowl shaped than other parts of the wadi side, but most of this terrace has been removed by lateral erosion.

Similarly, recent geomorphological and paleoenvironmental studies in the Wadi Faynan, a few kilometers to the south of the Hasa, indicate perennial flow in an aggrading channel above the current valley floor well into the early Holocene (Hunt et al. 2004). Hunt and colleagues additionally found evidence of much more humid conditions supporting a steppe/riparian forest environment until after approximately 7.4 ka, when increased precipitation did not result in increased arboreal vegetation. They attribute the absence of trees and an increase in alluviation after this time to the influence of Chalcolithic agropastoralism.

Major valley-floor developments in the Hasa may have been similar to those in adjacent drainages, and the intermediate terrace may have been a relatively stable surface throughout the early-middle Holocene. This surface and the watercourses associated with it would have been the resource of interest to Neolithic through Early Bronze Age populations in the Hasa. Most of this surface would have been lost to erosion following a dramatic period of incision in the Early Bronze Age IV. The higher elevation and more gentle profile of the valley floor during this period would account for the early Holocene occupation of the Tabaqa terrace, which would have been a more suitable settlement location in such conditions. The absence of early Holocene settlements at lower elevations may have been due to an avoidance of flooding in the valley bottom or to the subsequent erosion of archaeological remains at those elevations. Such a late date for large-scale erosion and channel incision in the Hasa is bolstered by and would help to explain other archaeological phenomena in this region.

Relatively little settlement is recorded in the Hasa for the Pottery Neolithic and Chalcolithic periods, when nearby areas were experiencing rapid settlement growth. Yet it has been suggested that in Transjordan there should be a counterpart to the western Beersheva and Ghassulian complexes (Hanbury-Tenison 1986; Lee 1973). If the intermediate terrace formed a more expansive surface in the Chalcolithic period, its current remnants represent a small fraction of its former extent. Extrapolating from the number of sites present on this remnant surface would suggest more Neolithic and Chalcolithic settlement in the Hasa than has previously been supposed. The potential for several dozen such Chalcolithic sites in the Wadi al-Hasa would be comparable to the number found in the Beersheva valley 60 kilometers to the west-northwest. The Beersheva valley shares some basic climatic and physiographic qualities with the Hasa, including being a major watercourse located at a desert/savanna ecotone (Levy and Goldberg 1987).

The land surface occupied by Chalcolithic settlers in the Beersheva valley remains relatively intact because it has not undergone the degree of channel incision that has occurred in the Hasa (Goldberg and Rosen 1987). The Beersheva and neighboring valleys have been the location of many of the best-known and most extensive archaeological sites from the Chalcolithic period (Levy 1992, 1995). If there was a significant Chalcolithic presence on the Transjordan plateau in places such as the Wadi al-Hasa, the absence of archaeological evidence there may be explained by the disappearance of the land surface most intensively used by the settlers. This possibility underscores the need for more archaeological research on the late-prehistoric periods in this part of the Levant.

Below the level of the intermediate terrace described earlier, at least three terraces date to the middle to late Holocene. Of these, only the second lowest or "Hasa" terrace is readily identifiable throughout the Wadi al-Hasa drainage system (Copeland and Vita-Finzi's [1978] Fill III). A second intermediate terrace is represented only by occasionally identifiable remnants approximately 8–12 meters above the current channel, and its date and extent are unclear at present. Likewise, the lowest terrace is found intermittently within the main channel and banked against the Hasa terrace deposits (Copeland and Vita-Finzi's [1978] Fill IV).

Some debate has appeared in the literature regarding the Hasa terrace and the lowest terrace. Copeland and Vita-Finzi (1978) dated the formation of the Hasa terrace (their Fill III) to the period from 8 to 2 ka based on buried archaeological materials and a single radiocarbon date. A recent radiocarbon date of 2.8 ka in the lowest 1 meter of the Hasa terrace is in general agreement with this conclusion (Schuldenrein and Clark 2001). Copeland and Vita-Finzi proposed that the Hasa terrace was incised at some point after 2 ka based on the position of a Nabatean/Roman retaining wall in the current channel, supporting terrace sediments against lateral erosion in the vicinity of a large Nabatean/Roman settlement (WHS 725, Umm Hraga) (MacDonald 1988).

Schuldenrein and Clark subsequently revised the date of the Hasa terrace based on an additional radiocarbon date of 1 ka near its surface (Schuldenrein 1998; Schuldenrein and Clark 1994). They proposed that it was still aggrading by 1 ka and that downcutting did not begin until four to five hundred years ago. The retaining wall predates Schuldenrein and Clark's radiocarbon date and supports Copeland and Vita-Finzi's date of incision at around 2 ka. This date is supported by evidence from a Roman bridge (WHS 535) downstream, dating to the early second century CE (MacDonald 1988), whose base is built in the current channel, below the level of the Hasa terrace. This bridge has alluvial sediments from Fill IV banked directly against it and subsequently incised, again supporting Copeland and Vita-Finzi's original interpretation of Fill IV deposition and incision during the Roman to medieval periods (Copeland and Vita-Finzi 1978).

The geomorphological and archaeological evidence presented here suggests that during the period from approximately 9 ka to 4.5 ka the Wadi al-Hasa valley was gradually incised from a late Pleistocene floodplain 20–60 meters above the current channel, forming a gentle basin 20–25 meters above the current channel. Between 4.5 ka and 2 ka, the Wadi al-Hasa landscape was transformed to a deeply incised state, with a relatively narrow floodplain and channel often at the level of bedrock. The deposition and incision of Fill IV represent a relatively minor fluctuation dating to the late Holocene. This interpretation stands in contrast to earlier views in which the major transformations were thought to date to the Pleistocene/Holocene transition, with a more recent period of degradation dating to the late-historic period (Schuldenrein 1998; Schuldenrein and Clark 1994). Present reconstructions of the terrace chronosequence are based on relatively brief field reconnaissance, and it is likely that more detailed studies will reveal a considerably more complex history, particularly of the middle Holocene (Schuldenrein and Clark 2001).

At various times in the past, the Hasa floodplain would have been a valuable agricultural resource that was effectively removed from productivity periodically by episodes of channel incision. Although the timing of the first major episode of Holocene channel incision that abandoned the Tabaqa terrace remains uncertain, present evidence suggests that this episode occurred by the Neolithic period 8–9 ka. There is no geological evidence that the floodplain was aggrading at this time, but evidence of Neolithic and Chalcolithic settlement behavior indicates that it was not as deeply incised as it is presently. If the analogy with neighboring wadis is correct, around 4.5 ka an episode of incision occurred that lowered the Hasa channel at least 20 meters, contributing to the lateral erosion of terrace sediments and lower water tables. The precise duration and extent of this episode of incision remains unknown, but no stable floodplain evidence is found again until the Hasa terrace, which is only 3–5 meters above the current channel and appears to have been aggrading by 4 ka (fig. 4.2).

It is interesting to note that, unlike the Early Bronze Age, the only Middle to Late Bronze Age materials identified on the WHS of the south bank of the Hasa were located in the far west end of the survey area at relatively low elevation in the proximity of the Hasa channel (MacDonald 1988). This renewed interest in the lowlands may have been related to a renewed floodplain and its agricultural resources. In general, settlement throughout the Iron Age was more closely associated with the Hasa channel and other permanent sources of water.

There is considerable evidence of settlement along the bottomlands of the Hasa and its major tributaries throughout the early-historic periods of the first millennium BCE (MacDonald 1988). Based on both the archaeological evidence of settlement activity and the geomorphological evidence, it appears that the Hasa channel was aggrading during this period. The formation of the Hasa floodplain would have offered a valuable agricultural resource as fluvial sediments accumulated and water sources remained in close proximity to this surface, thus facilitating irrigation.

The combination of retaining wall and Roman bridge built in the incised Hasa channel clearly indicates that incision of the Hasa terrace occurred sometime prior to the third century CE. If we assume that Nabatean settlers at Umm Hraga would not build a prominent site in the path of imminent destruction, the retaining wall in a 3-meter-deep channel at the edge of the site may suggest erosion was not considered a threat to that site during its early occupation, but became so later, during the Roman period. This chronology would bracket the end of the Hasa flood-

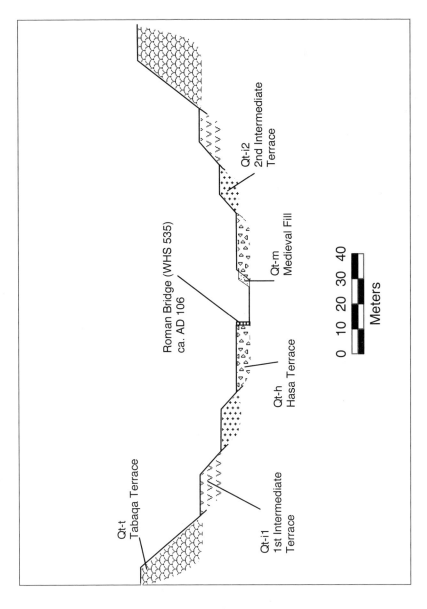

Figure 4.2
Valley-bottom cross section

plain aggradation and the beginning of its incision during the 100 BCE to 200 CE time range.

Settlement continued in the bottomlands, but the emphasis shifted to areas farther away during the Roman and Byzantine periods. Sometime after the Classical-period incision of the Hasa channel, a new period of aggradation deposited sediments in the channel up to an elevation near the level of the Hasa terrace. These deposits are now represented by small benches banked intermittently against the channel sides throughout the drainage (Fill IV) (Copeland and Vita-Finzi 1978). Although this episode of aggradation would not have significantly changed the form of most of the bottomland surfaces, it may have brought water flow in the channel up again to levels that facilitated irrigation and use of the Hasa terrace for agricultural purposes.

The channel appears to have again incised by the late sixteenth century CE, when the bridge associated with the Hajj road and the Qal'at al-Hasa were constructed. The foundations of this bridge are located in the channel bottom, as are the foundations of several mills in tributary streams attributed to the Ottoman period from the early sixteenth century to the early twentieth century (MacDonald 1988). This episode of incision is the last major change identified in the form of the Hasa drainage system.

Until the introduction of diesel pumps in the past few decades, the Hasa bottomlands would have been relatively difficult to cultivate because the water source typically lies in an incised channel 3–5 meters below the level of the arable Hasa terrace surface. Irrigation canals taken from the channel a sufficient distance upstream could still have been used in some places but would have required considerably more effort and organization than during periods of higher water levels. Numerous aqueducts have been recorded in the Hasa drainage system, and some undoubtedly were used to irrigate crops in addition to supplying water to mills and for other needs. There is no evidence for an extensive system of river irrigation, however, and it is likely that much of the bottomlands remained relatively underutilized during periods of incised channel.

The Timing and Causes of Terrace Formation

A few relevant insights may be gained into questions currently surrounding the evolution of the Hasa landscape by reference to the region's paleoenvironmental record. The major factors that contributed to changes in the valley-floor morphology include climate, base-level changes resulting from tectonic movement or fluctuating Dead Sea levels, and human actions. A drawback of many techniques of climate reconstruction has been that they are proxy measures of related processes. They consequently suffer from an equifinality that makes interpretation of the cause of change problematic. Conversely, analysis of multiple lines of evidence holds the potential for suggesting which factors were active at any particular time and for clarifying relationships among factors.

One method of climate reconstruction used in the Levant is based on measures of stable isotopes in speleothems, or stalagmite accretions, from sealed cave contexts in Israel (Bar-Matthews et al. 1999; Frumkin 1999). The isotopic data represent the most accurate and unbiased current record of climate change in the Levant for the period in question. Changing ratios of stable isotopes of ^{18}O and ^{13}C in both speleothems (Bar-Matthews et al. 1999; Frumkin 1999) and land-snail shells (Goodfriend 1999) have been used in recent years to establish records of climate change, including especially precipitation change, covering a period up to the past 170,000 years. These records offer distinct advantages over other methods. They appear to be sensitive to climate change and not very subject to changes in other environmental factors. They constitute a continuous and relatively well-dated record that is a reflection of local conditions because they are a measure of rainwater chemistry as it falls directly on the land surface.

The stable isotope record from Soreq cave speleothems in Israel (Bar-Matthews et al. 1999) provides a precise account of climate change throughout the Holocene. Generally speaking, high isotope values are indicative of relatively cool and dry conditions, whereas low values represent warmer temperatures and greater precipitation. An exception occurs where high values at 7–8 ka are probably associated with high precipitation extremes (Bar Matthews et al. 1999). Overall, these data reflect much greater climatic variability through the late Pleistocene and early Holocene, and relatively stable values from the middle Holocene to the present. In addition, these data provide a useful comparison both for other records of environmental change and for the archaeological record of land use.

Another technique applied to studies of climate change focuses on evidence of changing Dead Sea levels as they are reflected in sediment cores and cave deposits near the southern edge of the lake (Frumkin 1997; Neev and Emery 1995). The Dead Sea sedimentation record has traditionally been used to interpret past climate because it is thought to reflect the amount of freshwater entering the Dead Sea relative to the evaporation rate (Neev and Emery 1995).

The analysis of fluctuating levels of salt and marl sediments in cores from the Dead Sea floor provide a relatively sensitive and high-resolution account of the ratio of influx to evaporation in the basin. When precipitation is high, there is relatively more sediment deposited in the Dead Sea as tributary drainages experience higher flow and more water and sediment are added to the lake. When precipitation is low, relatively little water and sediment are added to the lake, and evaporation is relatively high, depositing more salt on the lakebed.

In large part, this ratio is indicative of past precipitation, but it also measures relative sedimentation in the Dead Sea through time. If a large amount of sediment were eroded from the Wadi al-Hasa in the late fifth millennium BP, as described earlier, it is logical to expect some record of deposition at its end point. The majority of that sediment is probably not to be found in the Dead Sea itself, but in alluvial fans where the Hasa opens onto the plain of the southern Ghor at present-day as-Safi. Extensive alluvial fans are found there, but their developmental history remains unclear at present. Although the coarser fraction would have been deposited at the alluvial fan, the Dead Sea and the locations of the sediment cores are only a few kilometers downstream. A massive episode of erosion in the middle Holocene in the Hasa should be identifiable there in fine sediments. A comparison of the most recent isotopic data with Dead Sea sedimentation levels suggests some interesting points with regard to the factors affecting valley morphology in the Hasa.

Overall, the record of Dead Sea sedimentation agrees fairly closely with other records of the paleoclimate during the late Pleistocene and early Holocene. However, the Dead Sea record indicates a large increase in sediment during the Early Bronze Age approximately 4–5.5 ka (see Donahue, Peer, and Shaub 1997 for calibrated date). The increase in sediment noted is comparable to the increase noted for the Pre-Pottery Neolithic, at 9–7 ka, but the evidence of Early Bronze Age precipitation increase is not nearly as great in other paleoclimate records documenting this time period. I suggest that in this instance the sediment record may also be evidence of a decrease in upland infiltration and the massive removal of sediment in channels such as the Wadi al-Hasa during the Early Bronze Age.

The isotope record from speleothems (Bar-Matthews et al. 1999) and land snails (Goodfriend 1999) as well as recent analyses of pollen in Mediterranean sapropel contexts (Rossignol-Strick 1999) are beginning to show a consistent pattern of climate change in the Levant. One of the more notable qualities of this climate record is that it indicates a great deal of variability in precipitation and temperature during the late Pleistocene and early Holocene. Following the last glacial maximum, approximately 20–18 ka, there was a sharp increase in precipitation and temperature.

This increase was punctuated by nearly two thousand years of cold, dry climate during the Younger Dryas and was then resumed, reaching the highest precipitation levels on record by the early Holocene, approximately 8.5–7 ka. It has also been argued that some evidence of changes in precipitation during the Neolithic is attributable to a shift from a monsoonal to a Mediterranean-type system (Bar-Yosef 1995; Simmons 1997). This shift to dry summers could have been a significant factor in landscape change at that time. Following this early Holocene peak, the climate record indicates temperature and precipitation levels similar to today, with numerous, relatively low-amplitude fluctuations. There was a drought at 5.2–5.1 ka, followed by moister conditions from 4.7 to 4.6 ka, and another drought at 4.1–4.0 ka. Fluctuations from 4 to 1 ka were relatively small, and the past one thousand years have been marked by moderate changes (Bar-Matthews et al. 1999).

A striking aspect of this reconstruction is that most of the very large fluctuations in climate that might have precipitated massive episodes of incision occurred in the period from 18 to 5 ka. During that span of thirteen thousand years, there were intense droughts followed by pluvial cycles lasting for centuries. Yet based on the archaeological evidence presented here, one of the largest cycles of erosion may have occurred as late as 4–4.5 ka, when the climate reached near modern levels, and fluctuations became relatively small in amplitude.

Another factor that contributed to channel incision would have been a changing base level. As noted earlier, the base level of the Hasa drainage system is the level of the Dead Sea. Water levels in the Dead Sea are known to have fluctuated dramatically during the late Pleistocene and the Holocene. The modern level of the Dead Sea is about 400 meters bmsl, but geomorphological evidence indicates that levels have dropped from Lake Lisan highs of 180 meters bmsl at 14 ka to as low as 700 meters bmsl at 10–11 ka (Frumkin 1997; Niemi 1997). Levels as high as 280 meters bmsl were attained during the Pre-Pottery Neolithic, approximately 9–8 ka, and possibly again during the Chalcolithic and Early Bronze Age, at 6.2–4.3 ka. There is evidence of an intermediate period at 7.2–6.8 ka during which levels dropped below 404 meters bmsl and the south basin of the Dead Sea was dry. This may have been the lowest level in the Holocene. Following an Early Bronze Age peak at 345 meters bmsl, levels appear not to have fluctuated more than 360 to 405 meters bmsl (Frumkin 1997). The high-amplitude fluctuations in the level of the Dead Sea during the late Pleistocene and early Holocene were obviously closely related to climate fluctuations noted earlier. Again we see abundant evidence that the largest fluctuations in base level for the Hasa drainage occurred over a seven-thousand-year span from approximately 14 ka to 7 ka.

Another base-level factor that has historically been assigned a causal role in channel incision along the eastern edge of the Dead Sea is tectonic lowering of the basin relative to the Transjordan plateau (Donahue 1985). More recently, however, the role of tectonic movement has been discounted primarily because current evidence indicates movement of only about 1 millimeter per year throughout the Holocene (Frumkin 1997; Niemi 1997). This much subsidence would result in only a total of approximately 10 meters of change throughout the entire epoch, in contrast to the hundreds of meters of change evident in a few millennia of lake-level fluctuation. Based on observations on the western shore of the Dead Sea, base-level fluctuations do not appear to have played a decisive role in the incision of upstream portions of tributary drainages (Bowman 1997). This conclusion is in accord with observations from elsewhere in the Mediterranean Basin (Schumm 1993).

The final factor that must be accounted for in evaluating the cause of channel incision in the Hasa is anthropogenic. Human actions are known to alter channel morphology in a number of ways, but the most likely activity of early Holocene settlers in the Hasa would have been devegetation and disruption of soil structure through agriculture and pastoralism. There is currently little archaeological evidence for these processes in the Hasa primarily because so little excavation has been done on post-Pleistocene sites. In neighboring areas, however, there is considerable evidence that Neolithic through Early Bronze Age agropastoralists altered local landscapes largely through deforestation, grazing, and construction activities (Baruch 1990; Hunt et al. 2004; Kohler-Rollefson 1988; Kohler-Rollefson and Rollefson 1990; Levy 1983a, 1983b; Rollefson and Kohler-Rollefson 1989, 1992; van Zeist and Bottema 1982).

By the Early Bronze Age, agropastoralist settlement in the Hasa reached an early peak with fifty-one potential settlement sites, a fivefold increase over the ten dating to the Chalcolithic period. Such settlement density may have constituted a significant new factor in landscape change. If settlers in the Hasa practiced agropastoralism and consumed wood fuel as they did elsewhere in the Levant during those periods, it is reasonable to infer that they might have played a part in the channel incision that followed. Activities such as deforestation, overgrazing, and trampling would have increased the quantity and velocity of overland flow of surface water, reducing infiltration of precipitation, entraining more sediment, and initiating channel formation. It should be noted that the introduction of pastoralism and construction activities in the southwestern United States have been clearly implicated in extensive arroyo incision of a similar magnitude in the late nineteenth and early twentieth centuries (Cooke and Reeves 1976).

This proposal is not meant to imply that humans are solely to blame for the degradation of the Hasa floodplain. In fact, it is almost certainly not the case, and it is unlikely that any single cause will be identified for that transformation. It is more likely, here as elsewhere, that human actions were one among multiple factors affecting change in the valley-floor morphology. Undoubtedly, both climatic and geological factors also contributed, but it merits acknowledgment that greater fluctuations in these two variables had come and gone for millennia without initiating such a rapid and dramatic period of incision as that suggested for the Early Bronze Age.

The Upland Plateau

The landscape history of the upland plateau is the least documented and perhaps the least changed of the three zones described here. From a geomorphological standpoint, landforms on the plateau are not as susceptible to significant changes as those in the lower elevations. The plateau is typified by topography of plains and rolling hills. There are important differences between the plateau to the north and south of the Hasa. The Kerak plateau in the north encompasses a much broader, less-dissected area than the Edomite plateau to the south, although the latter is equally high in elevation and precipitation. In many small areas, the southern plateau is probably equally fertile and has been a productive area comparable to the Kerak plateau. However, the southern plateau is cut by numerous quite large tributary canyons, creating a much more dissected and geomorphologically unstable terrain.

The uplands are currently dominated by cultivated fields of cereal grain, orchards, and patches of native grass and shrubs. Excavations by Mattingly and colleagues (1998) indicate that a broad variety of crops—including *Triticum durum/aestivum* (wheat), *Hordeum sativum* (barley), *Lens culinaris* (lentil), *Vicia ervilia* (bitter vetch), *Phoenix dactylifera* (date), and *Vitis vinifera* (cultivated grapes)—were grown in the vicinity of al-Mudaybi (ASKP 435) during the Byzantine through Late Islamic periods. A few small areas of remnant *Juniperus phoenica* (juniper) and *Quercus calliprinos* (evergreen oak) forest existed in the highest areas to the south, but they are nearly gone today (Harlan 1988). It is likely that the higher parts of the plateau supported more extensive woodlands in the past. The extent of these woodlands probably fluctuated here, as elsewhere in the Near East, during the late Pleistocene and early Holocene because of fluctuations in temperature and precipitation. By the early Holocene, woodlands were probably limited to the higher parts of the plateau and would have been composed predominantly of *Quercus boissieri* (deciduous oak) and some *Pistacia palestina* (pistachio) if the nearest pollen cores in the Dead Sea are representative. Cultivation of *Olea* (olive) may have begun as early as the Chalcolithic. Later, deciduous oak was replaced by *Pinus halepensis* (pine), which was subsequently dominated by evergreen oak of the type found presently.

These pollen data are subject to some chronological debate. In addition, they come from the western Dead Sea near Ein-Gedi (Baruch 1990; Falconer and Fall 1995). Thus, they may not be as directly related to conditions on the Transjordan plateau. They are, however, the nearest pollen record available for the Holocene time range, and it is reasonable to assume that vegetation on the western side of the Dead Sea was not extremely different from that on the east. Such changes in vegetation may have been significantly affected by developments in arboriculture and the harvesting of fuel wood during the Chalcolithic and Bronze Ages.

Harlan (1988) has shown that eighteenth- and nineteenth-century Europeans' descriptions are notably uniform in depicting the plateau as a treeless grassland as far as the eye could see, and he argues that it has probably been that way for a long time. Whatever woodlands once existed on the plateau had largely disappeared by the late-historic period, except for a few relict stands at the highest elevations.

The majority of the plateau has long been predominantly savanna and grassland and would have supported a rich fauna that was documented up into Classical time periods. Of primary interest to human subsistence, of course, would have been the large herds of ungulates that thrived there until at least the middle Holocene. Many species were probably diminished in number or were extinct by the middle Holocene, but some—such as gazelle, ibex, and ostrich—have been documented here into historic and even modern time periods (Harlan 1988; Jabbur 1995; Lawrence 1938). The number of these species would have fluctuated according to habitat availability and hunting pressure, but it appears to have remained high until the proliferation of modern firearms in the late nineteenth and early twentieth centuries, when it was drastically reduced (Jabbur 1995).

Following the early Neolithic, wild game was probably not the most significant natural resource found on the plateau. Rather, the availability of shrubs and grasses for domestic animals and upland soils for domestic crops would have been the most important resource throughout most of the Holocene. Undoubtedly, the nature and extent of these resources varied according to both human and climatic pressures. The most likely places to have been impacted were the steeper hillslopes, especially along the escarpments of the Dead Sea and major drainages. Many of these hillslopes are denuded of soil and vegetation today and may have been so for millennia. Most of the plateau area, however, is still agriculturally quite productive, supporting a human population as high or higher than it ever has. From an economic standpoint, the upland plains do not appear to be extremely degraded. It is worth noting that from an ecological standpoint, the destruction of natural grasslands and most of the native fauna may be considered a catastrophe with significant roots dating back to the Neolithic period and culminating in the modern era.

As late as the twentieth century, naturalists noted animals such as ibex, ostrich, leopard, hyena, jackal, and wild boar that are either extinct or very endangered today. Many animal species were able to recover their numbers after earlier periods of development when human populations entered decline. After hundreds of years of such decline during the late Ottoman period, for example, early European explorers noted an abundance of native habitat and wild animals in the nineteenth century (Harlan 1988). This recovery of wild species may have occurred repeatedly in the past as human settlement and agriculture waxed and waned with larger-scale political developments. It remains unknown whether or not many of the remaining endangered species will be able to recover from the current cycle of development.

A secondary resource of the uplands that was subject to anthropogenic pressure during the Holocene is the woodlands. Evidence of early exploitation of timber in the Hasa includes plaster floors documented at the Neolithic sites of Khirbet Hammam and el-Hemmeh (Makarewicz and Goodale forthcoming; Peterson 2004; Rollefson 1999; Rollefson and Kafafi 1985). Bossut, Kafafi, and Dollfus (1988) have noted a layer of colluvium at the Pottery Neolithic site of WHS 524 that they attribute to deforestation. If these interpretations are correct, the use of fuel wood for plaster production and other pyrotechnologies may have impacted woodlands as it did around Neolithic sites to the north.

A major source of copper located to the south of the Hasa in the Wadi Faynan was exploited by as early as the Chalcolithic period (Shalev and Northover 1987) and remained a source into the Classical periods. Wood from surrounding woodlands was used extensively as fuel for smelting copper at Faynan (Engle and Frey 1996). At times, the harvesting of fuel for this purpose may have extended as far as the uplands above the Wadi Dana just south of the present study area, but probably did not extend far into the Hasa area.

Finally, in the early twentieth century a great deal of timber was harvested from the uplands of the Transjordan plateau for use in building and powering the Hijaz railway constructed by German engineers in cooperation with the Ottoman Empire (Pick 1990). This harvest resulted in the destruction of most of the last remaining woodlands in west-central Jordan and was a source of bitterness among Jordanians. The overexploitation of local woodlands by imperial authorities for purposes unrelated to local needs stands as a recent example of the separation of motives between distant political elites and local producers that resulted in land degradation.

Wood for domestic fuel was undoubtedly used throughout the Holocene and is still used today in small measure. From at least the Early Bronze Age, when settled communities first appeared in large numbers on the plateau, there has been pressure on the small sources of wood in the area as an obvious choice for fuel and construction.

The spatially and temporally variable landscape of the Hasa described here was the setting for millennia of settlement, mobility, and abandonment. In each case, the decisions made by farmers and herders in this area were strongly affected by the combination of cultural and natural conditions they confronted. The following analyses address the evidence of decisions they made under different political and geographic constraints and possibilities. Chapter 5 focuses on the complex decisions of when and where to settle, and when to seek other options.

5

A History of Abandonment and Resettlement

As the natural and cultural environment of the Wadi al-Hasa has changed over the past several thousand years, human land use has also changed. People in the Hasa have moved from a mobile, hunter-gatherer way of life to a system in which some are settled and practice agriculture, while others are more mobile and practice pastoralism. In fact, there is a great deal of overlap and interaction between these two ways of life, and people have transitioned easily from one to the other depending on conditions (Jabbur 1995:32–38). Populations have frequently aggregated in the most economically productive areas and dispersed in conditions of political and climatic deterioration. The entire region has been transformed from a place free of suprafamily politics to one of contention among rival states and empires. And as the natural environment of the area changed, social, political, economic, and ideological forms came and went in great variety.

One consequence of the many cycles of changing circumstance throughout the Holocene is that human settlements have frequently been abandoned or relocated. In this chapter, I focus on the degree to which settlement abandonment may be attributed to declining landscape productivity owing to anthropogenic factors. A basic assumption here is that one reason people abandon a settlement location is that their ability to produce a livelihood from its surroundings has declined. When an area becomes sufficiently degraded through erosion or soil depletion and consequently through diminished vegetation, people will eventually be forced either to relocate or to enhance production technology. Technological solutions, including a variety of soil- and water-conservation techniques, have been utilized in the past to increase or maintain productivity in the Hasa (MacDonald 1988; Miller 1991). However, most of the area is agriculturally marginal, and many traditional technologies involve relatively high labor costs and a low return on investment. Terraces are one form of agricultural investment that does not appear as common in the Hasa as in neighboring parts of the Levant. For example, 115 terrace/checkdams were recorded by the surveys, in comparison with three hundred enclosures/corrals. This difference may be an indication of the lesser importance of agricultural intensification compared to the more extensive pastoral strategy. The location of the Hasa at the edge of the Arabian Desert and its generally low population create an opportunity for settlement mobility not seen in more densely inhabited regions. The presence of several hundred abandoned agropastoral sites in locations of marginal productivity are testament to people's willingness to redirect economic efforts rather than to intensify production in the same location.

If depletion of local land resources was a regular occurrence in the Hasa, and a common response was to relocate to more productive areas, this response should be manifest statistically in the spatial segregation of settlements from one time period to the next (Hill 2004a). Thus, I present a series of spatial statistical analyses in this chapter to quantify the degree and significance of settlement movement. However, establishing the simple relocation of settlements from one time period to the next does not adequately address the problem of equifinality. A number of possible explanations for settlement movement can be given that might have nothing to do with anthropogenic environmental degradation. These explanations include climatic, technological, and political changes, to name a few of the more obvious possibilities. To address the possibility of multiple causes I employ a control mechanism by evaluating areas with equivalent climatic and cultural conditions.

One of the most likely forms of landscape degradation to have occurred in this region is soil erosion (Goldberg and Bar-Yosef 1990; Naveh and Dan 1973). Soil erosion is a complex process affected by topography, precipitation, vegetation, and the actions of humans and other animals. To isolate individual factors it is necessary to establish controls for them. At the scale of these analyses, precipitation changes and consequent effects on vegetation are relatively constant throughout the study area, such that their effects are similar in equivalent climatic zones. For example, if the region experienced drought, its effects should be similar in locations of similar precipitation. Likewise, basic agropastoral economic activities should be similar in areas of comparable productive potential. By comparing settlement trends in adjacent areas, I identify differences in productivity and degradation attributable to differences in landscape stability.

If landscape degradation were a major factor in such population shifts, settlement would be more stable and enduring in locations of relatively low erosion potential. Conversely, in locations of high erosion potential, periodic degradation would necessitate settlement movement. The archaeological survey record of the Hasa presents the opportunity to make such comparisons between north and south. The areas included in the WHS (MacDonald 1988) and the WHNBS (Clark et al. 1992; Clark et al. 1994) provide broad coverage of lands ranging from high western plateau to canyons and eastern desert. Though the WHNBS technically covered the north bank of the Hasa, its actual extent was directly east of the WHS, so that in combination they provide west to east coverage. The ASKP (Miller 1991), however, provides broad coverage of the area directly to the north of the two Hasa surveys. It also includes a range of lands from high western plateau to eastern desert. It does not include much canyon area because its boundary was the edge of the Hasa gorge, and the large tributary drainages in the south are not found on the northern plateau.

This difference in terrain is at the heart of differences in landscape stability between the northern and southern survey areas. Both areas cover approximately the same range of elevation and precipitation. Both areas have been utilized by people practicing the same types of agropastoral economic behavior. But the south is typically considered a more marginal environment, whereas the north is more consistently productive (Harlan 1988; Knauf 1992). One of the most important reasons for this difference between areas so close together and so similar in other respects is the difference in topography. The south is dissected by numerous large tributary canyons and hills, whereas the northern landscape is much flatter and less dissected. Today, the soils in the more steeply sloped south are often thinner, less productive, and more easily eroded than those in the north (Willimott et al. 1963; Willimott et al. 1964).

If local erosion was a factor in settlement abandonment, it stands to reason that such movement would be more common in the south than in the north because of differences in soil stability. By evaluating frequency of settlement movement separately in these two areas, we can use the north as a control for understanding the cause of abandonment in the south. If change were due to climatic fluctuation, it would be expected to affect both areas in the same way, primarily along an east-west elevation gradient as precipitation increased or decreased. Likewise, if change were due to fluctuations in political or economic demands, it would also be expected to manifest in an east-west movement in both areas with respect to the eastern desert. If, however, settlement change were due to local land degradation, it would be expected to result in differences between areas of different susceptibility in the north and the south, with little east-west effect.

In this analysis, I employ a series of statistical measures of spatial correlation on sites from adjacent temporal periods to evaluate the relocation of settlement from one period to the next. In the absence of environmental change, an economically productive location would be utilized somewhat continuously, and settlement locations would show strong spatial association through time. Conversely, if environmental factors change, and productivity is diminished, settlements will be relocated to more productive areas. A high degree of settlement movement should be reflected in increased measures of spatial segregation between periods.

Data Considerations

Each of the archaeological surveys of this region was conducted with somewhat varying goals by researchers with different knowledge and interests. The use of these data together requires consideration of methodological differences among the surveys and of ways to extract reasonable common denominators from them. I developed a database of recorded sites based on copies of the original survey forms for the WHS and WHNBS projects and of the published data from the ASKP project. Data tables include sites and temporal components so that multiple components may be analyzed individually. I recorded a total of 1,664 individual sites and 3,714 components in this way.

One area of concern regarding these survey data is the accuracy of ceramic identifications. For example, the identification of Iron Age I ceramics in the area has been called into question by Bienkowski and colleagues (1997), who argue that the ceramics may actually be Iron Age II. The attribution of Early Bronze Age I sherds may be biased by the absence of diagnostics that would accurately place them into later Early Bronze Age periods. Likewise, the distinction between many Islamic period sherds and Early Bronze Age sherds is problematic, and the Early Islamic and Hellenistic periods in general are poorly understood in this area (Johns 1992; Smith 1990). There is no easy remedy to these problems outside further field research, and interpretation of the data must be cautious with respect to the more difficult time periods. However, in many cases it is possible to use the data with confidence by collapsing troublesome distinctions.

In these analyses, I avoid many dating problems by using broad temporal distinctions that obviate debates around finer-grained questions. For example, I do not address distinctions between Iron I and Iron II or between different divisions of the Early Bronze Age. For the purpose of these analyses, I utilize a division of twelve major periods as defined in the table given in this chapter.

Another potential source of concern in the comparison of these data is with regard to levels of coverage and intensity. The WHNBS was the only project to attempt full-coverage survey, and even that was occasion-

Table. Chronological divisions

Period—Abbreviation	Years
Pre-Pottery Neolithic—PPN	10,000–7600 BP
Pottery Neolithic—PN	7600–6250 BP
Chalcolithic—CH	6250–5300 BP
Early Bronze Age—EB	3300–1950 BCE
Middle/Late Bronze Age—ML	1950–1200 BCE
Iron Age—IR	1200–539 BCE
Hellenistic—HE	332–63 BCE
Nabatean—NB	312 BCE–106 CE
Roman—RO	106–324 CE
Byzantine—BZ	324–640 CE
Early Islamic—EI	640–1263 CE
Late Islamic—LI	1250–1918 CE

ally hindered by topography (Clark et al. 1992; Clark et al. 1994). The WHS utilized a combination of purposive and random transects stratified by plateau and gorge zones (Banning 1988). The ASKP indicated the intention to perform systematic survey but provided little detail concerning coverage or intensity (Miller 1991). Given the large area examined by the ASKP in only four survey seasons, it can be inferred that intensity was fairly low. The absence of any discussion of sampling strategy suggests coverage was somewhat purposive and nonsystematic. Stratification in the ASKP by geographic zone is not a concern because these data are used here only to represent the plateau.

Caution must be exercised in statistical use of data recorded by these surveys and especially in the comparison of such data across surveys. Spatial analyses including comparison of trends among different survey areas as well as the proximity of sites to other sites and geographical features are an important part of this research. The intensity and coverage of a survey project obviously affects the density of sites recorded and their proximity to other things on the landscape. Comparing survey data acquired using different methods poses potential problems for interpretation. This potential is minimized in statistical analysis by the use of randomizing techniques. For example, in the analyses presented here, the spatial segregation calculated is relative to what would be expected if the same number of points were randomly distributed in the survey area, or if points were randomly ascribed to the given locations. Thus, the fact that the WHNBS recorded a higher density of sites than the ASKP is statistically irrelevant in comparing spatial segregation in each survey area. The effects of purposive sampling are minimized by the fact that the quality being evaluated statistically is between-period segregation.

The lack of probabilistic sampling in the ASKP and to a lesser extent in the WHS presents the possibility of bias against some geographic zones and may affect analyses of differences in land use. It should be noted that the portion of the ASKP used here provides a control for analyses of land use in the rest of the Hasa. It is not used to analyze settlement variability on the Kerak plateau, but to provide a sample of sites for comparison with the Hasa settlement record. Although the WHS was not conducted entirely using probabilistic sampling methods, much of it was, and the rest provided a reasonably thorough cross section of land types throughout the area. If any bias were present, it would be against areas of very high topographic relief (Banning 1988). If sites are located in such areas and underrepresented by the survey, their presence would most likely strengthen the conclusions presented here.

Grab samples were the strategy common to all artifact collection and hence to dating techniques in these projects. In terms of dating components, only presence/absence of occupation during a given period is inferred. In this way, problems associated with unsystematic collection strategies are minimized. There are two exceptions to this rule. In many cases, very small samples were collected from individual periods, rendering unclear how important a temporal component was at a site. To minimize the effect of such small samples I systematically disregarded sherd counts below a number deemed to be significant. I used frequency distributions of sherd counts from each period to determine a significant number of sherds to qualify as a "presence." In most cases, there was an evident break in the frequency curves at between two and five artifacts, indicating a reasonable distinction between a small number of background sherds found at many sites and a larger number of sherds that might be interpreted as an occupation component.

A second exception to the presence/absence rule for temporal components occurs in the use of an upper-quartile sample of sites. Objective determination of the largest and most important sites from each period favored the use of a numerical attribute. Site size is problematic owing to widely varying methods of calculation and to its absence from many site records. Artifact counts were therefore the only numerical means of distinguishing relative size of temporal components at a site. As a means of identifying the largest sites, it is the best indicator available. In general, the upper-quartile distinction is a reasonable approximation of the largest sites from each period. The advantage of this approach is that it is a relatively objective technique for eliminating all but the most important sites for each time period from the analysis. The disadvantages are that it does not differentiate between site types, and component size is a difficult thing to determine from survey data.

In addition to the upper-quartile sample, analysis is based on a judgmental sample of sites deemed to be representative of agropastoral land use. Because this research addresses land use, I disregard a large portion of the survey data that less directly reflect immediate concern for agropastoral productivity. Many sites—such as forts, cemeteries, and roads—are obviously less directly related to agropastoral production than are villages, farms, and hamlets. I focused on sites indicating any kind of agropastoral production to address the relationships among people and soils most clearly. In most cases, the site type interpreted by the recorders is adequate to infer whether a site represents a locus of production. In some cases, I identified site types that would not clearly indicate production (e.g., towers), but for which closer consideration of the site description indicated the site's use as a Bedouin camp or possible fieldhouse.

Statistical Analyses

I use statistical analyses here to evaluate site longevity and the shifting of economic activity as a function of the continued productivity of the site catchment. If a location remains productive, and other cultural factors remain conducive to production there, a site should be utilized throughout successive periods. Long-term use of site locations is common throughout the Near East, as evidenced especially by tells representing settlement over many thousands of years in some cases. Many sites in the Hasa are multicomponent sites with evidence of use through at least two archaeological periods. If or when productivity declined beyond an acceptable rate, it stands to reason that the location would be abandoned in favor of an alternative.

Other factors, including cultural or climatic changes, could also affect the decision to abandon a location, and to control for these factors I include analyses of the Kerak plateau. The Hasa and the Kerak plateau are in such close proximity that farmers from the Kerak plateau are often seen tending fields in the Hasa that they reach either on foot or by donkey. Thus, cultural and climatic changes should be felt similarly in both areas, and it should be possible to control for their effects by comparing site abandonment in the two areas.

The spatial statistics used here are measures commonly employed in archaeology (Blankholm 1991; Kintigh 1990). Each of the techniques used is a measure of the proximity of points to other points relative to the expected proximity if the same number of points were randomly distributed. Each has respective strengths and weaknesses that complement each other and are used together to provide the most robust evaluation of trends.

Nearest-neighbor (NN) analysis was introduced to the archaeological literature as a means of evaluating the spatial association of artifacts in an assemblage (Whallon 1974). The NN coefficient provided by this analysis is a ratio of the actual average distance between the nearest neighbors among a set of points and the expected average distance if the same number of points were randomly distributed in the same area. Values around 1.0 indicate a random distribution, and values greater than 1.0 indicate spatial segregation.

This type of analysis has the advantage of being a relatively straightforward and simple statistic that is well known in the archaeological literature (Kintigh 1990). In the spatial analysis literature, it has been criticized primarily on two fronts: boundary and paired-point problems. Boundary problems arise from uncertainty about the exact area and boundaries being considered and from the possibility that actual nearest neighbors lie outside the boundaries and are not considered in the analysis. Paired-point problems arise from the possibility that the single nearest neighbors may be quite close, whereas in general pairs or small clusters may be widely distributed. Thus, the association measured is not indicative of global patterning, but only of the proximity of single points to one another. For these reasons, Kintigh (1990) advises the use of NN analysis in a relative rather than an absolute sense. In the present analyses, I emphasize the interpretation of the NN coefficient for between-period site distributions relative to within-period distributions and to between-period distributions in different survey areas.

An alternative to NN analysis is proposed by Hodder and Okell (1978), in which measures of distances between all points of each class are evaluated rather than a single nearest neighbor. Hodder and Okell's "A" (HOA) statistic is calculated as the product of the means of two intratype distances divided by the square of the mean distance between types. Values around 1.0 indicate a random distribution, and values less than 1.0 indicate spatial segregation.

An advantage of HOA is that it is not dependent on the boundary of the area being analyzed because it utilizes point locations as given. The HOA statistic with Monte Carlo randomization is a particularly useful measure of spatial segregation. Although the "A" statistic is useful as an absolute measure of spatial segregation among points, I emphasize the between-period segregation in relation to the mean of one hundred random runs and in relation to between-period segregation in different survey areas.

The final statistic used here is local density analysis (LDA) as proposed by Johnson (1984). The local density coefficient is the mean density of points of a given type found within a specified radius of a second point type, divided by the global density of the first type of points. The density of points is calculated as the number of points divided by (1) the area of the circle defined by the specified radius and (2) the area being analyzed. In this way, it provides a measure of the association or segregation of point types at a designated scale fixed by the radius used. Values around 1.0 indicate random distribution, and values less than 1.0 indicate spatial segregation.

Because LDA uses the total area being analyzed to calculate the global density, it is subject to some of the same boundary problems as NN analysis. In these analyses, I consider between-period local density coefficients in an absolute sense and between survey areas in a relative sense. Use of LDA offers the advantage of measuring spatial segregation at a user-defined scale. I used radii of 3, 4, 5, and 6 kilometers to assess segregation at the scale of a site catchment as it might be defined for agriculturalists (Chisholm 1968; Vita-Finzi and Higgs 1970). The area of such a site catchment would be the most likely radius affected by agropastoralists in this region. I used the computer program Tools for Quantitative Archaeology (Kintigh 1992) including the NEIG, HOA, and LDEN modules for all of the spatial statistical analyses presented here. The results of all analyses are listed elsewhere (Hill 2002), and I emphasize here the elements most relevant to the current discussion.

The statistics of most interest are the measures of spatial segregation between sites of one period and those of the immediately following period. I take this to be the best measure of settlement response to environmental change. A related question concerns the duration of avoidance once a location has been degraded and the implications for time of recovery. In addressing duration of avoidance, I consider spatial segregation through multiple succeeding periods to ascertain how long avoidance is maintained. In other words, I examine how long a high degree of spatial segregation endures before returning to a condition of spatial association or location resettlement.

Results

The Complete Data Set

I initially conducted analyses on all recorded site components, irrespective of size or type. Analyses of all recorded components show the least-significant patterning, which is certainly owing to the high density of archaeological material in the region not associated with agropastoral settlement. People engaged in a variety of activities have saturated the area with materials ranging from villages to graves to pot breaks. Measures of segregation among many noneconomic archaeological remains are probably only modestly affected by the productivity of the local landscape. Nonetheless, HOA does indicate a mild but consistently significant segregation between periods. In ten of eleven cases, the between-period "A" statistic is more than one standard error below the mean of one hundred random runs.

Dividing the component tables into all northern components (ASKP) and all southern components (WHS and WHNBS) illustrates an interesting aspect of structure in the settlement data. The between-period NN coefficients for the north show strong spatial association, indicating locational continuity through time. A comparison of between-period coefficients and within-period coefficients in the north indicates much more association between sites in successive periods than between contemporaneous sites. That is, agropastoral settlements have a greater tendency to cluster temporally than spatially. This tendency indicates continuity of land use on the northern plateau. In contrast, NN coefficients from the south indicate greater between-period spatial segregation than in the north in seven of eight comparable time periods. This difference between the north and south is likewise apparent in the HOA analyses. The between-period "A" statistics for all northern sites consistently indicate either mild association or are within one standard error of random. In the south, the between-period "A" statistic indicates segregation greater than one standard error from the random mean in ten of eleven cases. These statistics indicate significantly more location abandonment and subsequent avoidance in the south than in the north.

The Judgmental Sample

In the judgmental sample, we again see between-period NN coefficients from the north indicating more spatial association than within-period coefficients in all but one case. Figure 5.1 illustrates greater between-period than within-period spatial association, reflecting locational continuity through time in the north. In contrast, NN coefficients from the south indicate greater variability and as high, or higher, between-period than within-period segregation in six of ten cases. In six of eight comparable cases, between-period NN coefficients in the south indicate greater segregation than coefficients in the north (fig. 5.2). A t-test on the means of between-period NN from the north and the south indicates a probability of only 0.026 that such differences would occur randomly.

Likewise, between-period HOA analyses for the north indicate no between-period spatial segregation in six of eight cases, whereas between-period statistics for the south indicate significant segregation in every case. The HOA analysis with Monte Carlo simulation allows for comparison among actual distances between sites and distances among a random distribution of sites. Analysis of the actual site locations compared to the standard error among randomly distributed sites provides an indication of the significance of segregation.

In nine of ten cases, between-period "A" statistics in the south are more than three standard errors below the mean value of one hundred random runs. Figure 5.3 illustrates sites in the north with spatial association similar to the association occurring in one hundred random runs. In other words, there is no significant movement of site locations through time in the north. Conversely, figure 5.4 illustrates sites in the south as much more highly segregated from their predecessors than the same site locations would be in one hundred random runs. In other words, sites in the south are significantly situated to avoid the locations of their predecessors.

Local density analysis at the 3-, 4-, 5-, and 6-kilometer radius also indicates greater between-period segregation in the south than in the north in twenty-four out of thirty-two cases of comparable period and radius. The mean value of LDA coefficients in the north is 1.035, indicating a near-random between-period distribution of sites. In contrast, the mean value of LDA coefficients in the south is only 0.861, indicating general between-period spatial segregation of site locations. The mean LDA coefficient of all radii for each between-period comparison indicates that in six of eight comparable cases there was greater between-period segregation in the south than in the north (fig. 5.5).

The Upper-Quartile Sample

In the upper-quartile sample, comparison of between-period NN coefficients in the north and in the south indicates greater segregation in the south in

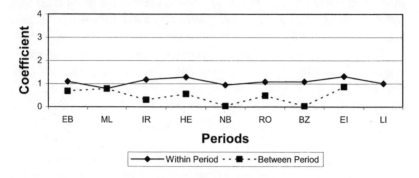

Figure 5.1 NN for northern area judgmental sample

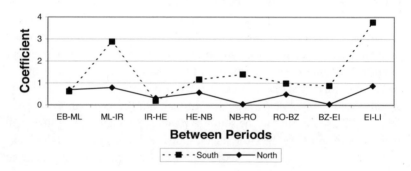

Figure 5.2 Between-period NN for southern and northern areas

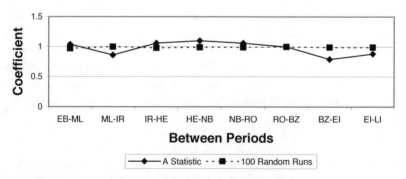

Figure 5.3 HOA for northern area judgmental sample

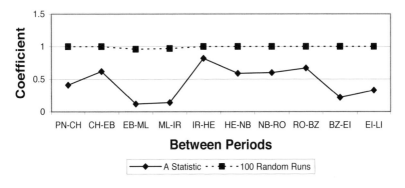

Figure 5.4 HOA for southern area judgmental sample

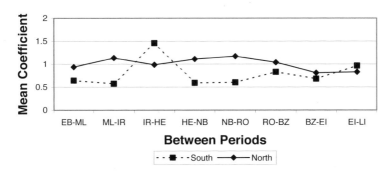

Figure 5.5 Mean LDA coefficient for northern and southern areas

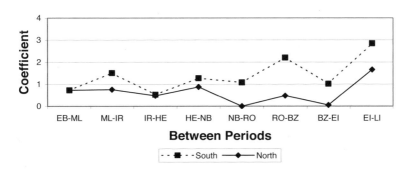

Figure 5.6 Between-period NN for upper-quartile sample

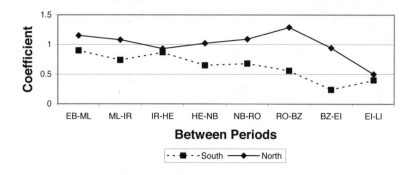

Figure 5.7 Between-period HOA for upper-quartile sample

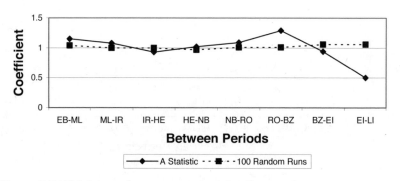

Figure 5.8 HOA for northern area upper-quartile sample

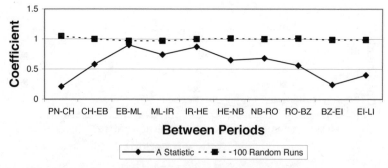

Figure 5.9 HOA for southern area upper-quartile sample

seven of eight cases, and identical values in the eighth case (fig. 5.6). A t-test on the means of between-period NN from the north and the south indicates a probability of only 0.019 that such differences would occur randomly.

Similarly, HOA analyses indicate greater segregation in the south than in the north in all cases (fig. 5.7). Values of the "A" statistic for the north are typically similar to values generated in one hundred random runs (fig. 5.8), whereas values for the south are more than one standard error below the mean of one hundred random runs in eight of ten cases (fig. 5.9).

Between-period LDA coefficients again indicate greater segregation in the south than in the north in twenty-four of thirty-two cases. The mean LDA coefficient for the northern area is 1.038, indicating a near-random distribution, whereas the mean for the south is 0.82, indicating overall betweenperiod segregation.

Discussion

The results of these statistical analyses indicate strongly that the sites recorded on the Kerak plateau experienced a different kind of locational continuity than those in the south. The consistent spatial segregation between temporal components of sites recorded by the WHS and WHNBS indicates that settlements in this southern area were less stable through time than their neighbors on the northern plateau. The statistics for the southern sites indicate greater than normal settlement abandonment and avoidance of previously occupied areas from one period to the next. The comparison between southern and northern areas provides a valuable control for understanding the causes of this movement.

If settlement movement was determined by changes in climate, technological development, or political situation, one would expect it to be of a more regional character, including both north and south. The survey universe on the Kerak plateau is directly adjacent to the southern universe. Sites on the Kerak plateau are at most only a few kilometers from comparable sites to the south and are in a comparable climate. Likewise, technological and political conditions have probably been approximately the same in the two areas over most of their history. The differences between site longevity in the two areas rule against the likelihood that long-term settlement mobility in the south was driven by climatic, technological, or political factors. The major difference between the two areas is their topography, which has a strong effect on the stability of their soils. Agropastoral activities in the south would have been more likely to degrade local soils than the same activities in the north.

Alternative Hypotheses

One factor that might bias these spatial analyses is the predominant site position within each area. The WHNBS recorded more sites in the eastern desert than did the survey of the Kerak plateau (ASKP). These eastern desert sites may not be comparable to the majority of ASKP sites that are located in the more humid and stable western plateau. Thus, even though the survey areas in the north and the south are roughly comparable in extent, the actual locations of most sites recorded are not equally distributed in the eastern and western parts of those areas. It might be argued that settlement movement in the south is biased by the large number of sites represented in the WHNBS.

Others have noted in discussions of human ecology in the Levant that areas on the desert margin are more susceptible to environmental change than either more humid or more arid locations (Gophna 1995; Tchernov and Horwitz 1990). An argument might be made that sites recorded by the WHNBS are in more marginal climatic conditions than those sites recorded by the ASKP and would therefore be more susceptible to small climatic fluctuations that lead to abandonment.

Another notable quality of the Hasa through history is its susceptibility to raiding from eastern desert tribes, especially during periods of declining political security in the area. If raiding by nomadic pastoralists was a common threat to security, it is likely that sites on the eastern edge of the study area, where it borders the open desert, would have been most susceptible. Settlements on the eastern border would have been the most likely to respond to this threat by abandoning their locations in favor of more defensible sites on the western plateau. Sites recorded by the WHNBS historically would have been the most vulnerable to attack from the east and hence the most likely to have a high degree of between-period spatial segregation caused by changing political situation. Such differences in susceptibility to climatic and political change are likely and require closer examination to evaluate their role in settlement movement.

One way to eliminate the possibility of an eastern WHNBS bias is to examine the spatial statistics for only the WHS data in comparison with the ASKP data. The WHS more closely mirrors the ASKP survey in extent and intensity and is not biased toward eastern, desert-margin sites. A quick look at the locations of sites in the judgmental sample reveals, for example, that WHS sites are on average slightly farther west than those recorded by the ASKP. Overall, a comparison of between-period spatial segregation indicates approximately the same patterns observed in the larger north-south comparisons discussed earlier.

For example, in the judgmental sample, LDA coefficients indicate greater between-period segregation among WHS sites than among ASKP sites in twenty-six of thirty-two comparable cases from the judgmental sample. In contrast, within-period LDA coefficients indicate more spatial association in the WHS than in the ASKP in twenty-two of thirty-six comparable cases. This contrast reflects both greater site clustering within a given period and a higher rate of site abandonment in the subsequent period in the WHS than in the ASKP.

The NN coefficients indicate greater between-period segregation among WHS sites than among ASKP sites in six of eight comparable cases in both the judgmental and the upper-quartile samples. The HOA also indicates greater between-period segregation in seven of eight comparable cases in both the judgmental and the upper-quartile samples.

Differences in between-period segregation in the ASKP and WHS areas are typically as robust as differences between the ASKP and the combined southern area described earlier. For example, the mean between-period LDA coefficient for the upper-quartile WHS sites is 0.76, indicating even greater segregation than the 0.82 figure noted earlier for the combined southern area. Overall, the distribution of WHS sites is similar to the distribution of ASKP sites with respect to the eastern desert margin. The differences in settlement longevity demonstrated between the WHS and the ASKP data rule against the likelihood that climate or political changes at desert-margin locations are the primary cause of site movement.

The effect of changes in climate or political situation or both, however, should not be ruled out completely as factors in settlement movement. Although comparisons between ASKP and WHS sites of comparable susceptibility to climatic and political change indicate these factors are not the primary cause of abandonment, segregation at eastern sites is notable. The LDA for WHNBS sites alone indicates the greatest between-period segregation in these analyses. The mean LDA coefficient for the judgmental sample is 0.46, whereas the mean for the upper-quartile sample is only 0.35. These numbers indicate a very high degree of settlement movement from one period to the next in the eastern Hasa. This level of mobility supports the idea that the eastern, desert margin sites have also been more susceptible to climate and political change than locations on the more humid and defensible western plateau. The eastern Hasa sites have probably been more vulnerable to a combination of factors including local degradation, climate, and security.

Duration of Abandonment

Evaluations of between-period segregation show a high degree of abandonment and location avoidance through time in the southern Hasa. A related question concerns the duration of such avoidance. If location avoidance is related to environmental degradation, the duration of avoidance will reflect the length of time before an area has recovered sufficiently to become economically useful again. I examine here evidence for the length of time settlers in the Hasa actively avoided a location once it was abandoned.

Monte Carlo simulation with the HOA analysis is particularly useful for quantifying the duration of avoidance because it provides a sense of the significance of segregation in any given period. The length of time before site segregation diminishes to a condition statistically indistinguishable from a random distribution is a measure of the duration of active avoidance. One reasonable indication that a location is no longer being avoided is when the "A" statistic returns to a value less than one standard error below the mean of one hundred random runs. Thus, a measure of no significant segregation of sites from previously occupied sites would indicate that no intentional avoidance of the location was observed. Figures 5.10 and 5.11 graph the span of time after abandonment in each period before no significant segregation is observed.

The horizontal bars for each period begin at the last date a site of the respective period was occupied and end at the earliest date of occupation for the period during which the "A" statistic returns to one standard error from the random mean. The duration of abandonment identified in both the judgmental sample (fig. 5.10) and the upper-quartile sample (fig. 5.11) are typically consistent for each period. The length of time varies in both samples from a maximum of almost three thousand years following the Chalcolithic to less than two hundred years following the Hellenistic period. Notably, the avoidance of site locations dating from the Nabatean to the Late Islamic period remained significant until the modern era.

Although the later periods show no significant decline in location avoidance through the last period analyzed, it is probably reasonable to infer that most locations have or will soon have been reoccupied. Modern populations are among the highest ever for this region, and modern technology is expanding production broadly throughout areas that have not been used for many years. If archaeological site locations were compared to modern land use, spatial segregation would probably be significantly reduced in most cases.

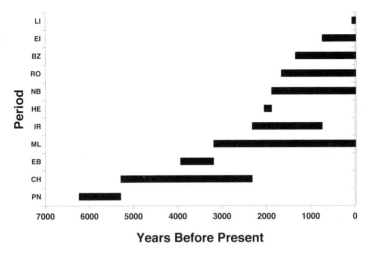

Figure 5.10 Duration of abandonment judgmental sample

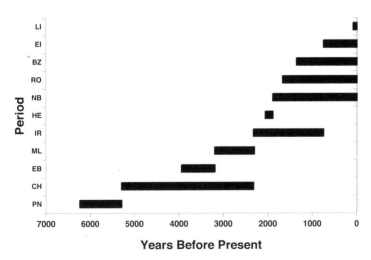

Figure 5.11 Duration of abandonment upper-quartile sample

Summary statistics of the duration of location avoidance following all periods may elucidate tendencies in the length of time necessary for landscape recovery. The mean duration of avoidance among sites in the judgmental sample is 1,399 years with a standard error of 307 years. The mean duration of avoidance among sites from the upper-quartile sample is 1,189 years with a standard error of 250 years.

Focusing on the Neolithic through the Iron Age is useful because they are the periods for which the segregation statistics are fairly robust, and we can identify the end of the cycle of avoidance. The mean duration of location avoidance for these periods is 1,890 years with a standard error of 508 in the judgmental sample, and 1,427 years with a standard error of 411 in the upper-quartile sample.

These statistics suggest that a span of roughly one to two thousand years is typically necessary for a location to recover from a cycle of agropastoral land use once it has reached a low threshold of productivity. Recovery periods are undoubtedly variable in different environments, and the arid dissected land of the Hasa probably takes longer to recover than more humid, gentle terrain. The fact that locations abandoned since the Nabatean period remained unattractive to settlers despite repeated cycles of land-use intensification is notable. It is a striking indication of the long-lasting effects of past land use in structuring settlement choices through time.

Analyses by Archaeological Period

The Neolithic

Characterization of settlement patterns throughout the Holocene provides powerful insights into long-term trends and factors affecting them. It is necessary, though, to examine individual periods in closer detail to refine these analyses and to understand exceptions to trends. The Neolithic is a period for which some of the earliest and most compelling evidence for anthropogenic environmental degradation has been documented at 'Ain Ghazal (Kohler-Rollefson and Rollefson 1990; Rollefson, Simmons, and Kafafi 1992; Simmons et al. 1988).

The sites of Khirbet Hammam (WHS 149) (Peterson 2000, 2004; Rollefson and Kafafi 1985) and el-Hemmeh (Makarewicz and Goodale forthcoming; Rollefson 1999) were comparable in some respects to 'Ain Ghazal. It is premature to infer the scale of degradation noted at 'Ain Ghazal and hypothesized for the region (Kohler-Rollefson 1988; Rollefson and Kohler-Rollefson 1989) because relatively little excavation has been done at Khirbet Hammam or el-Hemmeh. Nonetheless, they do appear to have been village sites in a steep valley with elements such as plaster floors that were implicated in deforestation at 'Ain Ghazal. Notably, the spatial segregation between Neolithic and Chalcolithic sites is among the highest recorded in the area.

The spatial segregation observed is certainly suggestive of anthropogenic degradation in the Neolithic leading to abandonment. It will be interesting in this regard to follow the research at Khirbet Hammam (Peterson 2000, 2004) and el-Hemmeh (Makarewicz and Goodale forthcoming). However, there are currently good reasons to be cautious about such an inference. In addition to a general lack of excavation data, relatively few sites from these early periods have been recorded, and those that have been found are typically fairly small. Khirbet Hammam is the largest, and it is thought to be about 4 hectares in extent, one-fourth to one-third the size of 'Ain Ghazal.

The Chalcolithic

Evidence of increasing pastoralism (Fall, Lines, and Falconer 1998), changing species use (Grigson 1995), and vegetation communities (Hunt et al. 2004) indicates the Chalcolithic was a time of anthropogenic environmental degradation in the southern Levant. The majority of the analyses presented here do indicate a significant amount of settlement movement between the Chalcolithic and the Early Bronze Age. This degree of abandonment and relocation in the Hasa is likely related to changing environmental conditions. The question remains how much of that change was anthropogenic and how much was natural.

Throughout the early Holocene, the climate of the Hasa was changing dramatically, with consequent changes for the geomorphology and vegetation of the area. However, the increase in aggregated settlement, agropastoral economic production, and the use of pyrotechnologies could not have failed to impact local environments and may also have affected the settlement movement documented here.

In short, settlement movement in the earliest periods is notable and may well be related to anthropogenic degradation such as that documented in neighboring areas. However, no Neolithic or Chalcolithic sites were recorded on the northern plateau, and thus there is no comparative settlement pattern to shed light on the causes of movement in these early periods. There is still a great deal to learn about the Neolithic and Chalcolithic periods in the Hasa, and more excavation data will clarify issues of settlement movement in the area.

The Bronze Age

The Early Bronze Age is the first period for which there is evidence of a large increase in settlement that may have had serious environmental impacts. In addition, van Zeist and Bottema (1982) have argued that the Early Bronze Age was a time of significant deforestation and replacement of wild arboreal species with economic species such as *Olea* (olive). There is notable settlement movement between the Early Bronze Age and the Middle and Late Bronze Ages in the southern area, which may be indicative of a response to a locally degraded landscape.

The statistical analyses indicate significant spatial segregation even for the small number of Middle and Late Bronze Age sites, and there may have been environmental reasons for reestablishing settlement in different locations. Moreover, there are other important differences between settlement trends in the northern and southern areas. In the south, settlement declined 89 percent, from forty-four potential settlement sites in the Early Bronze Age down to five in the Middle and Late Bronze Ages. In the north, settlement nearly doubled, from seven to thirteen sites during the same period. Given the probable absence of terracing, it is possible that Early Bronze Age expansion into the relatively steep uplands of the southern Hasa caused erosion in critical areas that altered cost-benefit calculations for settlers in that area. The difference in settlement movement between the northern and southern areas suggests that abandonment in the south is related to differences in the two areas rather than to regional climate change or to political insecurity.

The Iron Age

The Iron Age clearly represents a time of great settlement increase as well as agricultural intensification in the Hasa. It is also the first period for which there is good evidence of an increasing demand from external political powers for surplus production. All of these factors produce an expectation of environmental degradation during the Iron Age. Yet measures of spatial segregation between the Iron Age and the subsequent Hellenistic period are typically among the lowest in the southern area.

A number of factors should be considered with regard to this transition. First, the Hellenistic period is relatively poorly represented and poorly understood in the southern Levant. Survey data may not be entirely representative of actual site distributions owing to the lack of a clear ceramic chronology for this period. Second, the Hellenistic period is a relatively short transition period in this area between the Iron Age and the Nabatean period, with which the Hellenistic overlaps considerably. In other analyses (Hill 2000), I considered the combined Hellenistic and Nabatean periods and found statistically significant spatial segregation among sites in the WHS. Even though most analyses presented here indicate more settlement stability than for other periods, some such as the HOA still indicate statistically significant segregation between the Iron Age and the Hellenistic period.

One aspect of settlement change not addressed by statistical measures of spatial segregation is widespread abandonment without relocation in the area. Spatial segregation as measured here reflects movement within the area but does not measure movement out of the area. There was a 73 percent decline in recorded settlement from the Iron Age to the Hellenistic period, from 109 potential settlements to only 29. In the southern area, that decline is 81 percent, from 95 down to only 18. This represents the second largest percentage decline in settlement recorded for the area. Although many settlements that remained during this period may have stayed in the same locations, most settlements were abandoned. There does not appear to have been a dramatic change in climate during this period that would have caused previously arable locations to fail. This abandonment occurred after the decline of an episode of political intervention in the local economy. Mitigating factors, such as the poor ceramic chronology, may have been at play, but the Hasa apparently experienced a significant decline in agropastoral settlement for two to three centuries following the collapse of centralized authority in the late Iron Age. Declining agropastoral productivity after centuries of surplus production may well have been a factor in the abandonment of so many settlements.

The Classical Periods

The remainder of the Classical Age, including the Nabatean, Roman, and Byzantine periods, was the era of greatest population and economic intensification in the Hasa until modern times. Settlement sites reached their largest size and greatest number during this time, and the level of political organization involved in economic production reached its highest point. There was generally fairly high stability and security in the region. All of the elements leading to overexploitation of the landscape were in place, and the greatest response to local degradation should be expected during this time.

Measures of spatial segregation consistently indicate a high degree of settlement movement between the Nabatean, Roman, Byzantine, and Early Islamic periods. These statistics are among the most significant produced by the analyses and support the hypothesis that settlement relocation owing to local degradation was consistently greater in the south than in the north. There was a great deal of cultural continuity between the Classical periods, but relatively little evidence of major climatic change during this time span. Yet following each period there is significant settlement movement to a different part of the Hasa. It is probable that under conditions of high population density and surplus production for the support of central governments, agropastoralist producers in this area overexploited local landscapes, forcing abandonment and relocation through several centuries.

The Islamic Periods

The final transition period of note is between the Early and Late Islamic periods. Interpretation of these periods is ambiguous because both begin with a time of prosperity and economic expansion, followed by a decline. The resolution of most of the settlement data does not allow for analysis of these potentially interesting within-period trends. Nonetheless, most measures of segregation indicate significant settlement movement from the Early to the Late Islamic period. They indicate, furthermore, that such movement was greater in the south than in the north. These analyses again support the hypothesis that local environmental degradation following periods of intensive exploitation led to settlement abandonment and relocation. Analyses of historical records from the Ottoman period in particular show unequivocally that high population and overproduction led to land exhaustion, desertification, and the abandonment of settlements (Inalcik 1997).

In summary, the statistical analyses presented here provide strong evidence that periodic settlement movement was a common strategy in the Hasa. The comparison of politically and climatically similar areas in the north and the south indicate that this movement was much more prevalent in the south. The most likely factor to account for the difference in the two areas is topography and related differences in soil stability. The southern area is typified by greater topographic relief and thinner and less-stable soils. These aspects of the landscape contributed to greater local degradation around southern settlements, leading to abandonment.

Demonstrating that there was a high degree of site abandonment in the southern Hasa illustrates an important aspect of land management in this region. It provides compelling evidence that people regularly found it advantageous to surrender their investment in a location in favor of an alternative that must have often been uncertain and even risky. There have undoubtedly been many reasons over the millennia for abandoning a site, but the evidence suggests that local land degradation was a frequent reason. Thus far, the argument in favor of land degradation as a motive for abandonment has been based on the observation that some areas seem more vulnerable to erosion than others. Chapter 6 addresses that vulnerability explicitly by using a common measure of potential soil loss to evaluate different areas. Moreover, it addresses in a more explicit manner the association between exploiting vulnerable landscapes and the political climate shaping the decision-making process in each period of history.

6

A Geographic Information System Analysis of Potential Erosion

One of the most prevalent concerns in the discussion of anthropogenic landscapes around the world is soil erosion. Erosion is a problem in many places today and one of the most commonly cited environmental impacts in studies of the ancient world as well (e.g., Beaumont 1985; Bintliff 1992; Christopherson, Guertin, and Borstadt 1996; Davidson and Theocharopoulos 1992; Dobyns 1981; Goldberg and Bar-Yosef 1990; Hunt, Gilbertson, and Donahue 1992; Naveh and Dan 1973; O'Hara, Street-Perrott, and Burt 1993; Rice 1996; Schuldenrein 1986; Street-Perrott, Perrott, and Harkness 1989; Van Andel, Zangger, and Demitrack 1990; Vita-Finzi 1969; Wingard 1996). Erosion resulting from deforestation and overgrazing is a major cause of settlement abandonment by the Pre-Pottery Neolithic in the southern Levant (Kohler-Rollefson and Rollefson 1990; Rollefson, Simmons, and Kafafi 1992; Simmons et al. 1988). Changes in valley-floor morphology related to up-slope disturbances are recorded throughout the Holocene (Goldberg 1995; Goldberg and Bar-Yosef 1990; Mabry 1992), and soil erosion is often debated as an important factor in cultural developments throughout the region.

Though erosion itself is widely visible and relatively easy to document in the past, its causes are usually much more difficult to determine. This difficulty is owing to the complexity of the erosion process, in which multiple environmental factors are often in flux at any given time. For this reason, attempts to establish correspondence between cultural developments and increased erosion are beset by problems of equifinality. Even the most notable examples of ancient human impact on the environment and the scale of its effects are debated (e.g., Bar-Yosef 1995; Kohler-Rollefson and Rollefson 1990; Rollefson, Simmons, and Kafafi 1992). It is becoming increasingly clear that efforts to isolate the causes of ancient erosion are problematic both technically and theoretically. The ecology of the Levant has included humans as one interacting component among many for several hundred millennia.

An alternative approach to understanding erosion in the past is through modeling qualities of the landscape with respect to archaeological settlement patterns (Christopherson, Guertin, and Borstadt 1996; Wingard 1996). I use erosion modeling in these analyses to understand human land-use decisions in the past as they relate to the potential for erosion (see also Hill 2004a). The goal of this study is to elucidate aspects of the changing relationship between settlers in the Wadi al-Hasa and the soils critical to their livelihood.

One quality of land systems, including soils, important to understanding degradation is sensitivity. Blaikie and Brookfield define *sensitivity* as "the degree to which a given land system undergoes changes due to natural forces, following human interference" (1987:10). The susceptibility of land to erosion under conditions of cultivation and animal husbandry is one measure of its sensitivity. Over the past few decades, several attempts to model erosion sensitivity systematically have produced formulae suitable for GIS modeling. One of the best known of these attempts is the USLE developed by Wischmeier and Smith (1978; see also Renard et al. 1991 for the Revised USLE, used with more precise data). For these analyses, I used ArcView GIS software to calculate potential soil loss (PSL) in the Hasa as it is related to land use from the Neolithic through Ottoman periods.

These analyses focus on the proximity of archaeological sites to land resources, especially arable soils and water sources. The development of the GIS required the production and organization of relevant data from map and satellite image sources. The first objective was to identify and quantify the location and degree of land use. Maps of land-use intensity are based on the observation that settlement locations are closely related to land use and that land has been used most intensively in areas closest to settlements (Chisholm 1968; Netting 1968). The analysis of land-use intensity is closely related to site-catchment analysis in that it focuses on the area surrounding a site as a critical part of its economic context. Emphasis is shifted in use-intensity analysis to evaluate effects of settlement on the catchment rather than the products derived from the catchment.

I based the method of defining areas of land use on the location of sites and the topography of the surrounding area. Topography is the single most important variable determining the range of movement on foot for humans and their domestic animals in the Hasa. Thus, the analysis of topography, as represented by a digital elevation model (DEM), in relation to archaeological sites was the basis for creating maps of use intensity.

As a first step in modeling use intensity, I created a cost surface of the Wadi al-Hasa area for each period in question, based on slope values and site locations, to determine the cost of moving away from each site.

Producing a cost surface required a friction surface that was developed in the following way. The cost of moving up or down a slope for a given distance is equal to the work of walking over a flat surface for that distance plus the work of raising oneself a given elevation change. The work of walking over a flat surface was calculated using a formula derived by Cotterell and Kamminga (1990:195–96), wherein

work per stride = weight $\times$ p^2/8L,
where p = length of pace and L = length of leg

Based on an average adult leg length of 80 centimeters and pace length of L/1.65 or 48 centimeters, and weight of 65 kilograms, each stride takes 2.3 units of work. Because each cell in the DEM is 50 meters across or 104.2 strides, 239.7 work units are required for an adult to walk that distance. The work of elevating himself or herself up a given incline equals

weight $\times$ sine of slope $\times$ distance,
where distance = base distance (or 50 meters) $\div$ cosine of slope

Based on the DEM, I calculated the slope of each 50-meter cell and then performed the operations indicated by the formulae to produce a friction surface that reasonably approximates real-world conditions (see also Herhahn and Hill 1998; Hill 2000; Varien 1999). I calibrated the cost-surface model to a 2-degree slope because it is unlikely that empirical estimates were based on a perfectly flat surface. Thus, I determined the cost of walking 5 kilometers on a constant 2-degree slope and used that value as the maximum figure above which cells were removed from consideration. I then scaled the area remaining within the catchment of any site from a given period from 1, at locations nearest to sites, to 0 at the catchment perimeter, to reflect use intensity. The result is a map of approximated use intensity for each period. The use-intensity maps for each period are illustrated in figures 6.1 through 6.11.

I then overlaid additively the resulting maps, such that areas of repeated intensive use would receive values up to 11 (the number of periods), and areas on the perimeter of catchments used only briefly would receive a value approaching 0 (fig. 6.12). The result of this overlay procedure reflects cumulative use intensity for the entire duration of agriculture and pastoralism in this region.

The cumulative use-intensity map is valuable for understanding which areas would have been most affected by people through time. It

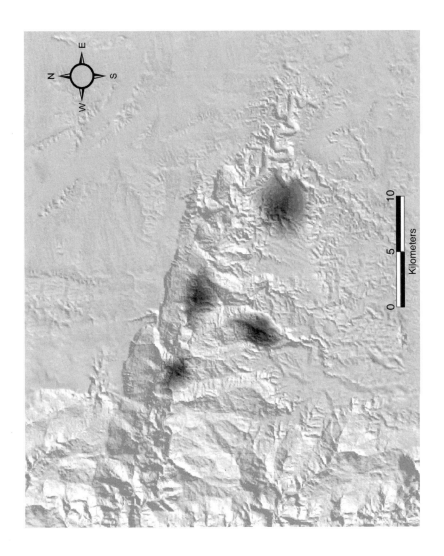

Figure 6.1 Pottery Neolithic use-intensity map

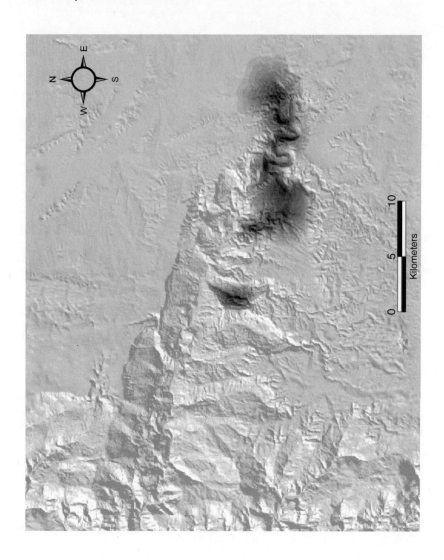

Figure 6.2 Chalcolithic use-intensity map

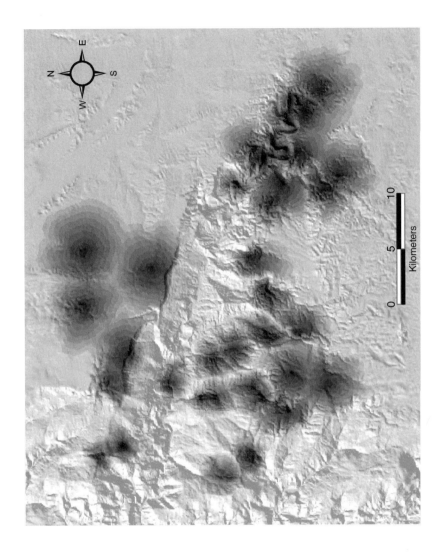

Figure 6.3 Early Bronze Age use-intensity map

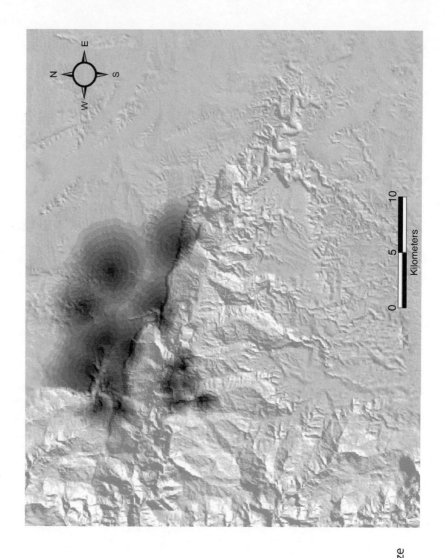

Figure 6.4 Middle/Late Bronze Age use-intensity map

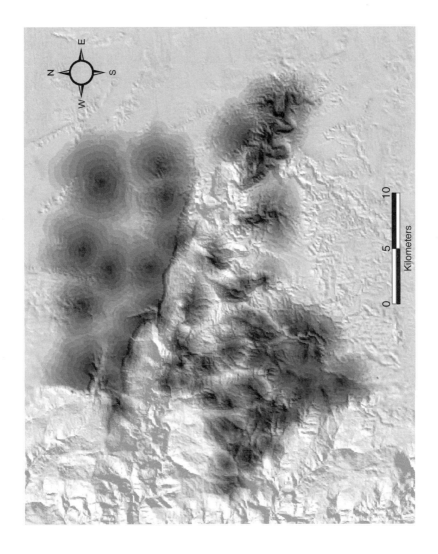

Figure 6.5 Iron Age use-intensity map

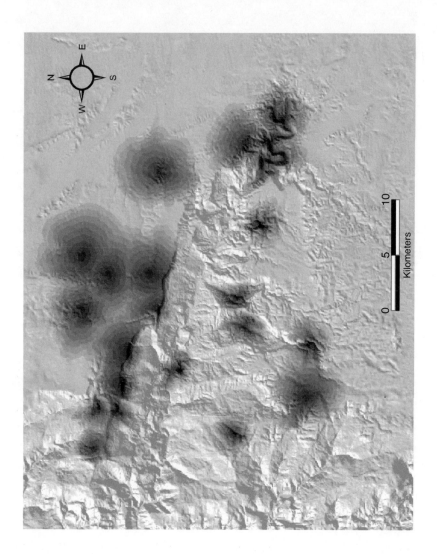

Figure 6.6 Hellenistic use-intensity map

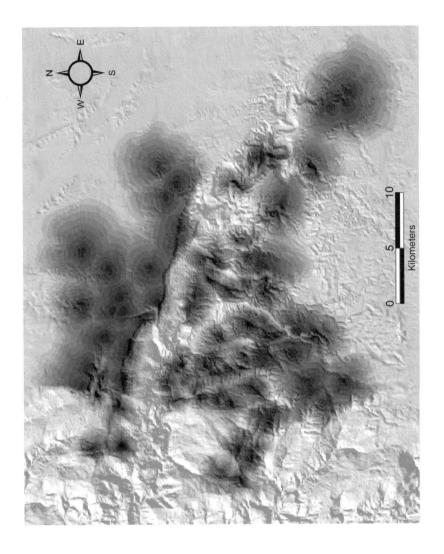

Figure 6.7 Nabatean use-intensity map

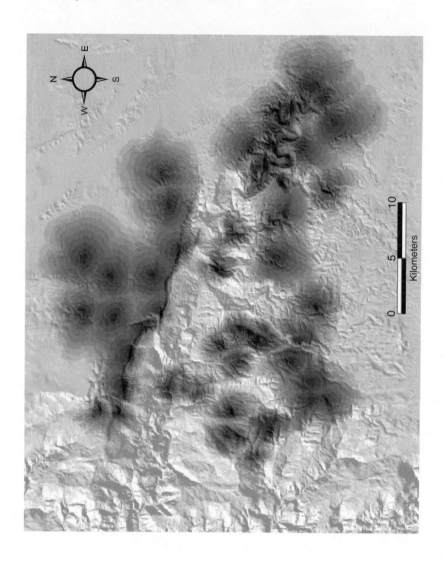

Figure 6.8 Roman use-intensity map

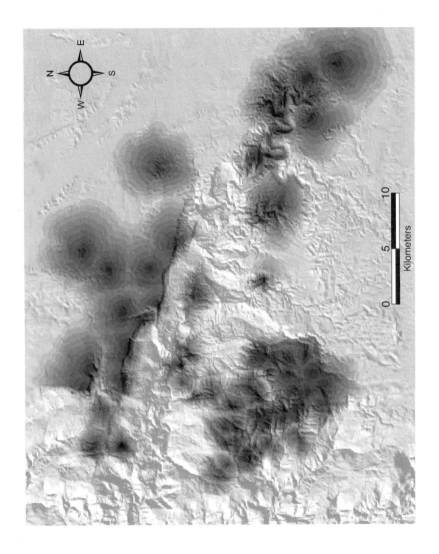

Figure 6.9 Byzantine use-intensity map

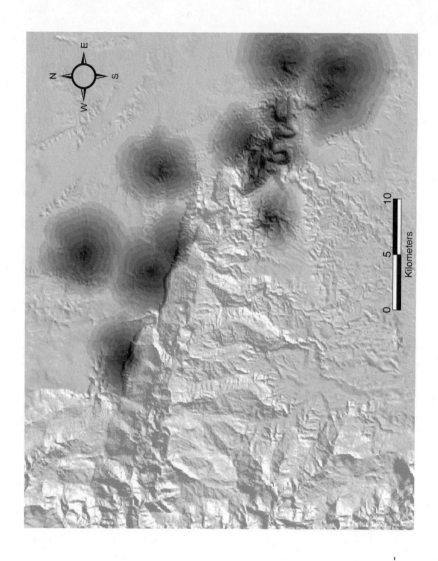

Figure 6.10 Early Islamic use-intensity map

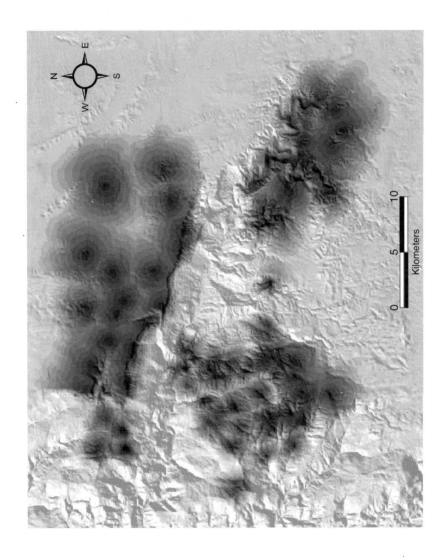

Figure 6.11 Late Islamic use-intensity map

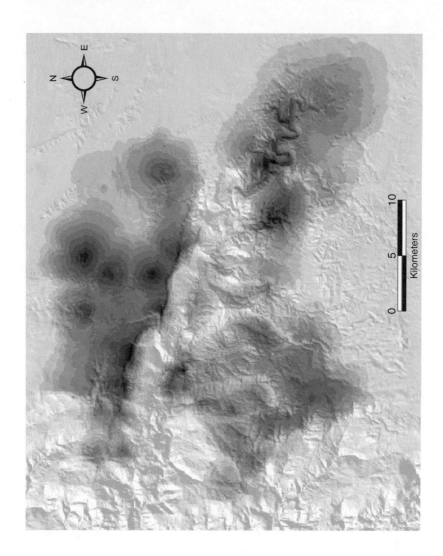

Figure 6.12 Cumulative use-intensity map

is also useful as a measure of settlement success. Given the multiple fluctuations in the natural and cultural environment of the region as well as
the obvious degradation that has occurred there, it is useful to understand which areas have been most successfully inhabited through time.
The measure of long-term use intensity might be considered a measure
of settlement success because sites occupied through multiple periods will
produce higher use-intensity values in their vicinity than those occupied
briefly and abandoned (Hill 2000).

In the second stage of GIS analysis, I used geographic variables to
model potential erosion in different locations. The variables required for
these analyses include topography, precipitation, and vegetation because
they are required to calculate the USLE (Wischmeier and Smith 1978).
Soil scientists developed the USLE to help farmers evaluate the erosional
consequences of different cultivation strategies (W. Graf 1988). The equation calculates the quantity of sediment that will be transported per unit
of land, given values for a range of parameters.

The equation is typically expressed as $A = R \times K \times S \times L \times C \times P$,
where

> A = tons per acre
> R = rainfall factor
> K = soil factor
> S = slope in percentage
> L = length of slope
> C = cropping-management factor
> P = erosion-control measures

Values used in this formula are derived from tables based on empirical observation and local topography. For instruction in the application
of this formula, I referred to Soil Conservation Service guidelines (U.S.
Department of Agriculture [USDA] 1976), publications by Wischmeier
and Smith (Wischmeier 1976; Wischmeier and Smith 1978), and indications for its use in the Near East by the Food and Agriculture Organization
(FAO) of the United Nations (1979). Applying numerical attributes as indicated by the formula permits calculation of soil movement, or PSL, in
each grid cell defined by the GIS.

I determined the slope "S" and slope length "L" values in the USLE calculation by using the DEM with the ArcView GIS program. The ArcView
program provides terrain and hydrologic-modeling functions that allow
for the simple calculation of slope between two grid cells of the DEM

and for the calculation of flow length, which is substituted here for slope length, as in the formula:

$LS = (L/72.6)^m (65.41 \sin a^2 + 4.56 \sin a + 0.065)$, where

L = slope length in feet

a = angle of slope

m = 0.5 if percent slope is 5 or more

0.4 if percent slope is 3.5–4.5

0.3 if percent slope is 1–3

0.2 if percent slope is less than 1

Using this formula, I calculated the combined "LS" factor as indicated by Wischmeier and Smith (1978) and removed from consideration any slopes greater than 35 degrees as probably weathering limited surfaces contributing little fine-grained material to sediment movement (Cooke and Warren 1973). Likewise, I removed from consideration anything with more than 35 hectares accumulated watershed as probably incised by gullies and hence not appropriate for the USLE.

I developed the rainfall factor "R" using FAO guidelines and meteorological data provided by the Royal Jordanian Geographic Centre. I used rainfall averages for the ten years from 1989 to 1998 from four weather stations at Kerak, Tafila, Qatrana, and Safi. These precipitation averages are somewhat greater than averages published previously for this area and may represent a period of relatively high rainfall (Harlan 1988). The advantage offered by data from the four stations is that they allow for the extrapolation of rainfall predictions to other areas based on elevation and geographic location. Given that precipitation has fluctuated considerably over the Holocene, the variability between mid- and late-twentieth-century calculations is probably insignificant, and any precipitation data are useful only in a relative sense.

I used multiple regression on the elevation, easting, northing, and precipitation from the four weather stations to extrapolate mean annual precipitation to other areas. Using four data points and four variables results in a saturated model with a coefficient of determination (r^2) equaling 1.0. The actual correlation is not perfect, of course, but even with any two of the independent variables and precipitation, the r^2 values are relatively high, indicating that elevation and geographic position are significant determinants of precipitation in this area. For example, the r^2 value for elevation and easting is 0.964, and for elevation and northing it is 0.726. Using grids of easting, northing, and elevation, I applied the multiple regression formula to produce a fourth grid of mean annual precipitation.

Using FAO and USDA guidelines for determining the "R" factor of the

USLE, I reclassified the precipitation grid to values of 20–50 for use in the USLE formula (FAO 1979; USDA 1976).

The inherent susceptibility of soil to erosion is designated as factor "K" in the USLE and is a function of soil attributes such as texture, permeability, etc. To produce a grid defining the "K" factor for the study area, I used a LandSat 7 ETM satellite image from September 1999, classified by land-surface type and rectified for topography. Classification was done with ERDAS Imagine image-analysis software using criteria from sixty ground control points described in the field in April 1999 (Hill 2001). I performed classification in an iterative manner using three subsets of the training sites, allowing for two stages of refinement.

The "K" factor of the USLE is based on soil parameters including texture, organic matter content, structure, and permeability. Based on soil studies by Willimott and colleagues (1963, 1964) and surface-texture observations made in the field, I categorized soils into three major types: Red Mediterranean soils, Yellow Mediterranean soils, and Yellow desert soils. These soils are derived primarily from chalk and limestone, with some basalt and sandstone contribution. Based on variability in soil texture, generally low organic matter, medium/course granular structure, and moderate permeability, I assigned a "K" value of 0.25 to Red Mediterranean soils and of 0.35 to Yellow Mediterranean and Yellow desert soils. I assigned other surface types—including various types of bedrock, channels, and urban settings—a null value to exclude them from analyses because they are not subject to erosion appropriate to calculation with the USLE.

The "C" factor of the USLE is the cover or management factor reflecting the effect of ground cover. I used tables prepared by the USDA for permanent pasture, rangeland, idle land, and grazed woodland (USDA 1976). Although vegetation was one of the categories I classified during LandSat image analyses, it is doubtful that conditions in 1999 are the same as those in the past. In fact, vegetation has varied considerably depending on climate and land use throughout the Holocene. For present purposes, I have scaled the "C" factor based on variability in precipitation, which has probably been the most significant nonanthropogenic factor affecting vegetation in the past. Field observations indicate more than 35 percent ground cover, with a 25 percent 0.5-meter weed and brush canopy in the most humid parts of the study area, ranging down to no ground cover in the most arid areas. Based on this range of ground cover and the assumption of a strong correlation with precipitation, I reclassified the precipitation grid from 0.12 to 0.45 to reflect lowest to highest ground cover respectively according to USDA (1976) guidelines.

Erosion-control measures are indicated by the "P" factor in the USLE and refer to terracing, contour cropping, and other techniques of slowing runoff to mitigate soil loss. Such techniques have been used in the Hasa since at least the Iron Age and are documented by various terrace and checkdam remains still found in the area. Unfortunately, relatively few of these remains are recorded, and they are difficult to date. For example, many such remains were noted but not recorded by the WHS because no temporal association could be assigned to them. I left the "P" value null in the present analyses because it cannot be effectively applied to soils throughout the area based on current evidence.

To calculate PSL for different periods in the Hasa I multiplied grids as described earlier to produce an overall grid of soil loss per year per hectare. This grid represents a general measure of the susceptibility of soils to erosion. Within each period, I calculated the amount of PSL within the catchments of sites identified for the period in order to evaluate differences in land use through time and in different parts of the study area.

It should be made clear that PSL as calculated here is an approximate measure of susceptibility to erosion under current conditions. Conditions today are obviously not the same as those in the past. Endeavors to better understand geographic conditions affecting soil loss in the past will undoubtedly be an important part of future research in this region. However, the current analyses should not be greatly affected by such differences in past conditions. Differences in factors such as precipitation probably varied relatively uniformly across the area. Thus, a change in the "R" factor would shift all PSL values in somewhat the same manner, and comparisons of PSL between local areas under different regional precipitation would remain valid.

Soils today are probably not significantly different in kind than those of the earlier Holocene. Soil loss is, however, an expectation of this research, and areas currently classified as bedrock were formerly covered with soil. The result of including such areas as erodible terrain would be to increase PSL values in areas identified here as highly sensitive. Most areas identified as bedrock and consequently removed from these analyses were in steep terrain that would have been among the first areas affected by erosion.

Finally, slope and slope length, or the "LS" factor, may have undergone some change through time, particularly in the valley bottoms (see chapter 4). Depending on how much erosion and channel incision occurred in the valley bottoms, current conditions there may be significantly different than those in the earliest periods. Although I argue that such changes in valley-bottom conditions were extremely important in the early human ecology of the area, they do not profoundly affect the PSL calculations presented here. The PSL calculations are typically summarized for an area such as a 5-kilometer catchment comprised largely of hillslopes in surrounding canyon sides. The actual valley bottom that may have been different in the past makes up a relatively small portion of the overall area evaluated. The calculations of PSL undoubtedly vary where they take place in valley bottoms affected by channel incision, but it is unlikely that such variations would overwhelm the values based on large areas presented here. Outside the valley bottoms, the topography of the area is probably not substantially different than it was in the past.

The objective in these analyses is to evaluate sensitivity to erosion in different parts of the Hasa as these areas were exploited through history. It is useful in this context to categorize use intensity, as described earlier, for graphing purposes. For each period, I divide the range of use-intensity values into ten intervals, from a highest value of 10 to a lowest value of 1. After adding individual period maps together to create cumulative use-intensity maps, I divided them into ten intervals in the same manner. With the use-intensity maps thus categorized, I summarized PSL values by use intensity. For example, in each of the ten categories of use intensity, I calculated summary statistics of PSL to evaluate variations in the sensitivity of lands used among different areas and different time periods.

It is also helpful to categorize PSL for the presentation of some analyses. In much of the discussion, I simply use tons per hectare per year (tons/hectare/year) as indicated by the USLE formula. As a relative measure, comparing the tons/hectare/year from one area to the next can be suggestive by itself, but for many questions it is useful to consider what is an acceptable rate of erosion. Wischmeier and Smith indicate that tolerances of approximately 5–12.4 tons/hectare/year are typical in the United States (Wischmeier and Smith 1978). The FAO (1979) suggests categorizing four levels of soil loss in North Africa and the Middle East as follows:

> less than 10 tons/hectare/year = none to slight
> 10–50 tons/hectare/year = moderate
> 50–200 tons/hectare/year = high
> greater than 200 tons/hectare/year = very high

For the purpose of graphing the present analyses, both tons/hectare/ year and the FAO categories are illustrative of variability in this area. For presentation, I focus on summaries of PSL by use-intensity category and on summaries of use intensity by PSL category to illustrate variability in land use among different areas and periods.

A final method of presenting the analyses with respect to individual periods is to calculate the total PSL within catchments of each period and geographic zone. No attempt has been made here to model erosion differently depending on the degree of use intensity. I present the total potential erosion within all catchments of each period and geographic area as a measure of the variability in exposure to land degradation. The PSL map is constant, meaning that the potential erosion as it is modeled is irrespective of land use. Rather, the variability charted is the exposure to that potential by settlers in different situations. I interpret this variability as the exposure of settlers in different periods to land degradation, and I evaluate those differences with respect to the political context of their decisions.

Susceptibility to erosion is, of course, not uniform throughout the Hasa. Its spatial variability is especially interesting because land use is also spatially variable through time. Land use in the Hasa has varied among different geographic zones and under different conditions of social and political development. This variability is important for two reasons. First, the analyses of settlement movement through time in the preceding chapter assume that lands in different areas had different levels of sensitivity to erosion. One goal of the USLE analyses is to address the validity of that assumption. Second, as noted previously, a common issue in studies of ancient environmental impact is the role of political hierarchy in mismanagement and overexploitation (Adams 1978; Blaikie and Brookfield 1987; Butzer 1996; McGovern 1994; McGovern et al. 1988; Redman 1999). A second goal of these analyses is to evaluate changes in the relationship between humans and soils as regional politics have changed.

Land-Use Intensity and Erosion

First, I examine intensity of land use in relation to sensitivity to erosion. I begin with a review of cumulative use intensity as it pertains to the issue of differential sensitivity to erosion in different geographic zones of the Hasa. This review is followed by a closer consideration of land use and sensitivity during specific periods. In each stage of analysis, I use a judgmental sample of the total survey database, as described in chapter 5, to more precisely reflect agropastoral land use. I further subdivided the sample by survey project to reflect the emphases on different geographic zones by those surveys. I also conducted analyses on the upper-quartile sample with similar results (Hill 2002), but in the interest of brevity these results are not presented here.

Patterns among Geographic Zones

The first distinction in land use to be evaluated is that between the northern area, encompassed by the ASKP, and the southern area, encompassed by the WHS and WHNBS. In chapter 5, I proposed that the higher degree of settlement abandonment and relocation documented in the south was owing to the relative instability of soils in that area compared to the north. Analyses of PSL indicate that land use in the south focused on more easily eroded soils than did land use in the north. Mean PSL in the catchments of northern sites is 13.4 tons/hectare/year, whereas the mean for southern sites is 25 percent greater at 16.8 tons/hectare/year.

The total defined use area extends into the eastern desert in areas that receive inadequate rainfall for nonirrigated agriculture. Thus, calculations of PSL are somewhat biased by large expanses of low-relief desert that were probably seldom, if ever, cultivated. Restricting analyses of PSL to the total use area that receives more than 200 millimeters of precipitation per year reveals even greater differences between the northern and southern areas. The mean PSL in that portion of the northern use area with more than 200 millimeters precipitation is still 13.4 tons/hectare/year, but the mean in a likewise restricted southern area is 47 percent greater at 19.7 tons/hectare/year.

Restricting analyses to areas receiving more than 200 millimeters of precipitation per year effectively excludes large areas that were often not economically significant. However, some areas receiving inadequate rainfall for dry farming have been irrigated using other means, including runoff techniques. Thus, eliminating these areas altogether from the analyses probably results in an underrepresentation of total erosion because runoff-irrigated lands may be among those most affected by cultivation.

Another means of restricting the analyses to reduce the eastern desert bias is to focus only on the areas in closest proximity to sites and having the highest use intensity. Isolating the catchment area within use-intensity zones 6–10 focuses on the area most heavily impacted, eliminating much of the eastern desert, but including areas that may have been subject to irrigation. The mean PSL in northern use-intensity zones 6–10 is 10.5 tons/hectare/year, whereas the mean PSL in southern use-intensity zones 6–10 is 60 percent greater at 16.8 tons/hectare/year.

Although the mean PSL reflects substantial differences between the

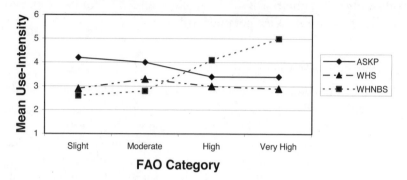

Figure 6.13 Mean use intensity by FAO categories of soil loss

two areas, it does not adequately convey the variability within each area. Analyses of cumulative use intensity summarized by FAO soil-loss categories indicate that areas of higher PSL are more intensively used in the south than in the north. Among ASKP sites, the highest cumulative use intensity is in areas of low to moderate PSL. Among WHS sites, use intensity is relatively evenly distributed with respect to PSL, whereas WHNBS sites exhibit the highest cumulative use intensity in areas of high to very high PSL (fig. 6.13).

The WHNBS area is in the easternmost part of the study area and manifests the highest settlement movement in these analyses (see chapter 5). The WHS area is intermediate between the ASKP and the WHNBS in terms of both PSL and settlement movement. These analyses of cumulative use intensity and PSL support the ideas that soils in the southern area are more easily degraded and that soil degradation has been a part of periodic settlement abandonment in the area. In general, soils are more erodable in the south, and the trend from low to high erodability among the three survey areas corresponds to the trend from low to high settlement movement in the three survey areas.

Evaluation of Individual Periods

I turn now to variability in exposure to potential erosion among geographic zones and time periods, especially as this variability is related to changes in the political environment of the area from the Early Bronze Age through Ottoman periods. These are the periods for which there is reason to believe changing social and political conditions, including the presence of strong centralized authority, might have affected land-use de-

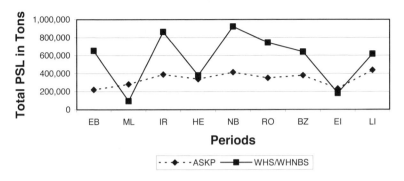

Figure 6.14 Total PSL for northern and southern areas by period

cisions. They are also the periods for which sites were recorded in both the northern and southern areas, allowing for comparison between geographic zones.

The principal hypothesis to be evaluated is that socially or spatially distant managers made land-use decisions with negative long-term consequences. One way to evaluate the effect of political hierarchy on land use is to examine the variability in exposure to high PSL values in times of different political organization. If elite authorities increased the demand for surplus production in the Hasa, this greater demand would result in the expansion of cultivation into new areas. Expansion of cultivation into lands with higher sensitivity to degradation would lead to short-term productive gains at the expense of long-term sustainability. Figure 6.14 is a graph of total PSL in the northern and southern areas during each period from the rise of the first political hierarchy in the area until the modern era. I calculated these values by summing the PSL within 5-kilometer use zones of all judgmental sample sites from the two geographic areas by chronological period.

Figure 6.14 is striking for its representation of the differences in PSL among areas used by people in the south versus the north in different time periods. In the north, land use was focused through time on areas having a fairly constant and comparatively low PSL level. This low variability is consistent with the idea that the northern plateau has been the location of stable and sustainable land use throughout the past five thousand years. Small fluctuations exist, reflecting expansion and contraction during different periods of political control, but overall land use was relatively constant.

In contrast, the exposure to high erosion by settlers in the south fluctuated markedly from one period to the next. The PSL levels there ranged from below levels in the north to more than twice as high as levels in the north. This fluctuation clearly represents fluctuation in the extent of land use in the southern area. The four major peaks in PSL represent pulses of expansion into the higher-sensitivity lands of the southern Hasa. Cultivation of these higher-sensitivity lands was generally less sustainable than cultivation in the north, and each peak of expansion was followed by a sharp drop in total PSL of occupied areas, indicating a relocation from the southern Hasa to less-sensitive locations. The high degree of land-use fluctuation in the south supports the hypothesis that expansion occurred periodically in association with changing political conditions in the area.

If such fluctuations were based on changes in climate, they would be expected to occur more uniformly throughout the area. Climate change significant enough to lead to large-scale settlement abandonment in the south would probably also be visible in land-use patterns a few kilometers to the north. Instead, the fluctuations documented here appear most likely to be related to changing land-use strategies from one period to the next.

If these fluctuations were only a result of local degradation, they would appear as movement from one part of the Hasa to another as local conditions varied. Instead, a pattern of widespread settlement followed by widespread abandonment suggests a correlation with changing regional political conditions. The decision to expand intensive land use into the Hasa or to revert to a more extensive nomadic economy is shown repeatedly in the historic literature to be associated with regional political conditions. The fluctuations in land use shown here support the hypothesis that political considerations affected land use.

One factor affecting the exposure to variable PSL is the rise and fall of the number of settlements recorded. The exposure to PSL measured here is the total amount within the use areas of sites from a given period. Thus, the more sites recorded, the more area included in the analysis. Yet the total PSL measured does not vary in accord with the number of settlements recorded. For example, the highest number of sites recorded in the southern area is ninety-four during the Iron Age, but the Nabatean period, with only seventy-five sites recorded, exhibits a higher level of PSL. Likewise, a relatively modest forty-four Early Bronze Age sites were recorded in the southern area, yet the PSL exhibited is greater than that for the Byzantine period with seventy-four sites recorded. Clearly, the PSL calculated is a function of more than simply the number of sites. Factors including site location and relative dispersal on the landscape also affect exposure during different periods.

The hypothesis that land mismanagement is associated with spatially or socially distant decision making is somewhat equivocally supported by these analyses. The greatest settlement expansion into high-sensitivity lands in the southern Hasa is recorded during the Nabatean period. The Nabatean period was certainly a time of political hierarchy and demand for surplus production, but other periods exhibited both more complex hierarchy and more distant authority. The Nabatean state was a relatively small, local polity in comparison to other systems. For example, the Roman and Byzantine periods were times of domination by very large empires with central authority located in distant regions. Yet both exhibit more modest exposure to degradation than the Nabatean period.

Likewise, the Iron Age was a period of increasing local hierarchy and periodic subjugation to Mesopotamian powers, but one does not gain the impression that Assyrian tribute demands and influence over land management were greater than those of Roman, Byzantine, or Ottoman powers. Yet the Iron Age exhibits the second-highest level of exposure to degradation in the history of the area.

Although the Early Bronze Age was a general time of rising political hierarchy and influence from Egypt in the Levant, it would be difficult to ascribe to distant authority the relatively high level of exposure to degradation during that time. It is not clear from either the archaeological or the historical records that there was a strong political presence in the Hasa during the Early Bronze Age. There is some indication that Egyptian military expeditions occasionally entered the area, but no evidence that they exerted any lasting authority over economic production there. The Middle and Late Bronze Ages were times of at least as much interference by Egypt, but they are marked by sparse settlement and very low exposure to degradation in the southern Hasa.

Likewise, presence and burdensome taxation by the Ptolemies in the Hellenistic period are not reflected in settlement expansion or exposure to degradation in the southern Hasa. The demand for taxes and tribute by distant authorities is present in nearly every period to some extent, and there is not adequate quantitative data on the exact rates to compare one period to the next. Anecdotes, however, indicate that some demands were more onerous than others.

For example, during the Hellenistic period the Ptolemies were particularly interested in resource extraction and had a notably high rate of taxation (Smith 1990). Evidence from the Roman period shows that the people of southern Transjordan considered the taxation excessive (D. Graf 1997b). And high rates of taxation were a factor among late Byzantine populations considering the options presented to them by their Muslim conquerors (Mayerson 1994b). Throughout much of the Early Islamic period, taxes were an issue of importance, but they appear to have been quite reasonable until the imposition of tax farming during the latter part of this period (Shaban 1976). Finally, the Ottoman period was a time in which excessive demands by tax farmers contributed to social upheaval and widespread economic collapse (Inalcik 1997).

These are not the periods in which we see the greatest expansion of settlement into highly sensitive lands. The Roman, Byzantine, and Ottoman periods exhibit moderately high exposure to erosion, but less than the Iron Age and the Nabatean period, for which we do not have any clear indication of excessive political intervention in economic production. Among the more notable characteristics of the Iron Age and Nabatean periods is the high level of peace and prosperity in the area. Likewise, the Early Bronze Age was probably relatively free of external political intervention and exhibits a relatively high exposure to erosion. In short, there is not a perfect connection between the spatial or social distance of managers and an increase in land degradation.

The expansion of settlement into marginal, highly sensitive lands in the Hasa is predicated on a variety of factors. Undoubtedly, elite demands were an important consideration in periods of expansion. But the demand alone for surplus production was not enough to lead to expansion when other considerations such as security and reasonable return on investment were in doubt. The greatest expansion of land use into marginal and sensitive areas occurred when there was both a demand for surplus production and a strong enough political presence to ensure the general security of rural producers. In addition, settlers in the Hasa have historically had alternative means of subsistence when elite demands became excessive. For example, when the tax burden became too great and expectation of reasonable benefit from cultivation diminished during the Ottoman period, there was widespread settlement abandonment and reversion to nomadic pastoralism.

The demand for surplus production would have been only one among many factors to consider in the past when individuals were making cost-benefit calculations regarding agricultural settlement. On several occasions, attempts by central authority to settle people in the Hasa for agricultural production were balanced by the threat of nomadic raiding or other conflict. When political authority was uncertain or unable to exert military control over the area, we see expansion of agriculture mitigated by the option to avoid authority through nomadism.

For example, much of the Hellenistic period was a time of contested military control over the Hasa. Although the exposure to potential erosion around Hellenistic sites was quite high, overall settlement was low, and there was widespread reliance on pastoralism. During the Roman and Byzantine periods, imperial authorities made major efforts to protect the region militarily, but there was also resistance to that authority. The relatively modest exposure to erosion during the Roman and Byzantine periods may have been affected by efforts to avoid imperial authority or by the declining productivity of high-sensitivity lands originally settled during the Nabatean period, or by both. During the Ottoman period, Turkish military authority declined as the area became of secondary economic importance to the empire. Although tax demands were quite high, there was little military defense of the region, and large numbers of people abandoned their farms and turned to pastoralism.

There have undoubtedly been many reasons for choosing a settlement site and subsequently abandoning it over the past several thousand years. The impetus to produce agricultural surplus for a centralized political authority has been one factor among many to consider. There is good reason to believe that at times political authorities have encouraged settlement in marginal areas. If we look at the long-term record of land use, however, it is evident that they have met with only partial success. Their efforts have been counterbalanced by other considerations, such as security, over which they have had limited control. One constant factor in the land-use decisions of rural people in the Hasa has been the option to abandon marginally productive locations either for alternative areas or for the alternative strategy of nomadic pastoralism. This multitude of considerations and options for settlers in the Hasa has resulted in a complex history of exposure to land degradation. Although elite authorities have often attempted to expand production in the Hasa, the power of local producers to resist has countered the mismanagement and overexploitation of a maladaptive political hierarchy.

Settlement Success and Landscape Stability

Another important trend in settlement and land use in the Hasa was first described by Donahue and Beynon (1988). They noted that the most successful long-term settlement seemed to be oriented around areas of relatively low topographic relief. They explained this tendency in terms

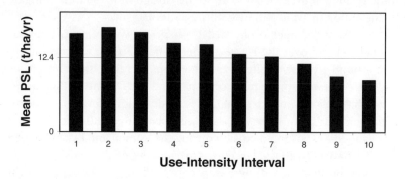

Figure 6.15 Mean PSL by use-intensity interval in upper-quartile sample (t/ha/yr = tons/hectare/year)

of geomorphological stability and the fact that low-relief lands were less susceptible to erosion and consequent declines in productivity.

The trend toward high use intensity in areas of low erosion is revealed most strongly around the upper-quartile sample of the largest sites. These analyses show the lowest PSL values in the highest use-intensity zones, as well as a distinct trend toward higher PSL in lower use-intensity zones (fig. 6.15). This trend supports the hypothesis that settlement success was greater in low-sensitivity lands.

Thus far, the discussion of erosion exposure by chronological period has been based on the total values of PSL in each period. Such an approach emphasizes the actual extent of land use and consequently the overall extent to which agropastoralists in the Hasa were exposed to the consequences of land use. An alternative is to evaluate the rate of erosion exposure by period. Analysis of the rate of PSL by period emphasizes the vulnerability of individual land managers to the consequences of erosion.

Several methods of evaluating erosion rates are possible, and I provide summary statistics of PSL by period elsewhere (Hill 2002). For the purpose of illustration, I focus here on the mean PSL value within the highest use-intensity zones of sites from each period. Figure 6.16 illustrates the mean PSL in use zones 6–10 for each period from the Pottery Neolithic to the Late Islamic from the judgmental sample. Examination of erosion rates in individual periods reveals the highest PSL in the use areas of Neolithic sites, followed by those of Chalcolithic sites. Sites from these earliest periods are strongly oriented around the valley bottomlands and are completely absent from upland areas. Butzer (1996) notes that the earliest periods of sedentary agricultural settlement in a region may be a time of trial and error with regard to land management. Early agriculturalists did not have a full understanding of the consequences of their actions and may have caused serious environmental degradation before they developed more sustainable practices in response to degradation.

Some have argued that the development of specialized pastoralism and the removal of herds to more distant locations were a response to early degradation in the vicinity of settlements (Kohler-Rollefson 1988; Levy 1983a, 1983b). The high rates of erosion in the vicinity of Neolithic and Chalcolithic sites in the Hasa are suggestive of a pattern of early mismanagement in this area.

Figure 6.16 suggests that the earliest periods of agropastoralism were times during which land use in the Hasa was focused on the most sensitive areas. The Pottery Neolithic and Chalcolithic periods show the highest rate of PSL followed by a decline to levels closer to the overall mean of 15.7 tons/hectare/year. This trend supports the idea that the use of more stable locations followed an early period of ignorance and mismanagement. Figure 6.16 also confirms that land use in the Iron Age and Nabatean resulted in both high overall levels of PSL and relatively high rates of PSL per site.

Although the Neolithic and Chalcolithic settlements were located in areas of high erosion potential, the total PSL within catchments of these periods remains lower than for later periods because relatively few early-period settlements were recorded in the surveys. If, as I suspect, many

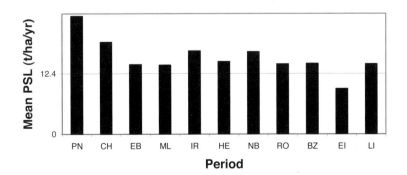

Figure 6.16 Mean soil loss in use zones 6–10 (t/ha/yr = tons/hectare/year)

more Neolithic and Chalcolithic sites were located in the valley bottom than we know of today, the actual erosion within the catchments of early-period sites may have been quite high. This high erosion would be in accord with the high degree of settlement movement following the Neolithic and Chalcolithic periods, as well as with the general trend toward greater use of upland areas by the Early Bronze Age.

In summary, the analyses presented here demonstrate that areas of the southern Hasa inhabited in the past were substantially more sensitive to land degradation than were areas in the north. This sensitivity resulted in significantly more site abandonment in the south because the soils in site catchments there would have been more easily eroded through use. A more interesting issue, though, is what led people to settle repeatedly in those unsustainable locations. Surely after several millennia of agropastoralism in the region, people have long been aware of the consequences of their actions in steep desert terrain.

One explanation is that distant but powerful political elites have demanded surplus production at the expense of sustainability. These analyses show expansion of land use into less-sustainable areas during periods of hierarchical political domination. But they also show that elite desire for expansion and increased production has not always been matched by reality. Without the combination of enforcement and prosperity to tip the cost-benefit scale, people in the Hasa may have chosen alternatives, including abandonment and mobility.

At the scale of political systems and individual land-use choices, a great deal of variability is evident, suggesting that multiple factors affect decision making in the short term. However, the long-term perspective illustrates strong trends suggestive of adaptation. A major element of every description of society in this area since the Neolithic is the role of specialized pastoralism and the relationship between nomadic pastoralists and sedentary peoples. This relationship has long been a basic factor of social and political organization here, and people have often moved between settled and mobile status. The archaeological and historical literature makes many references to the periodic settling of nomads followed by the reversion of settlers to nomadic pastoralism (see chapter 4).

Over time, the most successful and stable settlements were located in areas with more stable soils that were not as easily degraded. However, most settlements were relatively short lived and represent somewhat temporary periods of sedentism in a diversified and mobile economic strategy. Overall, there is no statistical clustering of sites in any one part of the

Hasa. On the contrary, every part of the area, including locations of high erodability, was equally likely to be settled at some time in the past.

In evolutionary terms, there is evidence of selection and adaptation. In the most stable uplands, we see settlements reproduced successfully through time from one period to the next. This differential reproduction of settlements through time results in a higher number of multicomponent sites in geomorphologically stable locations.

In less-stable terrain, we see relatively temporary settlement and frequent recourse to the flexible economic strategy of diversity and mobility. The maintenance of a resilient subsistence strategy throughout several thousand years of changing political conditions is easy to understand as an adaptation. The cultural traditions that encouraged rural people to maintain subsistence flexibility and diversity allowed them to survive in an environment where superimposed political and economic systems have failed repeatedly.

Adaptation has clearly influenced the long-term trends we see in settlement and land use. The marginal environment of this area has constrained the types of settlements and economic strategies that can be successfully reproduced over the long term. But we see these adaptations most clearly if we look at a span of time covering the past several thousand years. What the concept of adaptation explains here is long-term patterning in the archaeological record, not the actions of individuals at any given time. Thus, the combination of long-term analysis and examination of individual periods illustrates both adaptation and individual action in land use.

7

Reflections on the Significance and Causes of Environmental Degradation

Two issues are of central importance to an analysis of land use and environmental degradation in the Wadi al-Hasa. First, when did anthropogenic environmental degradation become a significant problem for people in this area? And second, under what kinds of social and political conditions was land use most inclined to degrade local resources? Settlement-pattern changes through time, in conjunction with archaeological and historical evidence of sociopolitical conditions, provide strong grounds for inferring anthropogenic degradation repeatedly throughout the Holocene.

One standard for identifying significant anthropogenic degradation is the transition from the dominance of natural causes to the dominance of human causes. Based on this standard, Goldberg and Bar-Yosef (1990) have argued that significant degradation did not occur in the southern Levant until at least the Chalcolithic period, approximately 5.5 ka. Previous degradation during the Neolithic was deemed to have been insignificant because it was local in scale, and because more serious environmental degradation probably resulted from a drought in the late Pre-Pottery Neolithic. The standard of dominance is one straightforward means of assessing the significance of human actions in forming the landscape as it appears today.

Likewise, other discussions of environmental degradation in the region have focused on evidence for large-scale processes that have contributed to the region's current appearance (e.g., Bottema, Entjes-Nieborg, and van Zeist 1990; Le Hourou 1981; Naveh and Dan 1973). However, for assessing the role of human actions in a complex and delicate ecosystem, the status of dominance is too strict a standard for determining significance. It is obvious from an ecological standpoint that a great deal of anthropogenic degradation might significantly alter ecosystem relations without being more important than regional climate fluctuations. Just because these anthropogenic factors are not the dominant factors shaping the landscape does not mean they are insignificant. *Significance* is a relative term in the context of environmental change. Factors that are insignificant in shaping millennial- and regional-scale environments may be quite significant to the humans and other organisms affected by them in local, seasonal, or annual interrelations.

On the other hand, one might argue that virtually any human activity has an environmental impact that may be detrimental to some aspect of the ecosystem at some scale. Too liberal a standard of significance, including very small-scale impacts, would not be useful to researchers interested in understanding the systematics of development and change in human ecology. Given adequate data resolution, anthropogenic environmental degradation might be documented in many cases that would not help to distinguish archaeologically and geographically important processes.

One of the first conceptual issues that must be clarified is the question of significance to whom. The simplest answer to this question is, of course, significance to humans. But the matter of scale remains unresolved. Do we mean individuals, social groups, or archaeological cultures? In recent decades, anthropologists have emphasized the role of individuals and human agency (Brumfiel 1992; Ortner 1984), and it is undoubtedly important to recognize archaeological processes as a function of individual actions. However, individual actions themselves and their effects on the environment are probably too random and too difficult to discern in the archaeological record to be very meaningfully interpreted. To draw valid inferences about cultural and environmental processes it is necessary to document change at the level of a population. Significant anthropogenic environmental degradation must affect a group of people at least at a suprahousehold level to be usefully interpreted in terms of human-ecological process.

A second issue to be resolved relates to the type of degradation that might be considered significant. It is easy to imagine Paleolithic foragers exploiting local resources to a point of diminished return, requiring movement to a new area. The depletion of local resources necessitating relocation would clearly be important to the people who have to seek subsistence in a new and unfamiliar territory. In most cases, however, this type of resource depletion would not interest researchers studying environmental degradation, for two reasons. First, the cyclical nature of predator-prey relationships is considered a normal part of ecosystem dynamics. If the depleted resources recover their former state once pressure is removed, the area would once again become a viable territory for them. Second, the relocation in most cases would not require a fundamentally different type of subsistence strategy. The basic properties of the population and the ecosystem presumably could remain unchanged.

G. Stone (1993) notes that in agrarian systems cultivation without intensification almost always degrades agricultural resources. For him, the question is why this degradation causes some groups to abandon their farms and others to intensify production to overcome the loss of resources. Both abandonment and intensification are common strategies to deal with degradation. Given land degradation as a constant, the focus of interest is directed toward variability among cultural factors that affect the use of different strategies. The question of significance, however, requires consideration of how land degradation affects change among cultural factors and vice versa. The significance of anthropogenic environmental degradation is a function of its role in causing fundamental changes in the development of cultural practice. People did not always practice agriculture, agricultural intensification, or agrarian abandonment as part of their subsistence strategies. The degree to which anthropogenic degradation influenced those developments is part of the calculation of the significance of degradation.

Thus, the issue of significance involves the scale of degradation and whom it impacts, as well as the type of change that results. For present purposes, I consider anthropogenic environmental degradation significant if it can be found to have affected suprafamily social groups in a permanent way or to have resulted in a change in basic economic activity, or both. Interestingly, such a standard potentially locates significant anthropogenic degradation earlier in time than some researchers would have it and renders some later degradation less significant. This is because some of the earliest degradation, such as overhunting and devegetation, appears to have resulted in profound economic changes for large numbers of people, including the rise of agriculture and nomadic pastoralism. Yet some more recent degradation such as soil nutrient depletion and erosion may occur on a larger scale, but not effect basic change in economic practice. To the extent that more recent degradation is a part of economic life in the region and is managed through established patterns of mobility and diversification, it may be considered less significant than earlier processes. Butzer (1996) proposes that the eastern Mediterranean landscape reached a new, degraded equilibrium up to four thousand years ago and that economic practice in the area today is part of a well-adapted system in that new equilibrium.

Some anthropogenic degradation is likely to predate the beginnings of agriculture in the Hasa. For example, such activities as overhunting may have occurred during the Epipaleolithic, contributing to the development of broad-spectrum subsistence strategies, sedentism, population growth, and the origins of agriculture (Neeley and Clark 1993). Although there is no specific evidence of overhunting in the area at such an early date, people there practiced similar strategies to those documented elsewhere and leading to Natufian and Neolithic cultures (Bar-Yosef and Belfer-Cohen 1989). Degradation of this date and type is not the focus of the present research, but it affected regional developments and establishes a baseline for consideration of Holocene economics. From the standpoint of early agropastoralists in the Levant, anthropogenic environmental degradation has always been significant.

The depletion of local resources and the need to mitigate the effects of degradation played a part in the early development of agriculture and pastoralism as they were practiced in the Hasa. By the Neolithic period, there is evidence for pyrotechnology and pastoralism at sites such as Khirbet Hammam and el-Hemmeh similar to that practiced with detrimental results elsewhere (Rollefson, Simmons, and Kafafi 1992; Simmons et al. 1988). A layer of colluvium associated with the upper levels of WHS 524 has been interpreted as a result of deforestation probably owing to human activities. At present, the lack of excavation data from large Neolithic sites in the Hasa precludes inference of degradation on a large scale. Following the abandonment of all Neolithic sites, however, a pronounced change in settlement type did occur during the Chalcolithic period.

The abandonment of Neolithic sites may have occurred in part because of late Neolithic drought, but during the Chalcolithic period precipitation returned to high levels. If climate change were the only factor preventing occupation of Neolithic sites, one would expect subsequent Chalcolithic occupations to be of a similar type and in similar locations. On the contrary, Chalcolithic sites were not located near Neolithic sites, nor were they of a similar type. The settlement pattern of relatively large Neolithic villages in valley-bottom locations was transformed to a more dispersed pattern of small, perhaps seasonally occupied farms and camps. This change in settlement type is associated with the transition to specialized pastoralism in response to herd pressures on agricultural lands.

The Chalcolithic again underwent a period of pronounced drought followed by a return to relatively high precipitation during the Early Bronze Age. Like the earlier transition, Early Bronze Age settlement patterns are quite different from their predecessors. Rather than small ephemeral sites typically associated with the large wadis, Early Bronze Age sites are often larger farms and villages and are more likely to be found in upland areas away from the major wadis. If climate change alone were responsible for the abandonment of Chalcolithic site locations, one would expect climate recovery to result in reoccupation of similar locations by people practicing similar economic strategies. On the contrary, we again find that settlements are in quite different locations and probably represent different types of activities. Pastoralism as practiced during the Chalcolithic may have degraded the landscape more than cultivation, particularly in desert fringe areas such as the Hasa (Fall, Lines, and Falconer 1998).

Analyses of potential erosion around Neolithic and Chalcolithic sites indicates that these areas would have experienced the highest rates of erosion of any sites occupied since the beginnings of agriculture. If early attempts at cultivation and domestic animal grazing in sensitive wadi terrain contributed to fundamental changes including economic diversification, the rise of specialized pastoralism, and settlement shifts to more stable upland areas, they must be considered archaeologically significant. If early incision of the Hasa floodplain is related to the rise of agropastoralism in this region, it would compound the significance of early anthropogenic degradation in shaping both the landscape and cultures of the region.

Subsequent degradation resulting from increased populations, market production, and tribute demands has undoubtedly had a quantitatively greater impact on the landscape of the Hasa. But within boundaries dictated by oscillating political and climatic conditions, economic practice remained remarkably consistent from the Early Bronze Age to the early twentieth century. The basic pattern of small village and farm agriculture complemented by varying degrees of nomadic pastoralism changed largely in the emphasis of one aspect or the other as drought and empires have come and gone.

Perhaps a more interesting and complex issue of land use and degradation in the Hasa is the relationship to politics. If we accept the idea that nature and society are inseparable (e.g., Goldman and Schurman 2000), the focus of environmental research is rightfully shifted toward the ways in which natural and cultural dynamics are reflexively intertwined. The object of studies of human impact on the environment can no longer be simply the point in time when humans as a discrete system began to dominate nature as a discrete system. The New Ecology's emphasis on nonequilibrium, variability, complexity, and uncertainty requires an appreciation of the dynamic processes involved in shaping the Hasa landscape (Kottak 1999; Scoones 1999). The growing recognition that nature is not an external variable in the study of society, but rather inextricably bound up with it, encourages movement beyond the documentation of instances of degradation.

Evidence of anthropogenic environmental degradation is turning out to be nearly ubiquitous in archaeological analyses of complex societies and surprisingly common even in analyses of smaller-scale societies (Redman 1999). The many valuable studies of past human impacts provide compelling evidence that our interesting question is no longer if or when people degraded their environment, but rather how cultural and natural dynamics interacted in particular ways and what the consequences were (McGlade 1995). Archaeologists are particularly well suited to close the "Great Divide" between society and nature (Goldman and Schurman 2000). Archaeology traditionally has a strong interest in the effects of environment on culture and more recently on the broad range of human impacts on the environment. Archaeological knowledge of human ecology in a variety of natural and cultural environments has great potential for elucidating the ways in which the two realms are interrelated (van der Leeuw and Redman 2002).

In the span of Holocene agropastoralism in the Hasa, three primary causal elements have contributed to environmental degradation. First, climate change has been a major factor in the disappearance of lakes, vegetation change, and changes in valley-floor morphology. Climate change was most pronounced during the late Pleistocene and early Holocene. Dramatic fluctuations in precipitation pattern and volume affected the distribution of resources in such a way that relatively large and concentrated populations of people were forced to respond with ever more creative and manipulative subsistence solutions. Beginning with economic diversification and the cultivation and husbandry of biotic resources, early settlers responded to declining hunting and gathering options by intervening directly in resource production. The development of domestication economies in turn had profound impacts on the landscape as this solution to climate and population predicaments created yet other problems. Through the early Holocene, formative agricultural societies were repeatedly confronted with climatic change unlike anything in the historical record (Bar-Matthews et al. 1999). But because of the effects of prior cultural responses, in each case it was impossible to resort to previous strategies. Each new climate shift and cultural development required a chain of new responses in a cycle of positive feedback. For example, the transition to a domestication economy in the Neolithic led to increased sedentism, population growth and aggregation, and declines in local wild plant and animal resources, thus preventing a return to hunting and gathering (Bar-Yosef and Belfer-Cohen 1989).

Since the middle Holocene, climate change has been considerably less pronounced, and, until the rise of capitalism and the modern era, economic response to climate change has been somewhat more predictable. There is some correlation between the rise and fall of archaeological and historical cultures, on the one hand, and the drought/pluvial cycles that have characterized the Levant, on the other (Issar 1995). But the underlying basis of the economic system fluctuated consistently between tributary and subsistence production based on diverse agropastoralism throughout this time. Unlike previous periods when each new development in economic strategy led to unknown consequences and engendered revolutionary new strategies in response, the later Holocene is characterized by the cyclical expansion and contraction of extant strategies, with somewhat more predictable results.

The second major causal element in anthropogenic environmental degradation has been human ignorance (see McGovern et al. 1988). Like climate change, ignorance of the consequences of new land-management strategies was probably a more important contributor to environmental degradation during the early Holocene. The development of revolutionary new techniques, such as agriculture and pastoralism, had consequences that could not have been foreseen in their early stages. Production technologies and settlement behaviors were undergoing unprecedented change at the same time that climate was undergoing at least unremembered change. The decline of wild species and the geomorphological change corresponding to early agropastoralism and the beginning of the Holocene would have been unforeseeable to people accustomed to mobile hunting and gathering in a Pleistocene landscape.

Moreover, many of the consequences of early domestication economies took place at a relatively small geographic scale and at a slow pace. For example, the deforestation posited in the vicinity of 'Ain Ghazal may have taken place over a span of nearly two thousand years and been relatively restricted in scope to the area around the site. It is unlikely, in the absence of historical records, that the inhabitants of late 'Ain Ghazal had a very clear sense of the earlier environment of the area or of the consequences of their ancestors' actions. What may appear catastrophic in an archaeological sense may not have even been perceptible as a consequence of human behavior to people at the time.

Ignorance has probably continued to be a problem in some contexts since the early Holocene. In the context of colonization by new groups of settlers unfamiliar with the local environment, ignorance may have periodically led to renewed episodes of degradation as people tried techniques that were successful in neighboring areas. Harlan (1988) discusses the repeated filling up and emptying out of the Hasa landscape as neighboring areas became more or less crowded. Many of the neighboring areas that supplied settlers to the Hasa have more humid and perhaps more stable landscapes.

During periods of settlement expansion in the Hasa, especially by populations from different environments, ignorance was likely a factor contributing to environmental degradation. The evidence presented in these analyses suggests that there were repeated and temporary cycles of increased settlement by agropastoralists throughout the Holocene. Settlements in the Hasa were typically abandoned by the following period as people either shifted locations or abandoned permanent settlement altogether in the area. The combination of higher rates of abandonment and higher rates of erosion in the Hasa, in contrast to the Kerak plateau, points toward land degradation as an important factor affecting settlement trends in the area. Ignorance of the consequences of particular land-use strategies in the Hasa may have contributed to settlers' willingness to take up unsustainable practices there.

It is also worth remembering that these cycles of expansion and abandonment span anywhere from two hundred years to more than a millennium. During most of this time, historical landscape records would have been sketchy or absent, and, again, much of the degradation may have occurred at a rate that was not easily recognizable to land managers at any specific time.

One might assume that climate change on the scale of the Pleistocene/Holocene transition and ignorance of the basic ecological consequences of human actions are problems of the past. However, such an assumption is likely unwarranted in view of current political and technological circumstances in the area. Informed climate observers widely share a view that weather conditions around the world are currently undergoing significant changes with unforeseeable results (Union of Concerned Scientists 2003). Among the probable results of the forecast global warming are extreme weather events including drought and flood. Areas such as the Levant are already in crisis regarding water management and availability, as limited resources are taxed beyond their potential. The disappearance of water sources, increased conflict over remaining sources, and hydrological and geomorphological change resulting from lower water tables and flooding—all have the potential to lead to ecological and human catastrophe in countries with rapidly growing populations. The effects of climate change will probably not be felt equally around the world, and less-developed nations with marginal ecological resources will suffer disproportionately the consequences of global warming.

Likewise, our understanding of the effects of extant land-management strategies may not be as sound as we would like. After literally millennia of relatively constant agropastoral technology, the Near East recently has experienced fundamental change in the way land is used. New technologies, largely imported from the West in the past few decades, have exposed landscapes to a degree of use and modification they have never before experienced. The recently completed Tannur Dam will alter the hydrology, fluvial geomorphology, and riparian habitat of the Hasa in an unprecedented manner. Diesel-powered pumps now irrigate soils in areas that were not readily irrigable using traditional gravity technologies, encouraging the cultivation of slopes and other areas that probably cannot sustain long-term use. Mechanized plowing has exposed thin, easily eroded soils to deeper disturbance and has extended cultivation into areas that might not have warranted the manual labor of traditional technologies. Water tanks hauled by truck allow more intensive grazing in areas where water limitations would have restricted pastoral use in the past. Finally, plastic-foam vegetable packaging and plastic pipe and sheeting, used in drip irrigation systems, are accumulating in large quantities among the riparian vegetation, following discard and floods.

All of these factors point toward the possibility that climate change and ignorance of the long-term consequences of human actions may once again contribute to social and economic change on a large scale in the Near East. Probably not since the early Holocene has the area undergone the kind of climate and technological change that is currently occurring or imminently to occur there. If so, it stands to reason that the consequences of current changes may rival in magnitude the origins of sedentary society and domestication economies that changed the course of human history there five to ten thousand years ago. The specifics of such change are, of course, impossible to predict and beyond the scope of the present research to attempt. By suggesting the possibility of large-magnitude changes in the future, however, I do not imply anything about the direction of those changes. There is nothing directional about the evolution of society, and the likelihood of total collapse seems about as great as the likelihood of ever more complex and sophisticated civilization. I predict neither one, but suggest that the evidence points toward dramatic change in the lives of the inhabitants of the Wadi al-Hasa in the coming decades. In truth, such a prediction is not very bold because the inhabitants of the Hasa are already in the midst of unprecedented technological developments that have changed their lives significantly over the past few decades. All that remains is to witness the long-term consequences of those developments as they are manifest through a multitude of feedback processes.

The final major causal element in environmental degradation in the Hasa over the past several thousand years is political. Archaeologists have long recognized the role of politics in human ecology. In more recent years, the field of political ecology has developed considerably in recognition of the fact that current political practice has a profound effect on the use and abuse of ecological resources. The interaction between politics and ecology can be seen in a number of ways, but my research has focused on the ways in which political organization has contributed to deleterious land management in the Hasa.

As noted previously, it has been widely hypothesized that when political organization becomes hierarchically differentiated, decision making is separated from its consequences. In centralized hierarchies with distant authority, the motivation and information to practice locally sustainable economic strategies are diminished. As a consequence, producers are pressured to overexploit resources, contrary to their own knowledge and self-interest. The Hasa is an area of marginal agricultural productivity that is susceptible to overexploitation with results such as erosion, as well as an area subject to cycles of conquest and decentralized local rule.

The implication of this hypothesis is that under conditions of increased hierarchy and foreign domination the Hasa should exhibit evidence of more exploitative, less-sustainable land management. As discussed in chapter 3, the political history of the Hasa can be divided into four major categories of hierarchical authority:

Lowest—Neolithic, Chalcolithic
Medium Low—Bronze Age, Hellenistic, 'Abbasid, Fatimid,
            Ayyubid, middle Ottoman
Medium High—Iron Age, Nabatean, Ummayad, Mamluk
High—Roman, Byzantine, early and late Ottoman

The implication of the political hierarchy hypothesis is that the most exploitative, least sustainable land management should be associated with the most hierarchical and most geographically distant center of political authority. In the present analyses, the highest exposure to erosion should have occurred during the Roman, Byzantine, and Ottoman periods. The lowest exposure to erosion should have occurred during the Neolithic and Chalcolithic periods.

The analyses in this study demonstrate that political hierarchy clearly cannot account for the full range of variability in land use. The highest PSL rates occurred during the lowest periods of hierarchy, the Neolithic and Chalcolithic. The highest total PSL exposure occurred during the medium-high periods of hierarchical but local authority such as the Iron

Age and Nabatean periods. The Roman, Byzantine, and Ottoman periods have relatively high total PSL values, but surprisingly not as high as
periods of local authority. The variability in land use demonstrated here
requires consideration of a fuller range of cultural factors than just the
social and geographical proximity of authority. This research suggests that
resistance, ethnic identification, and power over production decisions by
nonelites in the Hasa contributed substantially to variability in land use.
Moreover, these factors appear to have been important in the Hasa as long
ago as the Late Bronze Age and perhaps earlier.

The high rates of potential erosion in the vicinity of Neolithic and
Chalcolithic sites can probably be accounted for by the ignorance of settlers in developing new subsistence technologies without knowledge of
the long-term consequences of their actions. This phenomenon is discussed elsewhere and is more of a technological issue than a political one.
As noted earlier, it may have important lessons for current settlers in the
Hasa and elsewhere, but it probably does not bear on the issue of political
hierarchy and land exploitation.

However, the differences between the periods of local hierarchy and
foreign hierarchy may be indicative of an interesting aspect of the relationship between elites and producers. The discussion so far has assumed that
producers act as elite managers stipulate. Such a simplifying assumption
has the value of facilitating the modeling of systematic aspects of maladaptation in complex societies. Unfortunately, it obscures an important
aspect of actual behavior by assuming that power lies entirely with elite
decision makers. The model assumes that decision making is either in the
hands of local producers or in the hands of elite managers, when in reality
decision making is a complex process that all parties contribute to as their
abilities permit in a "dialectic of control" (Giddens 1984:14–16).

Many factors come into play in the land-management process, but I
wish to focus on the tension between elites and producers as they pursue
their separate goals. Adams (1978) noted that mobile populations in peripheral areas would be difficult for elites to control as they push for maximization. His discussion brings attention to the power that producers
have to resist domination and overexploitation of their land by evading
elite control. There are many ways for commoners to resist domination by
elite authorities, including abandonment of agricultural settlement and
the pursuit of mobile, diversified economic strategies (Netting 1993:284;
Scott 1985, 1990). One of the keys to both their desire and their ability to
evade elite control is the physical proximity of authority.

When authority in a local setting is manifested in people of common ethnic identity, there is less inclination to resist. Leadership is drawn from real or constructed kin networks, and the ideology justifying their position is often of local, traditional origin (Brumfiel 1994). This phenomenon is illustrated in Transjordan by the fact that considerably more statements of hostility to Roman authority are found than to Nabatean authority among inscriptions carved by nomadic herders (D. Graf 1997b). This difference exists even though both powers extracted surplus through similar state-level, centralized hierarchies. Hostility was aroused in part by the combination of Roman state demands and their reluctance to include Nabateans in positions of power. Similar inscriptions from the Nabatean period indicate closer, more amicable relations with Nabatean authorities.

Local producers' ability to resist is also strongly affected by the physical proximity of power. When elite authorities attempt to exert demands on producers, their demands must be accompanied by the power to enforce compliance. Mobilizing coercive power involves different considerations for local and foreign authorities. Coercive elements of state power such as the military are likely to be more effective when they are drawn from local populations because they have more knowledge of local conditions and practices. Likewise, local authorities are more likely to enforce their demands consistently if they rely on local production and cooperation to maintain their positions.

In contrast, military presence composed of foreign personnel, unfamiliar with and perhaps uninterested in local circumstances, would be less effective in enforcing compliance with foreign decrees. Perhaps more significant, the will to exercise coercive power in distant frontier areas such as the Hasa would fluctuate as an empire's attention was occupied with other political conflicts and as the importance of trade through Transjordan varied. In short, it would have been more difficult and more expensive for foreign political powers to enforce their will in frontier areas like the Hasa than it was for local powers such as the Iron Age and Nabatean kings to do so. Moreover, the motivation to enforce that will probably decreased when large empires were faced with other problems.

The present analyses highlight local inhabitants' power to resist elite attempts to settle them into surplus production. The spatial analyses demonstrate the willingness of people occupying the southern Hasa to abandon their settlements frequently. This tendency illustrates the options that inhabitants of a desert frontier such as the Hasa have in their interaction with elite authorities. When production declines or taxation increases to a point where a family's cost-benefit ratio is prohibitive to continued effort, they do have a choice. Unlike situations where producers are circumscribed in their settlement and subsistence options, inhabitants of the Hasa have always had the ability to take their flocks and disappear into the desert to the east and south.

These analyses support the hypothesis that political hierarchy affects land management, but conditionally. The elites in a political hierarchy are only one part of a complex interrelationship among multiple parties who have different avenues of power. The tendency for centralized authorities to mismanage land use through ignorance and greed is often countered by individuals' power to resist such efforts. The political complexities of land use require these two parts to be balanced in the analysis of maladaptation.

8
Conclusions

The research presented here covers an unusual chronological, theoretical, and methodological breadth. Most discussions of the archaeology and history of the Levant in post-Pleistocene times focus on a particular culture or time period. In addition to its sweeping temporal character, this research employs a broad range of theoretical and methodological approaches. Such eclecticism provides a diverse array of analytical tools and historical situations with which to evaluate trends among past human/landscape interaction. Following an analysis of this nature, however, it is necessary to draw the focus back down to a few essential qualities. I focus here on three major implications of the study, including the cultural historical, the methodological, and the theoretical.

One of the important questions in studies of anthropogenic environmental degradation in the Levant pertains to timing. When did such degradation become a significant problem? This question has typically been addressed through analysis of the temporal correlation among indices of degradation and cultural-historical developments. Moreover, such analysis has typically been focused on identifying significant degradation among the nonhuman components of the ecosystem. Such a focus is logical within the rubric of human impact on the environment. Most studies assume that environmental degradation is significant to people, and general discussions of degradation have made clear that it is a subjective problem, depending on the perspective of those using the land for economic gain. However, most analyses do relatively little actually to evaluate the effects of environmental degradation on human populations. I argue that from an anthropological perspective, the significance of environmental degradation to people is the most important question.

The present analyses pursue an alternative strategy, evaluating evidence of human response to degradation and its correlation with variable susceptibility to degradation. Such an approach focuses on the significance of degradation to human populations rather than to other ecosystem components such as soils or vegetation. Using this approach in the Wadi al-Hasa, I find evidence that human populations have been responding to local environmental degradation throughout the Holocene and probably previously. A multitude of interrelated factors, including human pressures on resources, combined to result in behavioral feedback leading to a diversified agropastoral economy by the Neolithic period. There is evidence that in virtually every period since that time, human pressure on landscape resources has been an issue for land managers to negotiate. Using neighboring areas to control for the effects of other pressures, I argue that erosion resulting from agropastoralism has been a significant factor affecting land-use decisions at least since the origin of domestication economies in this area.

The approach taken here to the problems of environmental degradation has been made possible through the use of a methodology that utilizes an extraordinary quantity of archaeological and geographic data. One of the most original aspects of this research is the serendipitous convergence of two decades of archaeological survey with the digital revolution, which has enabled me to contextualize millennia of human behavior in a single manageable database. The novelty of this achievement will be short-lived as even more powerful technology becomes available, but the research presented here would have been considerably more difficult even ten years ago and extremely difficult for an individual researcher fifteen years ago.

The methodological consequences of recent technology for the present research are twofold. First, it provided the analytical power to perform statistical and geographical modeling on large numbers of archaeological sites and their contexts using a range of critical environmental variables. Spatial statistical and PSL analyses incorporating billions of computations would not have been feasible without the use of sophisticated computers and software. Second, the ability to perform such analyses repeatedly for different temporal periods and using different samples has given these analyses a robust quality that is not available in smaller-scale studies.

Many debates around studies of anthropogenic environmental degradation hinge on the problem of equifinality. There is often not adequate temporal resolution among either the environmental indices or the archaeology in question to establish a precise human cause for the identified degradation. In addition, natural factors, such as climate, are rarely in stasis long enough to exclude them as possible contributors to the observed degradation. Thus, it is often difficult to determine with certainty what the human contribution to environmental degradation has been. An analysis of the available data from any particular period in the Hasa would be plagued by the same uncertainty.

However, the analysis of multiple periods in conjunction with an explicit control mechanism provides a degree of statistical confidence to the conclusions reached here. The fact that patterns of abandonment and location avoidance occur repeatedly over thousands of years is a strong indication that humans have often had to respond to local degradation. The fact that such patterns are restricted to areas of high susceptibility to erosion, whereas neighboring areas of lower susceptibility exhibit more stable long-term land use, is a strong indication that human action has been a significant cause of degradation. Although other factors have undoubtedly contributed to degradation over time, this study demonstrates that it is unlikely that these patterns of abandonment can be attributed entirely to natural environmental change. Humans have caused environmental degradation repeatedly through history and have had to respond to it each time. The confidence of these conclusions is directly related to the ability to observe correspondence among variables through multiple periods using multiple analytical techniques. A more detailed focus on any particular period or set of environmental circumstances would not provide the same robust conclusions.

The use of multiple scales of analysis necessitates a theoretical flexibility. Multiple theoretical considerations of human behavior and the material record left by it are employed to address the range of questions found in such a broad analysis. Two principal types of questions, equally important, are addressed in this research: those that seek to understand patterns in the archaeological record and those that seek to understand why people behaved they way they did in the past. Clearly, these questions are related, but satisfactory answers to them require somewhat different theoretical orientations. Using a combination of temporal perspectives from the long term of several thousand years to the short term of individual events, I have demonstrated that both evolutionary processes and immediate cost-benefit calculations structure patterns of land use.

The archaeological record as a whole consists of a complex palimpsest of material residue from activities spanning a geological epoch. A long-term diachronic view of that record illustrates patterns of differential reproductive success among those activities. Depending on environmental conditions, some activities are more successfully reproduced in successive generations than others. Of particular note in the Hasa are the differential successes of land-use practices in areas of variable susceptibility to erosion. Diversified agropastoralism with recourse to nomadism is a consistent feature of land use through the Holocene, despite numerous technological and economic fluctuations in the region. This pattern is in marked contrast to the practice in nearby areas, where agricultural land use has been successfully reproduced repeatedly through time in the same geomorphologically stable locations. I argue that these contrasting economic strategies are adaptations to a marginal environment that can sustain long-term agriculture only in a few areas, but that has repeatedly come under pressure to intensify production. What is visible in the archaeological record is the result of differential selection among strategies through time depending on environmental constraints.

Conversely, the actions of individual land managers at any particular time in the past are not likely to reflect adaptation. Instead, a short-term view of land use in the Hasa might as often show evidence of unsustainable intensification or abandonment, influenced by a variety of factors, including fluctuating socioeconomic demands and environmental degradation. Such relatively synchronic analyses illustrate not the cumulative record of selective processes, but the multitude of cost-benefit calculations that individuals make in the face of constantly changing conditions. Although evidence of adaptation is seen in a long-term view, it is not the dominant factor structuring land use at any particular time.

In summary, this examination of land use through the long term in a marginal environment illustrates how a variety of factors have affected decision making. The natural environment of the Hasa has posed considerable limitations on efforts at agropastoral exploitation. Likewise, the interests of the powerful have provided impetus for stability and intensification or for resistance and diversity. In combination, these factors have produced a dynamic history of alternating settlement and abandonment as the costs and benefits of different land-use strategies fluctuated. In each case, people's evaluation of those costs and benefits are structured by both contemporary circumstances and their predecessors' actions. In turn, their decisions structure their children's possibilities and constraints.

A century and a half ago Karl Marx said: "History is nothing but the succession of the separate generations, each of which exploits the materials, the capital funds, the productive forces handed down to it by all preceding generations, and thus, on the one hand continues the traditional activity in completely changed circumstances and, on the other, modifies the old circumstances with a completely changed activity" (quoted in Giddens 1971:23). The land resources of the Hasa are part of the means of production that have been handed from generation to generation, each time in modified form. And in each generation people have continued their traditional activity in both a new set of political circumstances and a landscape shaped by their ancestors. A multitemporal view of the Hasa illustrates the integration of structure and event as a succession of generations, bound by local tradition and ecological limitation, confronting political circumstances that offer both new meaning and new opportunities for land use. Processes lasting millennia are altered by daily decision making, while available choices and their consequences reflect those of previous eras. Thus, the landscape of the Hasa becomes a thing of time, a chronicle of living made and remade.

References

Adams, R. M. 1978. Strategies of Maximization, Stability, and Resilience in Mesopotamian Society, Settlement, and Agriculture. *Proceedings of the American Philosophical Society* 122: 329–35.

Adnanal-Bakhit, M. 1982. Jordan in Perspective: The Mamluk-Ottoman Period. In *Studies in the History and Archaeology of Jordan I*, edited by A. Hadidi, 361–62. Amman, Jordan: Department of Antiquities.

Akarli, E. D. 1986. 'Abdulhamid II's Attempt to Integrate Arabs into the Ottoman System. In *Palestine in the Late Ottoman Period: Political, Social, and Economic Transformation*, edited by D. Kushner, 74–92. Jerusalem: Yad Izhak Ben-Zvi Press.

Amiran, R. 1978. *Early Arad: The Chalcolithic Settlement and Early Bronze Age City I: 1st–5th Seasons of Excavation 1962–1966.* Jerusalem: Israel Exploration Society.

Amiran, R., and Ram Gophna. 1985. The Transition from the Chalcolithic to the Early Bronze Age. In *Biblical Archaeology Today*, 108–12. Proceedings of the International Congress on Biblical Archaeology. Jerusalem: Israel Exploration Society.

———. 1989. Urban Canaan in the EBII and EBIII Periods—Emergence and Structure. In *L'urbanization de la Palestine a l'Age du Bronze Ancien*, edited by P. de Miroschedji, 109–16. British Archaeological Reports International Series vol. 527. Oxford: British Archaeological Reports.

Atran, S. 1986. Hamula Organization and Masha'a Tenure in Palestine. *Man* 21(2): 271–95.

Avi-Yonah, M. 1977. *The Holy Land from the Persian to the Arab Conquests (536 B.C. to A.D. 640) A Historical Geography.* Grand Rapids, Mich.: Baker Book House.

Bailey, G. N. 1983. Concepts of Time in Quaternary Prehistory. *Annual Review of Anthropology* 12: 165–92.

Banning, E. B. 1986. Peasants, Pastoralists, and Pax Romana: Mutualism in the Highlands of Jordan. *Bulletin of the American Schools of Oriental Research* 261: 25–50.

———. 1987. De Bello Paceque: A Reply to Parker. *Bulletin of the American Schools of Oriental Research* 265: 52–54.

———. 1988. Methodology. In *The Wadi el Hasa Archaeological Survey 1979–1983, West-Central Jordan*, edited by B. MacDonald, 13–25. Waterloo, Ontario: Wilfred Laurier University Press.

———. 1995. Herders or Homesteaders? A Neolithic Farm in Wadi Ziqlab, Jordan. *Biblical Archaeologist* 58(1): 2–13.

Banning, E. B., D. Rahimi, and J. Siggers. 1994. The Late Neolithic of the Southern Levant: Hiatus, Settlement Shift, or Observer Bias? The Perspective from Wadi Ziqlab. *Paleorient* 20(2): 151–64.

Bar-Matthews, M., A. Ayalon, A. Kaufman, and G. J. Wasserburg. 1999. The Eastern Mediterranean Paleoclimate as a Reflection of Regional Events: Soreq Cave, Israel. *Earth and Planetary Science Letters* 166: 85–95.

Bartlett, J. R. 1979. From Edomites to Nabateans: A Study in Continuity. *Palestine Exploration Quarterly* 110–11: 53–66.

———. 1983. The "United" Campaign against Moab in 2 Kings 3:4–27. In *Midian, Moab, and Edom: The History and Archaeology of Late Bronze and Iron Age Jordan and North-West Arabia,* edited by J. F. A. Sawyer and D. J. A. Clines, 135–46. Sheffield: JSOT Press, Department of Biblical Studies.

———. 1992. Biblical Sources for the Early Iron Age in Edom. In *Early Edom and Moab: The Beginning of the Iron Age in Southern Jordan,* 7th ed., edited by P. Bienkowski, 13–19. Sheffield Archaeological Monographs. Oxford: Alden Press.

Baruch, U. 1990. Palynological Evidence of Human Impact on the Vegetation as Recorded in Late Holocene Lake Sediments in Israel. In *Man's Role in the Shaping of the Eastern Mediterranean Landscape,* edited by S. Bottema, G. Entjes-Nieborg, and W. van Zeist, 283–93. Rotterdam: A. A. Balkema.

Bar-Yosef, O. 1995. Earliest Food Producers—Pre-Pottery Neolithic (8000–5500). In *The Archaeology of Society in the Holy Land,* edited by T. E. Levy, 190–204. New York: Facts on File.

Bar-Yosef, O., and A. Belfer-Cohen. 1989. The Origins of Sedentism and Farming Communities. *Journal of World Prehistory* 3, no. 4: 447–98.

Bates, R. L., and J. A. Jackson. 1984. *Dictionary of Geological Terms.* 3rd ed. New York: Anchor Books, Doubleday.

Beaumont, P. 1985. Man-Induced Erosion in Northern Jordan. In *Studies in the History and Archaeology of Jordan II,* edited by A. Hadidi, 291–96. Amman, Jordan: Department of Antiquities.

Bender, F. 1974. *Geology of Jordan: Contributions to the Regional Geology of the Earth 7.* Berlin: Gebruder Borntraeger.

Bennett, C. M. 1983. Excavations at Buseirah (Biblical Bozrah). In *Midian, Moab, and Edom: The History and Archaeology of Late Bronze and Iron Age Jordan and North-West Arabia,* edited by J. F. A. Sawyer and D. J. A. Clines, 9–17. Sheffield: JSOT Press, Department of Biblical Studies.

Berlin, A. M. 1997. Between Large Forces: Palestine in the Hellenistic Period. *Biblical Archaeologist* 60(1): 2–51.

Bienkowski, P. 1990. Umm el-Biyara, Tawilan, and Buseirah in Retrospect. *Levant* 22: 91–109.

———. 1992a. The Beginning of the Iron Age in Southern Jordan: A Framework. In *Early Edom and Moab: The Beginning of the Iron Age in Southern Jordan,* 7th ed., edited by P. Bienkowski, 1–12. Sheffield Archaeological Monographs. Oxford: Alden Press.

———. 1992b. The Date of Sedentary Occupation in Edom: Evidence from Umm el-Biyara, Tawilan, and Buseirah. In *Early Edom and Moab: The Beginning of the Iron Age in Southern Jordan,* 7th ed., edited by P. Bienkowski, 99–112. Sheffield Archaeological Monographs. Oxford: Alden Press.

Bienkowski, P., R. Adams, R. A. Philpott, and L. Sedman. 1997. Soundings at

Ash-Shorabat and Khirbat Dubab in the Wadi Hasa, Jordan: The Stratigraphy. *Levant* 29: 41–70.

Bintliff, J. 1991. The Contribution of an Annaliste/Structural History Approach to Archaeology. In *The Annales School and Archaeology,* edited by J. Bintliff, 1–33. London: Leicester University Press.

————. 1992. Erosion in the Mediterranean Lands: A Reconsideration of Pattern, Process, and Methodology. In *Past and Present Soil Erosion: Archaeological and Geographical Perspectives,* edited by M. Bell and J. Boardman, 125–31. Oxford: Oxbow Books.

Blaikie, P., and H. Brookfield. 1987. *Land Degradation and Society.* New York: Methuen and Co.

Blankholm, H. P. 1991. *Intrasite Spatial Analysis in Theory and Practice.* Aarhus, Denmark: Aarhus University Press.

Bossut, P., Z. Kafafi, and G. Dollfus. 1988. Khirbet ed-Dharih (Survey Site 49/WHS 524), un nouveau gisement Neolithique avec Ceramic du Sud-Jordanien. *Paleorient* 14(1): 127–31.

Bosworth, C. E. 1967. *The Islamic Dynasties: A Chronological and Genealogical Handbook.* Islamic Surveys no. 5. Edinburgh: Edinburgh University Press.

Bottema, S., G. Entjes-Nieborg, and W. van Zeist, eds. 1990. *Man's Role in the Shaping of the Eastern Mediterranean Landscape.* Rotterdam: A. A. Balkema.

Bowersock, G. W. 1983. *Roman Arabia.* Cambridge, Mass.: Harvard University Press.

Bowman, D. 1997. Geomorphology of the Dead Sea Western Margin. In *The Dead Sea: The Lake and Its Setting,* 36th ed., edited by T. M. Niemi, Z. Ben-Avraham, and J. R. Gat, 217–25. Oxford Monographs on Geology and Geophysics. New York: Oxford University Press.

Braudel, F. 1980. History and the Social Sciences: The Longue Durée. In *On History,* edited by F. Braudel, translated by S. Matthews, 25–54. Chicago: University of Chicago Press.

Braun, E. 1989. The Transition from the Chalcolithic to the Early Bronze Age in Northern Israel and Jordan: Is There a Missing Link? In *L'urbanization de la Palestine a l'Age du Bronze Ancien,* edited by P. de Miroshedji, 7–28. British Archaeological Reports International Series vol. 527. Oxford: British Archaeological Reports.

Brockelmann, C. 1948. *History of the Islamic Peoples.* Translated by Joel Carmichael and Moshe Perlman. London: Routledge and Kegan Paul.

Brumfiel, E. M. 1992. Distinguished Lecture in Archeology: Breaking and Entering the Ecosystem—Gender, Class, and Faction Steal the Show. *American Anthropologist* 94 (3): 551–67.

————. 1994. Ethnic Groups and Political Development in Ancient Mexico. In *Factional Competition and Political Development in the New World,* edited by E. M. Brumfiel and J. W. Fox, 89–102. Cambridge: Cambridge University Press.

Bunimovitz, S. 1995. On the Edge of Empires—Late Bronze Age (1500–1200 BCE). In *The Archaeology of Society in the Holy Land,* edited by T. E. Levy, 320–32. New York: Facts on File.

Butzer, K. W. 1994. The Islamic Traditions of Agroecology: Cross-Cultural Experience, Ideas, and Innovation. *Ecumene: Journal of Environment, Culture, Meaning* 1: 7–50.

———. 1996. Ecology in the Long View: Settlement Histories, Agrosystemic Strategies, Ecological Performance. *Journal of Field Archaeology* 23(2): 141–50.

Childe, V. G. 1971. The Neolithic Revolution. In *Prehistoric Agriculture,* edited by S. Struever, 15–22. Garden City, N.Y.: Natural History Press.

Chisholm, M. 1968. *Rural Settlement and Land Use.* 2d ed. London: Hutchinson and Co.

Christopherson, G. L., D. P. Guertin, and K. A. Borstadt. 1996. *GIS and Archaeology: Using ARC/INFO to Increase Our Understanding of Ancient Jordan.* Palm Springs, Calif.: Environmental Systems Research Institute. Available at: http://gis.esri.com/library/userconf/proc96/TO150/PAP119/P119.HTM.

Clark, G. A., M. P. Neeley, B. MacDonald, J. Schuldenrein, and K. 'Amr. 1992. Wadi al Hasa Paleolithic Project—1992: Preliminary Report. *Annual of the Department of Antiquities of Jordan* 36: 13–23.

Clark, G. A., D. I. Olszewski, J. Schuldenrein, N. Rida, and J. D. Eighmey. 1994. Survey and Excavation in the Wadi al-Hasa: A Preliminary Report of the 1993 Season. *Annual of the Department of Antiquities of Jordan* 38: 41–55.

Cole, D. P. 1985. Bedouin and Social Change in Saudi Arabia. In *Arab Society Social Science Perspectives,* edited by S. E. Ibrahim and N. S. Hopkins, 286–306. Cairo: American University in Cairo Press.

Cooke, R. U., and R. W. Reeves. 1976. *Arroyos and Environmental Change in the American Southwest.* Oxford Research Studies in Geography. Oxford: Clarendon Press.

Cooke, R. U., and A. Warren. 1973. *Geomorphology in Deserts.* Berkeley and Los Angeles: University of California Press.

Copeland, L., and C. Vita-Finzi. 1978. Archaeological Dating of Geological Deposits in Jordan. *Levant* 10: 10–25.

Cotterell, B., and J. Kamminga. 1990. *Mechanics of Pre-industrial Technology.* Cambridge: University Of Cambridge Press.

Crumley, C. L. 1994. Historical Ecology: A Multidimensional Ecological Orientation. In *Historical Ecology: Cultural Knowledge and Changing Landscapes,* edited by C. L. Crumley, 1–16. Santa Fe, N.Mex.: School of American Research Press.

Danin, A. 1995. Man and the Natural Environment. In *The Archaeology of Society in the Holy Land,* edited by T. E. Levy, 24–39. New York: Facts on File.

Davidson, D. A., and S. P. Theocharopoulos. 1992. A Survey of Soil Erosion in Viotia, Greece. In *Past and Present Soil Erosion: Archaeological and Geographical Perspectives,* edited by M. Bell and J. Boardman, 149–54. Oxford: Oxbow Books.

Dever, W. G. 1980. New Vistas on the EB IV ("MB I") Horizon in Syria-Palestine. *Bulletin of the American Schools of Oriental Research* 237: 35–64.

———. 1987. The Middle Bronze Age: The Zenith of the Urban Canaanite Era. *Biblical Archaeologist* 50: 149–77.

———. 1995. Social Structure in the Early Bronze IV Period in Palestine. In *The Archaeology of Society in the Holy Land,* edited by T. E. Levy, 282–97. New York: Facts on File.

Dickson, D. B. 1987. Circumscription by Anthropogenic Environmental Destruction: An Expansion of Carneiro's (1970) Theory of the Origin of the State. *American Antiquity* 52, no. 4: 709–16.

Dobyns, H. F. 1981. *From Fire to Flood: Historic Destruction of Sonoran Desert Riverine Oases*. Socorro, N.Mex.: Ballena Press.

Donahue, J. 1985. Hydrologic and Topographic Change during and after the Early Bronze Occupation at Bab edh-Drah and Numeira. In *Studies in the History and Archaeology of Jordan II*, edited by A. Hadidi, 131–40. Amman, Jordan: Department of Antiquities.

Donahue, J., and D. E. Beynon. 1988. Geologic History of the Wadi el Hasa Survey Area. In *The Wadi el Hasa Archaeological Survey 1979–1983, West-Central Jordan*, edited by B. MacDonald, 26–40. Waterloo, Ontario: Wilfred Laurier University Press.

Donahue, J., B. Peer, and R. T. Shaub. 1997. The Southeastern Dead Sea Plain: Changing Shorelines and Their Impact on Settlement Patterns through Historical Periods. In *Studies in the History and Archaeology of Jordan VI: Landscape Resources and Human Occupation in Jordan throughout the Ages*, edited by G. Bisheh, M. Zaghloul, and I. Kehrberg, 127–36. Amman, Jordan: Department of Antiquities.

Donner, F. M. 1981. *The Early Islamic Conquests*. Princeton, N.J.: Princeton University Press.

Engle, T., and W. Frey. 1996. Fuel Resources for Copper Smelting in Antiquity in Selected Woodlands in the Edom Highlands to the Wadi Arabah/Jordan. *Flora* 191(1): 29–39.

Esse, D. L. 1989. Secondary State Formation and Collapse in Early Bronze Age Palestine. In *L'urbanization de la Palestine a l'Age du Bronze Ancien*, edited by P. de Miroshedji, 81–96. British Archaeological Reports International Series vol. 527. Oxford: British Archaeological Reports.

Falconer, S. E., and P. L. Fall. 1995. Human Impacts on the Environment during the Rise and Collapse of Civilization in the Eastern Mediterranean. In *Late Quaternary Environments and Deep History: A Tribute to Paul S. Martin*, edited by D. W. Steadman and J. I. Mead, 3: 84–101. Hot Springs, S.Dak.: Mammoth Site of Hot Springs, South Dakota, Inc., Scientific Papers.

Falconer, S. E., and S. H. Savage. 1995. Heartlands and Hinterlands: Alternative Trajectories of Early Urbanization in Mesopotamia and the Southern Levant. *American Antiquity* 60(1): 37–59.

Fall, P. L., L. Lines, and S. Falconer. 1998. Seeds of Civilization: Bronze Age Rural Economy and Ecology in the Southern Levant. *Annals of the Association of American Geographers* 88(1): 107–25.

Faroqhi, S. 1997. Part II. Crisis and Change, 1590–1699. In *An Economic and Social History of the Ottoman Empire*, edited by H. Inalcik and D. Quataert, 2: 409–636. Cambridge: Cambridge University Press.

Fiema, Z. T. 1991. Economics, Administration, and Demography of the Late Roman and Byzantine Southern Transjordan. Ph.D. diss., University of Utah.

Finkelstein, I. 1995. The Great Transformation: The "Conquest" of the Highlands Frontiers and the Rise of the Territorial States. In *The Archaeology of Society in the Holy Land*, edited by T. E. Levy, 349–62. New York: Facts on File.

Food and Agriculture Organization (FAO) of the United Nations. 1979. *A Provisional Methodology for Soil Degradation Assessment*. Rome: FAO.

Frumkin, A. 1997. The Holocene History of Dead Sea Levels. In *The Dead Sea: The Lake and Its Setting*, 36th ed., edited by T. M. Niemi, Z. Ben-Avraham, and J. R.

Gat, 237–48. Oxford Monographs on Geology and Geophysics. New York: Oxford University Press.

———. 1999. Continental Oxygen Isotopic Record of the Last 170,000 Years in Jerusalem. *Quaternary Research* 51: 317–27.

Gebel, H. G., M. S. Muheisen, H. J. Nissen, N. Qadi, and J. M. Starck. 1988. Preliminary Report on the First Season of Excavations at the Late Aceramic Neolithic Site of Basta. In *The Prehistory of Jordan: The State of Research in 1986,* edited by A. N. Garrard and H. G. Gebel, 101–34. British Archaeological Reports International Series vol. 396(i). Oxford: British Archaeological Reports.

Giddens, A. 1971. *Capitalism and Modern Social Theory: An Analysis of the Writings of Marx, Durkheim, and Max Weber.* Cambridge: Cambridge University Press.

———. 1984. *The Constitution of Society: Outline of the Theory of Structuration.* Berkeley and Los Angeles: University of California Press.

Gilead, I., ed. 1995. *Grar: A Chalcolithic Site in the Northern Negev.* Beer-Sheva Studies by the Department of Bible and Ancient Near East no. 7. Beer-Sheva: Ben-Gurion University of the Negev Press.

Glueck, N. 1937. The Nabatean Temple of Khirbet et-Tannur. *Bulletin of the American Schools of Oriental Research* 67: 6–16.

———. 1939. *Explorations in Eastern Palestine, III.* Annual of the American Schools of Oriental Research nos. 18–19. New Haven, Conn.: American Schools of Oriental Research.

Goldberg, P. 1995. The Changing Landscape. In *The Archaeology of Society in the Holy Land,* edited by T. E. Levy, 40–57. New York: Facts on File.

Goldberg, P., and O. Bar-Yosef. 1990. The Effect of Man on Geomorphological Processes Based upon the Evidence from the Levant and Adjacent Areas. In *Man's Role in the Shaping of the Eastern Mediterranean Landscape,* edited by S. Bottema, G. Entjes-Nieborg, and W. van Zeist, 71–86. Rotterdam: A. A. Balkema.

Goldberg, P., and A. M. Rosen. 1987. Early Holocene Paleoenvironments of Israel. In *Shiqmim I: Studies Concerning 4th Millennium Societies in the Northern Negev Desert, Israel,* edited by T. E. Levy, 23–34. British Archaeological Reports International Series vol. 356. Oxford: British Archaeological Reports.

Goldman, M., and R. A. Schurman. 2000. Closing the "Great Divide": New Social Theory on Society and Nature. *Annual Review of Sociology* 26: 563–84.

Goodfriend, G. A. 1999. Terrestrial Stable Isotope Records of Late Quaternary Paleoclimates in the Eastern Mediterranean Region. *Quaternary Science Reviews* 18: 501–13.

Gophna, R. 1995. Early Bronze Age Canaan: Some Spatial and Demographic Observations. In *The Archaeology of Society in the Holy Land,* edited by T. E. Levy, 269–82. New York: Facts on File.

Gophna, R., N. Liphschitz, and S. Lev-Yadun. 1986. Man's Impact on the Natural Vegetation in the Central Coastal Plain of Israel during the Chalcolithic and Bronze Ages (circa 4000–1600 B.C.). *Tel Aviv* 13: 69–82.

Graf, D. F. 1997a. The Origins of the Nabateans. In *Rome and the Arabian Frontier: From the Nabateans to the Saracens,* 45–75. Varorium Collected Studies Series. Brookfield, Vt.: Ashgate.

———. 1997b. Rome and the Saracens: Reassessing the Nomadic Menace. In *Rome and the Arabian Frontier: From the Nabateans to the Saracens,* 341–400. Varorium Collected Studies Series. Brookfield, Vt.: Ashgate.

———. 1997c. The Saracens and the Defense of the Arabian Frontier. In *Rome and the Arabian Frontier: From the Nabateans to the Saracens,* 1–26. Varorium Collected Studies Series. Brookfield, Vt.: Ashgate.

Graf, W. L. 1988. *Fluvial Processes in Dryland Rivers.* Heidelberg, Germany: Springer-Verlag.

Grigson, C. 1995. Plough and Pasture in the Early Economy of the Southern Levant. In *The Archaeology of Society in the Holy Land,* edited by T. E. Levy, 245–68. New York: Facts on File.

Hammond, P. C. 1973. *The Nabateans—Their History, Culture, and Archaeology.* Studies in Mediterranean Archaeology no. 37. Gothenburg, Sweden: Paul Astroms Forlag.

Hanbury-Tenison, J. W. 1986. *The Late Chalcolithic to Early Bronze I Transition in Palestine and Transjordan.* British Archaelogical Reports International Series vol. 311. Oxford: British Archaeological Reports.

Harlan, J. R. 1985. The Early Bronze Age Environment of the Southern Ghor and the Moab Plateau. In *Studies in the History and Archaeology of Jordan II,* edited by A. Hadidi, 125–29. Amman, Jordan: Department of Antiquities.

———. 1988. Natural Resources. In *The Wadi el Hasa Archaeological Survey 1979–1983, West-Central Jordan,* edited by B. MacDonald, 40–48. Waterloo, Ontario: Wilfred Laurier University Press.

Hart, S. 1992. Iron Age Settlement in the Land of Edom. In *Early Edom and Moab: The Beginning of the Iron Age in Southern Jordan,* 7th ed., edited by P. Bienkowski, 93–98. Sheffield Archaeological Monographs. Oxford: Alden Press.

Hawting, G. R. 1987. *The First Dynasty of Islam: The Ummayad Caliphate AD 661–750.* Carbondale: Southern Illinois University Press.

Henry, D. O. 1994. Prehistoric Cultural Ecology in Southern Jordan. *Science* 265: 336–41.

Herhahn, C. L., and J. B. Hill. 1998. Modeling Agricultural Production Strategies in the Northern Rio Grande Valley. *Human Ecology* 26: 469–87.

Herr, L. G. 1997. The Iron Age II Period: Emerging Nations. *Biblical Archaeologist* 60(3): 114–83.

Hill, J. B. 2000. Decision Making at the Margins: Settlement Trends, Temporal Scale, and Ecology in the Wadi al Hasa, West-Central Jordan. *Journal of Anthropological Archaeology* 19: 221–41.

———. 2001. Geoarchaeological Research of Holocene Occupations in the Wadi Al-Hasa: A Preliminary Report on the 1999 Season. *Annual of the Department of Antiquities of Jordan* 44: 11–17.

———. 2002. Land Use and Land Abandonment: A Case Study from the Wadi al-Hasa, West Central Jordan. Ph.D. diss., Arizona State University.

———. 2004a. Land Use and an Archaeological Perspective on Socio-Natural Studies in the Wadi al-Hasa, West-Central Jordan. *American Antiquity* 69(3): 389–412.

———. 2004b. Time, Scale, and Interpretation: 10,000 Years of Land Use on the Transjordan Plateau, amid Multiple Contexts of Change. In *Mediterranean Archaeological Landscapes: Current Issues,* edited by E. F. Athanassopoulos and

L. Wandsnider, 125–42. Philadelphia: University of Pennsylvania Museum Publications.

Hillel, D. 1991. *Out of the Earth: Civilization and the Life of the Soil.* Berkeley and Los Angeles: University of California Press.

Hodder, I., and E. Okell. 1978. A New Method for Assessing the Association between Distributions of Points in Archaeology. In *Simulation Studies in Archaeology,* edited by I. Hodder, 97–107. Cambridge: Cambridge University Press.

Hole, F., K. Flannery, and J. Neeley. 1969. *Prehistory and Human Ecology of the Deh Luran Plain: An Early Village Sequence from Khuzistan, Iran.* Memoirs of the Museum of Anthropology no. 1. Ann Arbor: University of Michigan.

Holt, P. M. 1986. *The Age of the Crusades: The Near East from the Eleventh Century to 1517.* History of the Near East series. London: Longman Group Ltd.

Hopkins, D. 1993. Pastoralists in Late Bronze Age Palestine: Which Way Did They Go? *Biblical Archaeologist* 56(4): 200–211.

Hughes, D. 1983. How the Ancients Viewed Deforestation. *Journal of Field Archaeology* 10: 437–45.

Humphreys, R. S. 1977. *From Saladin to the Mongols: The Ayyubids of Damascus, 1193– 1260.* Albany: State University of New York Press.

Hunt, C. O., H. A. Elrishi, D. D. Gilberston, J. Grattan, S. McLaren, F. B. Pyatt, G. Rushworth, and G. W. Barker. 2004. Early-Holocene Environments in the Wadi Faynan, Jordan. *The Holocene* 14(6): 921–30.

Hunt, C. O., D. D. Gilbertson, and R. E. Donahue. 1992. Paleoenvironmental Evidence for Agricultural Soil Erosion from Late Holocene Deposits in the Montagnola Senese, Italy. In *Past and Present Soil Erosion: Archaeological and Geographical Perspectives,* edited by M. Bell and J. Boardman, 163–74. Oxford: Oxbow Books.

Hüttermann, A. 1999. *The Ecological Message of the Torah: Knowledge, Concepts, and Laws Which Made Survival in a Land of "Milk and Honey" Possible.* South Florida Studies in the History of Judaism no. 199. Atlanta, Ga.: Scholars Press.

Hütteroth, W. 1975. The Pattern of Settlement in Palestine in the Sixteenth Century: Geographic Research on Turkish Defter-i Mufassal. In *Studies on Palestine during the Ottoman Period,* edited by M. Ma'oz, 3–10. Jerusalem: Magnes Press, Hebrew University, and Yad Izhak Ben-Zvi.

Hütteroth, W., and K. Abdulfattah. 1977. *Historical Geography of Palestine, Transjordan, and Southern Syria in the Late 16th Century.* Erlangen Geographische Arbeiten, Herausgegeben vom Vorstand der Frankischen Geographischen Gesellschaft no. 5. Erlangen: Selbstverlag der Franischen Geographischen Gesellschaft in Komission bei Palm und Enke.

Ilan, D. 1995. The Dawn of Internationalism—The Middle Bronze Age. In *The Archaeology of Society in the Holy Land,* edited by T. E. Levy, 297–320. New York: Facts on File.

Inalcik, H. 1997. Part I. The Ottoman State: Economy and Society, 1300–1600. In *An Economic and Social History of the Ottoman Empire,* edited by H. Inalcik and D. Quataert, 1: 1–409. Cambridge: Cambridge University Press.

Issar, A. S. 1995. Climate Change and the History of the Middle East. *American Scientist* 83: 350–55.

Jabbur, J. S. 1995. *The Bedouins and the Desert—Aspects of Nomadic Life in the Arab*

East. Translated by Lawrence I. Conrad. State University of New York Series in Near Eastern Studies. Albany: State University of New York Press.

Joffe, A. H. 1993. *Settlement and Society in the Early Bronze I and II, Southern Levant: Complementarity and Contradiction in a Small-Scale Complex Society.* Monographs in Mediterranean Archaeology no. 4. Sheffield, England: Sheffield Academic.

Johns, J. 1992. Islamic Settlement in Ard al-Karak. In *Studies in the History and Archaeology of Jordan IV,* edited by M. Zaghloul, K. 'Amr, F. Zayadin, R. Nabeel, and N. R. Tawfiq, 363–68. Amman, Jordan: Department of Antiquities.

Johnson, I. 1984. Cell Frequency Recording and Analysis of Artifact Distributions. In *Intrasite Spatial Analysis in Archaeology,* edited by H. J. Hietala, 75–96. Cambridge: Cambridge University Press.

Kaegi, W. 1992. *Byzantium and the Early Islamic Conquests.* Cambridge: Cambridge University Press.

Kempinski, A. 1989. Urbanization and Metallurgy in Southern Canaan. In *L'urbanization de la Palestine a l'Age du Bronze Ancien,* edited by P. de Miroshedji, 163–68. British Archaeological Reports International Series vol. 527. Oxford: British Archaeological Reports.

Kennedy, H. 1981. *The Early Abbasid Caliphate: A Political History.* London: Croom Helm Ltd.

———. 1991. Nomads and Settled People in Bilad a-Sham in the Fourth/Ninth and Fifth/Tenth Centuries. In *Bilad al-Sham during the Abbasid Period,* edited by M. A. al-Bakhit and R. Schick, 105–13. Amman, Jordan: History of Bilad al-Sham Committee.

Kintigh, K. W. 1990. Intrasite Spatial Analysis: A Commentary on Major Methods. In *Mathematics and Information Science in Archaeology: A Flexible Framework,* 3rd ed., edited by A. Voorrips, 165–200. Bonn: Studies in Modern Archaeology.

———. 1992. *Tools for Quantitative Archaeology.* Tempe, Ariz.: K. W. Kintigh.

Kirkebride, D. 1966. Five Seasons of Excavation at the Pre-Pottery Neolithic Village of Beidha in Jordan. *Palestine Exploration Quarterly* 98: 8–72.

Kitchen, K. A. 1992. The Egyptian Evidence on Ancient Jordan. In *Early Edom and Moab: The Beginning of the Iron Age in Southern Jordan,* 7th ed., edited by P. Bienkowski, 21–34. Sheffield Archaeological Monographs. Oxford: Alden Press.

Knapp, A. B. 1992. Archaeology and Annales: Time, Space, and Change. In *Archaeology, Annales, and Ethnohistory,* edited by A. B. Knapp, 1–22. Cambridge: Cambridge University Press.

Knauf, E. A. 1983. Midianites and Ishmaelites. In *Midian, Moab, and Edom: The History and Archaeology of Late Bronze and Iron Age Jordan and North-West Arabia,* edited by J.F.A. Sawyer and D.J.A. Clines, 135–46. Sheffield: JSOT Press, Department of Biblical Studies.

———. 1992. Assyrian Involvement in Edom. In *Early Edom and Moab: The Beginning of the Iron Age in Southern Jordan,* 7th ed., edited by P. Bienkowski, 47–54. Sheffield Archaeological Monographs. Oxford: Alden Press.

Kohler-Rollefson, I. 1988. The Aftermath of the Levantine Neolithic Revolution in the Light of Ecological and Ethnographic Evidence. *Palorient* 14(1): 87–93.

———. 1993. Camels and Camel Pastoralism in Arabia. *Biblical Archaeologist* 56(4): 180–88.

Kohler-Rollefson, I., and G. O. Rollefson. 1990. The Impact of Neolithic Subsistence Strategies on the Environment: The Case of 'Ain Ghazal, Jordan. In *Man's Role in the Shaping of the Eastern Mediterranean Landscape,* edited by S. Bottema, G. Entjes-Nieborg, and W. van Zeist, 3–14. Rotterdam: A. A. Balkema.

Kottak, C. P. 1999. The New Ecological Anthropology. *American Anthropologist* 101(1): 23–35.

Kuijt, I., and N. Goring-Morris. 2002. Foraging, Farming, and Social Complexity in the Pre-Pottery Neolithic of the Southern Levant: A Review and Synthesis. *Journal of World Prehistory* 16(4): 361–440.

LaBianca, O. S., and R. W. Younker. 1995. The Kingdoms of Ammon, Moab, and Edom: The Archaeology of Society in the Late Bronze Age/Iron Age Transjordan (CA 1400–500 BCE). In *The Archaeology of Society in the Holy Land,* edited by T. E. Levy, 399–416. New York: Facts on File.

Lambton, A. K. S. 1985. *State and Government in Medieval Islam, an Introduction to the Study of Islamic Political Theory: The Jurists.* London Oriental Series no. 36. Oxford: Oxford University Press.

Lawrence, T. E. 1938. *Seven Pillars of Wisdom.* Deluxe ed. Garden City, N.Y.: Garden City Publishing.

Lee, J. R. 1973. Chalcolithic Ghassul: New Aspects and Master Typology. Ph.D. diss., Hebrew University.

Le Hourou, H. N. 1981. Impact of Man and His Animals on Mediterranean Vegetation. In *Mediterranean Type Ecosystems,* edited by F. Di Castri and H. A. Mooney, 479–521. Berlin: Springer-Verlag.

Leonard, A. 1989. The Late Bronze Age. *Biblical Archaeologist* 52: 4–39.

Levy, T. E. 1983a. Chalcolithic Settlement Patterns in the Northern Negev Desert. *Current Anthropology* 24(1): 105–7.

———. 1983b. The Emergence of Specialized Pastoralism in the Southern Levant. *World Archaeology* 15(1): 15–36.

———. 1986. Archaeological Sources for the Study of Palestine: The Chalcolithic Period. *Biblical Archaeologist* 49: 82–108.

———. 1992. Transhumance, Subsistence, and Social Evolution in the Northern Negev Desert. In *Pastoralism in the Levant: Archaeological Materials in Anthropological Perspectives,* edited by O. Bar-Yosef and A. Khazanov, 65–82. Monographs in World Archaeology vol. 10. Madison, Wisc.: Prehistory Press.

———. 1995. Cult, Metallurgy, and Rank Societies—Chalcolithic Period (CA. 4500–3500) BCE. In *The Archaeology of Society in the Holy Land,* edited by T. E. Levy, 226–45. New York: Facts on File.

Levy, T. E., and P. Goldberg. 1987. The Environmental Setting of the Northern Negev. In *Shiqmim I: Studies Concerning 4th Millennium Societies in the Northern Negev Desert, Israel,* edited by T. E. Levy, 1–22. British Archaeological Reports International Series vol. 356. Oxford: British Archaeological Reports.

Lindner, M., and E. A. Knauf. 1997. Between the Plateau and the Rocks: Edomite Economic and Social Structure. In *Studies in the History and Archaeology of Jordan VI: Landscape Resources and Human Occupation in Jordan throughout the Ages,* edited by G. Bisheh, M. Zaghloul, and I. Kehrberg, 261–64. Amman, Jordan: Department of Antiquities.

Liphschitz, N., R. Gophna, and S. Lev-Yadun. 1989. Man's Impact on the Vegetational Landscape of Israel in the Early Bronze Age II–III. In *L'urbanization de la Palestine a l'Age du Bronze Ancien,* edited by P. de Miroschedji, 263–68. British Archaeological Reports International Series vol. 527. Oxford: British Archaeological Reports.

Liver, J. 1967. The Wars of Mesha, King of Moab. *Palestine Exploration Quarterly* 99(Jan.–June): 14–31.

Mabry, J. B. 1992. Alluvial Cycles and Early Agricultural Settlement Phases in the Jordan Valley. Ph.D. diss., University of Arizona.

MacDonald, B. 1984. A Nabatean and/or Roman Military Monitoring Zone along the South Bank of the Wadi el Hasa in Southern Jordan. *Echos du Monde Classique / Classical Views* 28: 219–34.

———, ed. 1988. *The Wadi el Hasa Archaeological Survey 1979–1983, West-Central Jordan.* Waterloo, Ontario: Wilfred Laurier University Press.

———. 1999. The Tafila-Busayra Archaeological Survey: Phase 1. *Annual of the Department of Antiquities of Jordan* 44: 507–22.

MacDonald, B., and C. D'Annibale. 1983. The Classical Period (332 B.C.–A.D. 640) Sites of the Wadi el Hasa Archaeological Survey, Southern Jordan: A Preliminary Report. *Echos du Monde Classique / Classical Views* 27: 149–58.

MacDonald, B., L. Herr, M. P. Neeley, S. Quaintance, and A. Bradshaw. 2001. The Tafila-Busayra Archaeological Survey: Phase 2 (2000). *Annual of the Department of Antiquities of Jordan* 45: 395–411.

MacDonald, B., and C. Vibert-Gogue. 1980. The Hermitage of John the Abbott at Hammam Afra, Southern Jordan. *Liber Annuus* 30: 351–64.

Makarewicz, C. A., and N. B. Goodale. Forthcoming. Results from the First Excavation Season at el-Hemmeh: A Pre-Pottery Neolithic Site in the Wadi el-Hasa, Jordan. *Neo-Lithics 01/05: A Newsletter of Southwest Asian Lithics Research.*

Mattingly, G. L. 1996. Al-Karak Resources Project 1995: A Preliminary Report on the Pilot Season. *Annual of the Department of Antiquities of Jordan* 40: 349–67.

Mattingly, G. L., J. I. Lawlor, J. D. Wineland, J. H. Pace, A. M. Bogaard, and M. P. Charles. 1998. Al-Karak Resources Project 1997: Excavations at Khirbat al-Mudaybi. *Annual of the Department of Antiquities of Jordan* 42: 127–44.

Mayerson, P. 1994a. The Desert of Southern Palestine According to Byzantine Sources. In *Monks, Martyrs, Soldiers, and Saracens: Papers on the Near East in Late Antiquity (1962–1993),* edited by P. Mayerson, 40–52. Jerusalem: Israel Exploration Society in association with New York University.

———. 1994b. The First Muslim Attacks on Southern Palestine (A.D. 633–634). In *Monks, Martyrs, Soldiers, and Saracens: Papers on the Near East in Late Antiquity (1962–1993),* edited by P. Mayerson, 53–98. Jerusalem: Israel Exploration Society in association with New York University.

———. 1994c. Saracens and Romans: Micro-Macro Relationships. In *Monks, Martyrs, Soldiers, and Saracens, Papers on the Near East in Late Antiquity (1962–1993),* edited by P. Mayerson, 313–21. Jerusalem: Israel Exploration Society in association with New York University.

———. 1994d. Towards a Comparative Study of a Frontier. In *Monks, Martyrs, Soldiers, and*

Saracens: Papers on the Near East in Late Antiquity (1962–1993), edited by P. Mayerson, 327–39. Jerusalem: Israel Exploration Society in association with New York University.

McGlade, J. 1995. Archaeology and the Ecodynamics of Human-Modified Landscapes. *Antiquity* 69: 113–32.

McGovern, T. H. 1994. Management for Extinction in Norse Greenland. In *Historical Ecology: Cultural Knowledge and Changing Landscapes,* edited by C. L. Crumley, 127–54. Santa Fe, N.Mex.: School of American Research Press.

McGovern, T. H., G. Bigelow, T. Amorosi, and D. Russell. 1988. Northern Islands, Human Error, and Environmental Degradation: A View of Social and Ecological Change in the Medieval North Atlantic. *Human Ecology* 16(3): 225–70.

McGowan, B. 1997. Part III. The Age of the Ayans, 1699–1812. In *An Economic and Social History of the Ottoman Empire,* edited by H. Inalcik and D. Quataert, 2: 639–758. Cambridge: Cambridge University Press.

Mellart, J. 1975. *The Neolithic of the Near East.* New York: Charles Scribner and Sons.

Millard, A. 1992. Assyrian Involvement in Edom. In *Early Edom and Moab: The Beginning of the Iron Age in Southern Jordan,* 7th ed., edited by P. Bienkowski, 35–39. Sheffield Archaeological Monographs. Oxford: Alden Press.

Miller, J. M., ed. 1991. *Archaeological Survey of the Kerak Plateau.* Atlanta, Ga.: Scholars Press.

———. 1992. Early Monarchy in Moab. In *Early Edom and Moab: The Beginning of the Iron Age in Southern Jordan,* 7th ed., edited by P. Bienkowski, 77–91. Sheffield Archaeological Monographs. Oxford: Alden Press.

Moumani, K. A. 1996. Quaternary Sediments of the Jurf Ed Darawish Area, Central Jordan. Master's thesis, University of Wales.

———. 1997. *The Geology of Al Husayniyya Al Janubiyya (Jurf ed Darawish) Area: Map Sheet No. 3151-II.* Amman, Jordan: Geological Directorate, Amman Mapping Division.

Moumani, K., J. Alexander, and M. D. Bateman. 2003. Sedimentology of the Late Quaternary Wadi Hasa Marl Formation of Central Jordan: A Record of Climate Variability. *Palaeogeography, Palaeoclimatology* 191: 221–42.

Mousa, S. 1982. Jordan: Toward the End of the Ottoman Empire 1841–1918. In *Studies in the History and Archaeology of Jordan I,* edited by A. Hadidi, 385–92. Amman, Jordan: Department of Antiquities.

al-Muheisen, Z., and F. Villeneuve. 1992. Khirbet ed-Dharih 1992. *Liber Annuus* 42: 356–59.

———. 1994. Khirbet ed-Dharih. *American Journal of Archaeology* 98: 540–42.

Naveh, Z. 1990. Ancient Man's Impact on the Mediterranean Landscape in Israel: Ecological and Evolutionary Perspectives. In *Man's Role in the Shaping of the Eastern Mediterranean Landscape,* edited by S. Bottema, G. Entjes-Nieborg, and W. van Zeist, 43–50. Rotterdam: A. A. Balkema.

Naveh, Z., and J. Dan. 1973. The Human Degradation of Mediterranean Landscapes in Israel. In *Mediterranean Type Ecosystems: Origin and Structure,* edited by F. di Castri and H. A. Mooney, 373–89. Berlin: Springer-Verlag.

Neeley, M. P., and G. A. Clark. 1993. The Human Food Niche in the Levant over the Past 150,000 Years. In *Hunting and Animal Exploitation in the Later Paleolithic and Mesolithic of Eurasia,* edited by G. Peterkin, H. Bricker, and P. Mellars, 4: 221–40. Washington, D.C.: AP3A.

Neeley, M. P., J. D. Peterson, G. A. Clark, S. K. Fish, and M. Glass. 1998. Investigations at Tor al-Tareeq: An Epipaleolithic Site in the Wadi el-Hasa, Jordan. *Journal of Field Archaeology* 25: 295–317.

Neev, D., and K. O. Emery. 1995. *The Destruction of Sodom, Gomorrah, and Jericho: Geological, Climatological, and Archaeological Background.* Oxford: Oxford University Press.

Nelson, M. C. 2000. Abandonment: Conceptualization, Representation, and Social Change. In *Explorations in Social Theory,* edited by M. B. Schiffer, 52–62. Salt Lake City: University of Utah Press.

Netting, R. M. 1968. *Hill Farmers of Nigeria: Cultural Ecology of the Kofyar of the Jos Plateau.* Seattle: University of Washington Press.

———. 1986. *Cultural Ecology.* 2d ed. Prospect Heights, Ill.: Waveland Press.

———. 1993. *Smallholders, Householders: Farm Families and the Ecology of Intensive, Sustainable Agriculture.* Stanford, Calif.: Stanford University Press.

Niemi, T. M. 1997. Fluctuations of Late Pleistocene Lake Lisan in the Dead Sea Rift. In *The Dead Sea: The Lake and Its Setting,* 36th ed., edited by T. M. Niemi, Z. Ben-Avraham, and J. R. Gat, 226–36. Oxford Monographs on Geology and Geophysics. New York: Oxford University Press.

Nissen, H., M. Muheisen, H. Gebel, C. Becker, R. Neef, H. Pachur, N. Qadi, and M. Schultz. 1987. Report on the First Two Seasons of Excavations at Basta (1986–1987). *Annual of the Department of Antiquities of Jordan* 31: 79–120.

O'Brien, M. J., and T. D. Holland. 1992. The Role of Adaptation in Archaeological Explanation. *American Antiquity* 57: 3–59.

O'Hara, S. L., F. A. Street-Perrott, and T. P. Burt. 1993. Accelerated Soil Erosion around a Mexican Highland Lake Caused by Prehispanic Agriculture. *Nature* 362: 48–51.

Oleson, J. P. 1995. The Origins and Design of Nabatean Water Supply Systems. In *Studies in the History and Archaeology of Jordan V: Art and Technology throughout the Ages,* edited by K. 'Amr, F. Zayadine, and M. Zaghloul, 707–20. Amman, Jordan: Department of Antiquities.

Olszewski, D. I., N. R. Coinman, J. Schuldenrein, T. Clausen, J. B. Cooper, J. Fox, J. B. Hill, M. Al-Nahar, and J. Williams. 1998. The Eastern al-Hasa Late Pleistocene Project: A Preliminary Report on the 1997 Season. *Annual of the Department of Antiquities of Jordan* 42: 53–74.

Olszewski, D. I., and J. B. Hill. 1997. Renewed Excavations at Tabaqa (WHS 895), an Early Natufian Site in the Wadi al-Hasa, Jordan. *Neo-Lithics: A Newsletter of Southwest Asian Lithics Research* 3: 11–12.

Ortner, S. B. 1984. Theory in Anthropology since the Sixties. *Society for the Comparative Study of Society and History* 26(1): 126–66.

Papalas, C. A. 1997. A Chronological Study of Chalcolithic and Early Bronze Architectural Forms in the Wadi al Hasa of West-Central Jordan. Master's thesis, Arizona State University.

Parker, S. T. 1986. *Romans and Saracens: A History of the Arabian Frontier.* American Schools of Oriental Research Dissertation Series no. 6. Winona Lake, Ind.: American Schools of Oriental Research.

———. 1987. Peasants, Pastoralists, and Pax Romana: A Different View. *Bulletin of the American Schools of Oriental Research* 265: 35–51.

———. 1999. The Byzantine Period: An Empire's New Holy Land. *Near Eastern Archaeology* 62(3): 134–80.

Patrich, J. 1995. Church, State, and the Transformation of Palestine—the Byzantine Period. In *The Archaeology of Society in the Holy Land,* edited by T. E. Levy, 470–87. New York: Facts on File.

Peake, F. G. 1958. *A History of Jordan and Its Tribes.* Coral Gables, Fla.: University of Miami Press.

Peterson, A. D. 1986. Early Ottoman Forts on the Hajj Route in Jordan. Master's thesis, University of Oxford.

Peterson, J. D. 2000. The Origins and Development of an Early Agricultural Village in West-Central Jordan: Mapping and Preliminary Test Excavations at Khirbet Hammam in the Wadi el-Hasa. *American Schools of Oriental Research Newsletter* 50: 24.

———. 2004. Khirbet Hamman (WHS 149): A Late Pre-Pottery Neolithic B Settlement in the Wadi el-Hasa, Jordan. *Bulletin of the American Schools of Oriental Research* 334: 1–17.

Pick, W. P. 1990. Meissner Pasha and the Construction of Railways in Palestine and Neighboring Countries. In *Ottoman Palestine 1800–1914: Studies in Economic and Social History,* edited by G. G. Gilbar, 179–218. Leiden: E. J. Brill.

Quataert, D. 1997. Part IV. The Age of Reforms, 1812–1914. In *An Economic and Social History of the Ottoman Empire,* edited by H. Inalcik and D. Quataert, 2: 761–943. Cambridge: Cambridge University Press.

Rappaport, R. A. 1978. Maladaptation in Social Systems. In *The Evolution of Social Systems,* edited by J. Friedman and M. J. Rowlands, 49–87. Pittsburgh: University of Pittsburgh Press.

Rast, W. E., and R. T. Schaub. 1974. Survey of the Southeastern Plain of the Dead Sea, 1973. *Annual of the Department of Antiquities of Jordan* 19: 5–53.

Redman, C. L. 1992. The Impact of Food Production: Short-Term Strategies and Long-Term Consequences. In *Human Impact on the Environment: Ancient Roots, Current Challenges,* edited by J. E. Jacobsen and J. Firor, 35–49. Boulder, Colo.: Westview Press.

———. 1999. *Human Impact on Ancient Environments.* Tucson: University of Arizona Press.

Renard, K. G., G. R. Foster, G. A. Weesies, and J. P. Porter. 1991. RUSLE: Revised Universal Soil Loss Equation. *Journal of Soil and Water Conservation* 46(1): 30–33.

Rice, D. 1996. Paleolimnological Analysis in Central Petén, Guatemala. In *The Managed Mosaic: Ancient Maya Agriculture and Resource Use,* edited by S. L. Fedick, 193–206. Salt Lake City: University of Utah Press.

Richard, S. 1987. The Early Bronze Age: The Rise and Collapse of Urbanism. *Biblical Archaeologist* 50(1): 22–43.

Rollefson, G. O. 1989. The Late Aceramic Neolithic of the Levant: A Synthesis. *Paleorient* 15(1): 168–73.

———. 1999. El-Hemmeh: A Late PPNB–PPNC Village in the Wadi el-Hasa, Southern Jordan. *Neo-Lithics* 2: 6–8.

Rollefson, G. O., and Z. Kafafi. 1985. Khirbet Hammam: A PPNB Village in the Wadi el Hasa, Southern Jordan. *Bulletin of the American Schools of Oriental Research* 258: 63–69.

Rollefson, G. O., and I. Kohler-Rollefson. 1989. The Collapse of Early Neolithic Settlements in the Southern Levant. In *People and Culture in Change: Proceedings of the Second Symposium on Upper Paleolithic, Mesolithic, and Neolithic Populations of Europe and the Eastern Mediterranean Basin,* edited by I. Hershkovitz, 59–72. British Archaeological Reports International Series vol. 508. Oxford: British Archaeological Reports.

———. 1992. Early Neolithic Exploitation Patterns in the Levant: Cultural Impact on the Environment. *Population and Environment* 13: 243–54.

Rollefson, G. O., A. H. Simmons, and Z. Kafafi. 1992. Neolithic Cultures at 'Ain Ghazal, Jordan. *Journal of Field Archaeology* 19: 443–70.

Roller, D. W. 1983. The 'Ain La'ban Oasis: A Nabatean Population Center. *American Journal of Archaeology* 87: 173–82.

Rosen, S. A., and G. Avni. 1993. The Edge of the Empire: The Archaeology of Pastoral Nomads in the Southern Negev Highlands in Late Antiquity. *Biblical Archaeologist* 56(4): 189–99.

Rossignol-Strick, M. 1999. The Holocene Climatic Optimum and Pollen Records of Sapropel 1 in the Eastern Mediterranean, 9000–6000 BP. *Quaternary Science Reviews* 18: 515–30.

Royal Jordanian Geographic Centre. 1986. *National Atlas of Jordan—Part II—Hydrology and Agrohydrology.* Amman: Royal Jordanian Geographic Centre.

Sauer, J. A. 1987. Transjordan in the Bronze and Iron Ages: A Critique of Glueck's Synthesis. *Bulletin of the American Schools of Oriental Research* 263: 1–26.

Schaub, R. T. 1982. The Origins of the Early Bronze Age Walled Town Culture of Jordan. In *Studies in the History and Archaeology of Jordan I,* edited by A. Hadidi, 67–75. Amman, Jordan: Department of Antiquities.

Schick, R. 1994. The Settlement Pattern of Southern Jordan: The Nature of the Evidence. In *The Byzantine and Early Islamic Near East: Land Use and Settlement Patterns,* edited by G. R. D. King and A. Cameron, 133–54. Studies in Late Antiquity and Early Islam vol. 2. Princeton, N.J.: Darwin Press.

Schuldenrein, J. 1986. Paleoenvironment, Prehistory, and Accelerated Slope Erosion along the Central Israeli Coastal Plain (Palmahim): A Geoarchaeological Case Study. *Geoarchaeology* 1: 61–81.

———. 1998. Geoarchaeological Observations on the Wadi Hasa, West Central Jordan. In *Survey and Excavation in the Wadi al-Hasa, West Central Jordan,* edited by G. A. Clark and N. Coinman, 1: 205–28. Arizona State University Anthropological Research Papers no. 50. Tempe: Arizona State University.

Schuldenrein, J., and G. A. Clark. 1994. Landscape and Prehistoric Chronology of West-Central Jordan. *Geoarchaeology* 9(1): 31–55.

———. 2001. Prehistoric Landscapes and Settlement Geography along the Wadi Hasa, West-Central Jordan. Part I: Geoarchaeology, Human Palaeoecology, and Ethnographic Modelling. *Environmental Archaeology* 6: 23–38.

Schumm, S. A. 1993. River Response to Baselevel Change: Implications for Sequence Stratigraphy. *Journal of Geology* 101: 279–94.

Scoones, I. 1999. New Ecology and the Social Sciences: What Prospects for a Fruitful Engagement? *Annual Review of Anthropology* 28: 479–507.

Scott, J. C. 1985. *Weapons of the Weak: Everyday Forms of Peasant Resistance.* New Haven, Conn.: Yale University Press.

———. 1990. *Domination and the Arts of Resistance: Hidden Transcripts.* New Haven, Conn.: Yale University Press.

Shaban, M. A. 1976. *Islamic History: A New Interpretation 2, A.D. 750–1055 (A.H. 132–448).* Cambridge: Cambridge University Press.

Shalev, S., and P. J. Northover. 1987. Chalcolithic Metal and Metalworking from Shiqmim. In *Shiqmim I: Studies Concerning 4th Millennium Societies in the Northern Negev Desert, Israel,* edited by T. E. Levy, 357–71. British Archaeological Reports International Series vol. 356. Oxford: British Archaeological Reports.

Sharon, M. 1975. The Political Role of the Bedouins in Palestine in the Sixteenth and Seventeenth Centuries. In *Studies on Palestine during the Ottoman Period,* edited by M. Ma'oz, 11–30. Jerusalem: Magnes Press, Hebrew University, and Yad Izhak Ben-Zvi.

Simmons, A. 1997. Ecological Changes during the Late Neolithic in Jordan. In *The Prehistory of Jordan, II: Perspectives from 1997,* 4th ed., edited by H. G. K. Gebel, Z. Kafafi, and G. O. Rollefson, 309–318. Studies in Early Near Eastern Production, Subsistence, and Environment. Berlin: ex oriente.

Simmons, A., I. Kohler-Rollefson, G. Rollefson, R. Mandel, and Z. Kafafi. 1988. 'Ain Ghazal: A Major Neolithic Settlement in Central Jordan. *Science* 240: 35–39.

Smith, R. H. 1990. The Southern Levant in the Hellenistic Period. *Levant* 22: 123–30.

Stone, C. D. 1993. *The Gnat Is Older Than Man: Global Environment and Human Agenda.* Princeton, N.J.: Princeton University Press.

Stone, G. D. 1993. Agricultural Abandonment: A Comparative Study in Historical Ecology. In *Abandonment of Settlements and Regions,* edited by C. M. Cameron and S. A. Tomka, 74–84. Cambridge: Cambridge University Press.

Street-Perrott, F. A., R. A. Perrott, and D. D. Harkness. 1989. Anthropogenic Soil Erosion around Lake Patzcuaro, Michoacan, Mexico, during the Preclassic and Late Postclassic Hispanic Periods. *American Antiquity* 54(4): 759–65.

Tchernov, E., and L. K. Horwitz. 1990. Herd Management in the Past and Its Impact on the Landscape of the Southern Levant. In *Man's Role in the Shaping of the Eastern Mediterranean Landscape,* edited by S. Bottema, G. Entjes-Nieborg, and W. van Zeist, 207–16. Rotterdam: A. A. Balkema.

Tversky, A., and D. Kahneman. 1974. Judgment under Uncertainty: Heuristics and Biases. *Science* 185: 1124–131.

———. 1981. The Framing of Decisions and the Psychology of Choice. *Science* 211: 453–58.

Union of Concerned Scientists. 2003. The State of Climate Science: October 2003. Letter from U.S. Scientists to the U.S. Senate. Available at: http://www.ucsusa.org/global_envi ronment/global_warming.

U.S. Department of Agriculture (USDA), Soil Conservation Service (SCS). 1976. *Conservation Planning Note No. 11—Arizona: Universal Soil Loss Equation.* Phoenix: USDA, SCS.

Van Andel, T. H., and E. Zangger. 1990. Landscape Stability and Destabilization in the Prehistory of Greece. In *Man's Role in the Shaping of the Eastern Mediterranean*

Landscape, edited by S. Bottema, G. Entjes-Nieborg, and W. van Zeist, 139–158. Rotterdam: A. A. Balkema.

Van Andel, T. H., E. Zangger, and A. Demitrack. 1990. Land Use and Soil Erosion in Prehistoric and Historical Greece. *Journal of Field Archaeology* 17: 379–98.

Van der Leeuw, S. E. 1998. *The ARCHAEOMEDES Project: Understanding the Natural and Anthropogenic Causes of Land Degradation and Desertification in the Mediterranean Basin.* Luxembourg: Office of Publications of the European Union.

Van der Leeuw, S. E., and C. L. Redman. 2002. Placing Archaeology at the Center of Socio-natural Studies. *American Antiquity* 67(4): 597–605.

van Zeist, W., and S. Bottema. 1982. Vegetational History of the Eastern Mediterranean and the Near East during the Last 20,000 Years. In *Paleoclimates, Paleoenvironments, and Human Communities in the Eastern Mediterranean Region in Later Prehistory,* edited by J. L. Bintliff and W. van Zeist, 277–323. British Archaeological Reports International Series vol. 133. Oxford: British Archaelogical Reports.

Varien, M. 1999. *Sedentism and Mobility in a Social Landscape: Mesa Verde and Beyond.* Tucson: University of Arizona Press.

Vita-Finzi, C. 1966. The Hasa Formation: An Alluvial Deposition in Jordan. *Man* 1: 386–90.

———. 1969. *The Mediterranean Valleys: Geological Changes in Historical Times.* Cambridge: Cambridge University Press.

Vita-Finzi, C., and E. S. Higgs. 1970. Prehistoric Economy in the Mount Carmel Area: Site Catchment Analysis. *Proceedings of the Prehistoric Society* 36: 1–37.

Walmsley, A. 1991. Architecture and Artifacts from Abbasid Fihl: Implications for the Cultural History of Jordan. In *Bilad al-Sham during the Abbasid Period,* edited by M. A. al-Bakhit and R. Schick, 135–59. Amman, Jordan: History of Bilad al-Sham Committee.

———. 1997. Land Resources and Industry in Early Islamic Jordan (Seventh–Eleventh Century): Current Research and Future Directions. In *Studies in the History and Archaeology of Jordan VI: Landscape Resources and Human Occupation in Jordan throughout the Ages,* edited by G. Bisheh, M. Zaghloul, and I. Kehrberg, 345–52. Amman, Jordan: Department of Antiquities.

Weippert, M. 1987. The Relations of the States East of the Jordan with Mesopotamian Powers during the First Millennium BC. In *Studies in the History and Archaeology of Jordan III,* edited by A. Hadidi, 97–106. Amman, Jordan: Department of Antiquities.

Whallon, R. 1974. Spatial Analysis of Occupation Floors II: The Application of Nearest Neighbor Analysis. *American Antiquity* 39: 16–34.

Whitcomb, D. 1992. Reassessing the Archaeology of Jordan of the Abbasid Period. In *Studies in the History and Archaeology of Jordan IV,* edited by M. Zaghloul, K. ʿAmr, F. Zayadin, R. Nabeel, and N. R. Tawfiq, 385–90. Amman, Jordan: Department of Antiquities.

White, L., Jr. 1967. The Historical Roots of Our Ecological Crises. *Science* 155: 1203–207.

Wilkinson, T. J. 2003. *Archaeological Landscapes of the Near East.* Tucson: University of Arizona Press.

Willimott, S. G., B. P. Birch, R. F. McKee, K. Atkinson, and B. S. Nimry. 1964. *Conservation*

Survey of the Southern Highlands of Jordan. Submitted to Environmental Survey for Agricultural Assessment. Durham, England: Durham University.

Willimott, S. G., D. W. G. Shirlaw, R. A. Smith, and B. P. Birch. 1963. *The Wadi el Hassa Survey.* Durham, England: Department of Geography, University of Durham.

Wingard, J. D. 1996. Interactions between Demographic Processes and Soil Resources in the Copán Valley, Honduras. In *The Managed Mosaic: Ancient Maya Agriculture and Resource Use,* edited by S. L. Fedick, 207–35. Salt Lake City: University of Utah Press.

Wischmeier, W. H. 1976. Use and Misuse of the Universal Soil Loss Equation. *Journal of Soil and Water Conservation* 31: 5–9.

Wischmeier, W. H., and D. D. Smith. 1978. *Predicting Rainfall-Erosion Losses—A Guide to Conservation Planning.* U.S. Department of Agriculture (USDA) Agriculture Handbook no. 282. Washington, D.C.: USDA.

Younker, R. W. 1997. Moabite Social Structure. *Biblical Archaeologist* 60(4): 229–36.

Index

abandonment: duration of, 101, 110–12; as cause of environmental degradation, 23–24; due to environmental degradation, 4, 23–26, 35, 148, 153, 165–66; as resistance, 14, 30, 60–62, 152, 160; as spatial phenomenon, 6, 92–117, 139–44, 157

'Abbasid: Islamic dynasty, 57–58, 66, 159

Adadnirari: Assyrian king, 45

Adams, Robert M., 15–16, 160

adaptation: and broad spectrum subsistence in Epipaleolithic, 73; as cumulative process, 16–22; and land use in the Hasa, 148–49, 166. *See also* maladaptation

aggregation of population, 155

agriculture, 3–5; effects of early, 152–56; in historical periods, 36–59; and productivity, 8, 42; strategies of, 14; and sustainability, 24–25

agropastoralism: and effects through history, 147–65; and environmental degradation, 24, 42, 80; as strategy, 28, 63

'Aila (Modern Aqaba), 55

'Ain al-Buhira, 72–73

'Ain Ghazal: as example of early environmental degradation, 25–27, 112–13, 156; as notable Neolithic site, 33–34

alluvial deposits: as alluvial fans, 40, 86; in the Beersheva Valley, 26, 80; in the Wadi al-Hasa, 69–70, 74–76, 81

Annales school of history, 20–21

aqueducts, 49, 85

Arabian Desert: and occupation by nomadic pastoralists, 46, 94; and Saracen nomads, 51

Arabs and Arab ethnicity, 46–65

Arad, 38

arboriculture: and effects on pollen profiles, 40, 90. *See also* orchards

archaeology: and contributions to human ecology, 3, 22, 155, 163–64; and spatial analysis, 100–101

Ashurbanipal: Assyrian king, 45

ASKP 304 (Mu'ta), 55

ASKP 420 (Nakhl), 48

ASKP 435 (al Mudaybi), 89

ASKP 436 (Mhai), 48

Assyria: and Iron Age incursions in Transjordan, 45

Atagartis: Nabatean Goddess, 49

Ayyubid: Islamic dynasty, 57–59, 66, 159

Bab edh-Dhra: and evidence of channel incision, 40; as important Early Bronze Age site, 38

Babylonia: Neo-Babylonian conquest, 45–47

Banning, Edward B., 35, 51–52, 77

Basta, 33

Bedouin: and domestic mode of production, 29–30; and relationships with other historical polities, 42, 53–62

bedrock: and geology of the Hasa, 74, 81; and Universal Soil Loss Equation (USLE), 135–36

Beersheva valley: and Chalcolithic sites, 37, 80; and fluvial geomorphology, 26

Hodder and Okell's "A" statistics,
100–101
Holocene: degradation, 150–57; geology,
67–104; as temporal unit; 5, 25–28,
32–33
Hula Basin, 26, 39
human Ecology, 3–4, 108; and theoretical concepts, 18, 30, 151–59
hunting and gathering, 36, 155–56
hydraulic technology, 49–50

ideology: and attitudes about land use,
14, 24; and resistance, 20, 54, 161
indeterminacy: and scale, 21
intensification: as land use strategy,
14–15, 20, 64, 151–52, 166; periods
of, 112–15
Iron Age: and chronology, 96–97; culture
history of, 43–48, 64–66; and land
use, 82, 114–15, 125, 142–47, 159,
161; and tribal organization, 29
irrigation, 8, 24, 50, 82–84, 158
Islam, 20, 24, 55–62. *See also* Early
Islamic period; Late Islamic period
Israel: and paleoenvironmental studies, 23, 27, 85; and relations with the
Hasa, 44–46
Istanbul, 61, 65

Judah, 46
Judea, 49
Judham, 55
Jurf ad-Darawish, 62, 70

Kerak: as prominent site in region, 58–
59, 65, 134; Plateau as part of study
area, 11, 41, 47, 55–56, 89–92, 98–99,
107–8, 157; revolt, 62. *See also* Wadis
Kerak and Numeira
Khirbet et Tannur, 48–49
Khirbet Hammam, 33–34, 78, 91,
112–13, 153
Kushu, 41

Lacustrine deposits, 70–75
Lake Hasa, 69–75
Lake Kinneret, 26
Lakhm, 55
land capital, 30
land exhaustion, 60, 116
LandSat: satellite photos, 70, 72, 135
Late Bronze Age. *See* Middle/Late Bronze
Age
Late Islamic period: and chronology, 97;
and crops produced, 89; culture his-
tory of, 58–62; and environmental
degradation, 60; and land use, 116,
131
"Limes" defense, 51
Local Density Analysis, 101–9
longue durée, 21

Ma'an, 55
MacDonald, Burton, 11, 32, 44, 49, 51,
58, 72
maladaptation: and resistance to authority, 160–62; and scale, 16–17
Mamluk: Islamic dynasty, 58–66, 159
market economy: and environmental
degradation, 154; and land use, 28,
48, 65
Marls, 85
Mecca, 60
Mesha stele, 44
Mesopotamia: and land use, 15; and relations with the Hasa, 41–45, 64, 143
Mhai, 48
Middle/Late Bronze Age: and chronology, 97; culture history of, 40–43, 66,
159–60; and environmental degradation, 26; and land use, 82, 114, 124,
141–43
mills, 84
Moab, 40–47, 64
mobility: and land use, 14–15, 28–30, 77,
93–94, 148–49, 152; and resistance to
authority, 42–43, 160
Mohammed, 56, 65
monsoon: precipitation pattern, 35, 87

About the Author

J. Brett Hill has conducted archaeological fieldwork in several areas of the Near East, Europe, and the North American Southwest. He received his B.A. (1984) from the University of Colorado and his M.A. (1995) and Ph.D. (2002) from Arizona State University (ASU). He is continuing his research on spatial analysis and human ecology at the Center for Desert Archaeology in Tucson, Arizona. His ongoing study of the ecological, economic, and political aspects of long-term land use in desert environments has resulted in several recent publications, including articles in *American Antiquity, Journal of Field Archaeology, Journal of Anthropological Archaeology,* and *Human Ecology.* He has conducted numerous projects using geographic information system technology to evaluate how environment structured the economic and social opportunities available to ancient farmers and herders and how people degraded their environment. In the Mediterranean Basin, he is working with a multidisciplinary team to conduct comparative analyses between areas of similar natural environment but different culture history in Jordan and Spain. In Arizona, he is using macroregional data to evaluate settlement patterns and demography from the Early Agricultural period to the collapse of the Classic period Hohokam. The macroscale view of human ecology in both cases affords new perspectives on concepts such as adaptation, resilience, and sustainability that are critical to understanding contemporary environmental dilemmas. He is currently a visiting assistant professor of anthropology at Hendrix College, Conway, Arkansas.